After the **Ego**

Also from Phoenesse

BLINDED BY FEAR
Insights From the Pathwork® Guide on
How to Face Our Fears

GET A BETTER BOAT
Trustworthy Teachings
for Difficult Times

WALKER
A Memoir

LIVING LIGHT
On Seeking and Finding True Faith

WORD FOR WORD
An Intimate Exchange Between a Couple of Kindred Souls
By Jill Loree and Scott Wisler

The *Real. Clear.* seven-book series offers a fresh approach to timeless spiritual teachings, conveying profound ideas by way of easier-to-read language. It's the Pathwork Guide's wisdom in Jill Loree's words.

HOLY MOLY
The Story of Duality, Darkness and a Daring Rescue

FINDING GOLD
The Search for Our Own Precious Self

BIBLE ME THIS
Releasing the Riddles of Holy Scripture

THE PULL
Relationships & Their Spiritual Significance

PEARLS
A Mind-Opening Collection of 17 Fresh Spiritual Teachings

GEMS
A Multifaceted Collection of 16 Clear Spiritual Teachings

BONES
A Building-Block Collection of 19 Fundamental Spiritual Teachings

NUTSHELLS
Snippets from *Pearls*, *Gems* and *Bones*

SPIRITUAL LAWS
Hard & Fast Logic for Forging Ahead

The *Self. Care.* How-to-Heal series offers a bird's-eye view of the Pathwork Guide's teachings and shows us how to apply them in working with others and ourselves.

SPILLING THE SCRIPT
A Concise Guide to Self-Knowing

HEALING THE HURT
How to Help Using Spiritual Guidance

DOING THE WORK
Healing Our Body, Mind & Spirit by Getting to Know the Self
By Jill Loree with Scott Wisler

www.phoenesse.com

The *Guide Speaks* website delivers spiritual truths by way of thousands of questions posed to the Pathwork Guide and answered with candor and insight.

THE GUIDE SPEAKS
The Complete Q&A Collection
By Eva Pierrakos with Jill Loree

KEYWORDS
Answers to Key Questions Asked of the Pathwork® Guide
By Eva Pierrakos with Jill Loree

www.theguidespeaks.com

After the **Ego**

Insights From the Pathwork® Guide
on How to Wake Up

Jill Loree

Published by Phoenesse LLC
www.phoenesse.com

ISBN: 978-1732735873

Cover image by Rudy and Peter Skitterians from Pixabay.

Phoenesse® is a registered service mark of Phoenesse LLC.
Pathwork® is a registered service mark of the Pathwork Foundation.
Quotation from the Pathwork Guide Material © 2000, 2009, 2013
are reprinted by permission of the Pathwork Foundation.

Contents

Introduction

There is so much phenomenal information packed into this book. To help you get the most from these teachings, I would like to offer an orientation regarding some of the Pathwork Guide's word choices. According to the Guide, human beings have a tendency to get used to particular words. Over time, certain words can become so abused and misunderstood they become negatively charged. As a result we develop an allergy to them. "Sin" and "evil" are two such words.

Other times, we will hear a word so often, we come to think we know what it means and then don't think any further about all it represents. The word "ego" is in this category. So as you read along, the Guide will regularly change up the word he uses, even though he is still essentially pointing to the same thing. Here are other words the Guide uses to refer to our ego:

Ego-self
Ego mind
Conscious mind
Conscious awareness
Dualistic consciousness
Immediate consciousness
Limited consciousness
Limited mind
Mind
Outer mind
Superimposed mind
Objective Observer

In this collection of teachings, the Guide will be presenting ideas regarding the awakened state—about how to wake up—which is something your ego may not yet be familiar with. In truth, every incarnated being on this planet has the same long-term goal: to wake up. So understanding more about it is incredibly important.

Here are some of the words the Guide uses to point to the part of our being that relates to the awakened state:

Real self (Higher Self and Lower Self)
True self (Higher Self)
Inner self
Inner mind
Inner universe
Unitive consciousness
Universal intelligence
Universal self
Universal force
Universal life
Universal life force
Universal consciousness
Greater universal consciousness
Greater consciousness
Great universal power
Greater self
Godself
God-consciousness
Greater mind
Inner divinity
Deep mind
Unlimited mind
Infinite mind
Infinite consciousness
Expanded consciousness
Divine consciousness
Awakened consciousness

As these teachings unfold, you will come to see how this word-changing strategy, if you will, helps us break up rigid structures in our mind—so our mind can expand beyond itself. For the ego mind has a tendency to believe it knows. But there is much the limited ego mind does not yet know, especially if we have not yet experienced this larger aspect of ourselves.

In many lectures, the Guide refers to the mind's tightly held beliefs as "images." It's as though we took a picture of a thought, and then put it in frame and set it on the shelf of our mind. By now we've looked at it for so long, we don't even notice it is there.

In our work, we must come to see our images, and take them out of the precious frames we have put them in. For they hold misconceptions and, being untrue, lead us into traps and painful life situations. But I'll let the Guide tell you more about that. For now, just know that the Guide will point to our images in different ways, and when he does, we need to take notice. Here are alternative words used for images:

Misconceptions
Misunderstandings
Mistaken beliefs
Limited beliefs
Limiting beliefs
Fixed beliefs
Tightly held convictions
Wrong conclusions
Wrong thinking
Misguided thinking

Finding our images is key for unlocking our limited world and setting us free. Make no mistake, we are now prisoners—not of an unfair world, but of our own mind. And yet there is so much more to life we can experience, once we open to the truths presented in this book. There is so much more to discover about life—after the ego.

–Jill Loree

Chapter 1

The Function of the Ego in Relationship to the Real Self

What is the endgame of being human? Where are we all heading? What's the point of life? Our goal is always one thing: to become our Real Self. All the many teachings from the Pathwork Guide are approaching this same task, each coming at it from a different angle.

As we work in this direction, it will help if we understand how our inner self, or Real Self, differs from our outer self, or ego. What is the relationship between these two? For many of us, having heard various conflicting theories, we're confused about the function of the ego. Some postulate the ego is essentially negative and therefore undesirable. So then the goal of spirituality is to get rid of it, right? Other theories—particularly from a psychological point of view—say our ego is important, for we cannot be mentally healthy without an ego.

Which of these viewpoints is correct? Let's find out. For if our vision on this is not clear, it will be difficult to reach our all-important goal of self-realization. First, let's clarify the Real Self and its essence. This is our inner self and it is an integral aspect of nature. As such, we are bound to the laws of nature. And nature is something we can trust. It's not reasonable then, to not trust ourselves—to not trust our *innermost* selves. If it seems to us that nature is our enemy, this is only because we don't understand the natural laws that nature is following.

So our inner self *is* nature. Our Real Self *is* life. We are creation. This is a better way to say it than to say we are "a part" of nature, or part of creation. Our Real Self and nature are one and the same thing.

Whenever we function from our Real Self, we are in truth and we are joyful. Our most constructive and creative contributions to life arise from our inner self. So everything that expands life—everything wise and beautiful and generous—comes from here. This is worth contemplating, as it cannot be emphasized too much. It's essential we understand this truth, not only with our

1

mind—we need to feel this.

If this is so, then what is the function of our outer personality—our ego? This is the part of us that operates on a level we have direct access to. Since we are directly, or consciously, aware of our ego, this is our conscious awareness. This is the part of us that thinks, acts, sorts and makes decisions.

If we have a weak ego, we'll have a hard time coping with life. If we have an overgrown ego, we'll be lost from our Real Self. In other words, both extremes of ego-weakness and ego-inflation will result in being separated from our inner essence. And this essentially is our problem. All our conflicts in life stem from having too big an ego, or too small an ego.

Most often, it's not that one person has a big ego and another has too small an ego, but that both have an imbalance within themselves. We're underdeveloped in one area of our personality and overdeveloped in another. So nature will take its course and try to reestablish a balance. Overdevelopment of our ego, then, may be nature's way of straightening out the disturbance caused by having a weak ego in another area of our lives.

It's only after we've sufficiently developed our ego that we can be done with them. Maybe this sounds like a contradiction, but it's not. Because if our ego is not well-developed, all our efforts to compensate for this will wind up leading to more weakness. So we're kidding ourselves if we think we can dispense with our ego before we've learned to walk straight in the world. For as long as we lack a strong enough ego, we lack the ability to think, sort, decide and act appropriately in any situation that comes up.

If we hope to reach the holy grail of our Real Self by rejecting the effort needed to develop a healthy ego, we're coming at things from a place of poverty. The correct way forward is to fully own and operate our outer selves first. If we hope to skip the creation of a healthy ego—perhaps because we're too lazy—we're in error. And this is going to cost us, as all errors do. Make no mistake, developing a healthy ego is no easy thing. But this work simply can't be avoided. Doing so only delays reaching our goal.

To restate the situation: Only when we are in full possession of our outer ego-self can we let go of it and reach our inner self. This is not a theory; this is a spiritual law. And it's actually a logical law that pushes us to act from a place of strength and abundance, rather than from a place of neediness and poverty. Then, once we reach this mini-mountaintop—when we are in full possession of our outer ego—we'll have the much-needed perspective that, hey, this is not the final answer. This is not the end-all and be-all of who we are. Now, with the use of an ego that's neither underdeveloped nor overemphasized, we can start to transcend ourselves and reach a higher state of consciousness. But not before then.

So as we make our way along our spiritual path, we'll begin—perhaps through meditating—by applying the faculties of our ego. In practical terms, we'll use our ego mind to absorb what's going on in our life and sort out the truth of the situation. Only later will we be able to grasp things on a deeper level of our being, in our greater consciousness.

Many people don't even realize there is anything beyond their ego. They think the goal of life is to cultivate a strong ego—although they may not think about things in these terms. And that's how an overdeveloped ego comes into play. But this is a dead-end street. It misses the whole point. Instead of reaching the stage of having a powerful ego that can be transcended, the person further aggrandizes it. But the scope of the ego is so limited and the possibilities so puny, there's nothing great happening here at all.

It's super important to understand the spiritual law at work here. It's the law stating we must fully reach a certain state of being before we can abandon it for something better. Too often, we totally ignore this law. Our Real Self knows that the universe is unlimited, and that absolute perfection exists—that we can ultimately expand and reach the sky. And when we get there—when we're fully living from our real inner selves—we will become the master of all natural laws.

We all deeply yearn to live in this final reality, and to reach our full potential. But if we hear the call of this message from our deepest inner selves without the benefit of a healthy ego, the meaning will be distorted. Then we will childishly strive for perfection.

Think of a baby at birth who has no ego. It only wants one thing: total pleasure. Babies seek omnipotence, without frustration or lack of fulfillment. To go on with such strivings though, without the development of an ego, is to be unrealistic and even destructive. And so it is that on a spiritual path, we learn that we must let go of our forceful demands before we can come to our desires, fresh and new, and actually realize them.

The long and short of it is this: We must accept our limitations as human beings before we can tap into the unlimited fount of power sitting in our core, waiting for us to find it. We must accept our imperfections, as well as the imperfections of life on Earth, before we can reach our destiny, which is filled with absolute perfection.

And the thing stopping most of us from getting there is this: We must shed the childish notion that we can have all this and not work for it—that we can get there without the aid of a well-developed ego. We have to let go of our outdated desire for pleasure supreme and figure out how to make do with limited pleasure, before we can discover all that can be ours. To accept less is to accept life as it is right now, in this earthly reality. And to do this, we're going to need to have an ego.

Once our ego is well-equipped for dealing adequately with what this earthly realm offers—which is where our body and soul now lives—then we can deeply comprehend our greater faculties. But we must walk before we can run. So yes, our ultimate goal is perfection, unlimited power and full pleasure, and these aren't things to only hope for in a faraway future, after we've left our body. The measure is not time, but quality. And these qualities can exist at any time. In particular, they will exist the moment we awaken to truth—the moment we wake up. Yet we can awaken to truth only when we've found and let go of our childish demands for utter perfection, utter power and utter pleasure.

When we still have a weak ego, these are selfish desires that are also destructive. So our work—if we want to attain our desires—must be to abandon them. This is the same basic spiritual law that says: If we work from abundance, we'll create more abundance; if we work from poverty and need, we'll create more poverty and need.

When we have a strong, healthy ego, we can relax into our current reality without being upset that we may not get to experience fulfillment right now. We realize that there must be obstructions within ourselves that must give way before bounty can come. But when we have a weak ego, we can't wait. We think we'll just die if our wish to rule the world doesn't happen. Our wish, then, is a negative one. We'll cling to the limited laws and conditions of the little ego, and doing so will distort the greater laws.

From our weakness and our neediness, our undeveloped ego will avoid the work necessary to create strength and fullness. Instead of adequately dealing with what's in front of us, we'll try to bypass it. But once we get a taste of our Real Self, we'll no longer fear it and we'll stop over-emphasizing our ego. We will no longer neglect the important work of developing our ego faculties, which too often are slumbering, left untended.

Best of all, we'll trust life, because we'll begin to trust ourselves. Trust, after all, is an essential key for living a good life.

The Ego's Job Description

False ideas and ego-directed self-will are a natural part of the ego world. They are not, however, natural aspects of our Real Self. Fortunately, all egos come equipped with the innate ability to give up both false ideas and self-will. In fact, *only* the ego has the power to do so. The ego is also given the important task of changing its own mind and its intention.

It plays a necessary part in realizing that it is holding onto a false idea and that it does seem to harbor a surprising amount of self-will. Then it's up to the ego to decide whether to continue down the road it's on, or try a new path and abandon these two burdens.

The ego alone enjoys the job of exchanging a false idea for a truthful one. Doing so typically involves letting go of tense, anxious self-will and swapping it out for a flexible, free-flowing will that is relaxed. This critical work will, of course, require the use of the ego's well-developed reasoning powers, along with a willingness to call upon the intuitive levels of the self for higher inner guidance.

"All the blessings are extended to every one of you. These blessings are a reality that transcend and envelop you. They are the universal love, responding to your valiant efforts of self-expansion. Be in peace, be in God!"
–The Pathwork® Guide

Chapter 2

What Blocks the Ego from Connecting with the Real Self

Our attempts to find ourselves—to understand who we are, where we belong in the world, and how we can fulfill ourselves—require a certain amount of insight and strength. Whether we lead meaningful and fulfilling lives also depends entirely on the relationship between our ego and our Real Self. If this relationship is in balance, everything falls nicely into place. All of these teachings from the Pathwork Guide are pointing to this same thing, prying at it from a multitude of directions to help us open to this truth as our personal experience.

Our Real Self can also be called the universal life principle, which manifests in each and every one of us. It is life itself. It is unending consciousness in both the deepest and the highest sense. It is pleasure supreme and infinite movement all rolled into one. Since it *is* life, it can never die. It's the very essence of everything that moves and breathes. It is eternal vibration. It knows everything and since it can only be true to its own nature, it is constantly creating and furthering itself.

Each person—each individual consciousness—*is* this universal consciousness. We're not just part of it, for that would imply we are just a little drop of it. No, we actually *are* universal consciousness. And this original consciousness, or creative life principle, can take many forms. When we each incarnate as those various forms, we forget our connection with the origin. At that point, a disconnection occurs. We continue to exist and we still contain the universal consciousness, but we become oblivious to our own nature. We lose track of basic spiritual laws and we lose sight of our potential. This, in a nutshell, describes the general state of human consciousness.

When we start becoming aware of this Real Self, we realize that in fact it's always been there. We just haven't noticed it because we were under the impression we were cut off from it. So it's not quite right to say our Real Self "manifests." More correctly, we begin to notice it. We may pick up on its energy or its self-directing consciousness. Of course our separated ego also comes bundled with energy and consciousness, but the intelligence of the ego alone is far infe-rior to the universal intelligence at our disposal. The same is true for the energy.

These two things—consciousness and energy—are not separate aspects of the Real Self. They are one. But some of us tend to be more receptive to consciousness while others are more receptive to energy. Nonetheless, they are both part of the experience of self-realization.

One of our Real Self's fundamental characteristics—as it expresses itself through both consciousness and energy—is spontaneity. So it can't possibly re-veal itself through a laborious process or through a cramped state of hyper-fo-cus. And it always shows itself indirectly as the byproduct of making an effort. In short: It shows up when it is least expected.

As we move along on our spiritual path, our work is to dig deep and round up all the courage and strength we can find to overcome our own resistance to facing ourselves in truth. We will do this by admitting to our shortcomings, owning up to our problems, and working through our illusions. And let's not kid ourselves, doing so will require a significant amount of effort.

But with our nose pressed to the grindstone, so to speak, we must also not lose sight of our goal: to see the truth about ourselves. We need to see past particular illusions, and we need to disassemble our barriers to being construc-tive—so we can stop being so destructive. Our sights, however, must not be set on self-realization itself and some theoretical promise to feel good. For if we arduously force our search to find our Real Self, it won't come. It can't. It can only come about indirectly, even though our Real Self and all its yummy good-ness holds everything we could ever wish for.

How Fear Derails Us

Every step we take in the direction of truth is a step toward freedom. So if we truly have a genuine desire to be constructive and to participate in the creative process of life, this is the way we must go. What gets in the way is our fear of the unknown and our reluctance to let go. And yet the less open we are to seeing and knowing the truth, the less possibility there is to experience our spontaneous Real Self.

Let's back up a step. What might it look like for this universal life principle to show up? We might suddenly receive wisdom for solving a personal problem that we previously hadn't imagined before. Or maybe we'll experience life in a new, vibrant way we hadn't known before, adding flavor to what we're doing and seeing.

This isn't a trick. The Real Self is always safe and always holds out justified hope that we aren't going to be disappointed. There's no reason to fear this new way of experiencing life, and yet this isn't something we can push, force or manipulate. It will happen all by itself, to exactly the same degree we no longer fear the involuntary processes.

Humanity now finds itself wrestling with deeply wanting the fruits of the Real Self and its involuntary processes, while at the same time fearing and battling them. This is a terrible conflict to be trapped in, and deeply tragic. The only way to resolve it is to let go of our fear. And all of life is moving us towards this resolution.

Our work begins by finding and understanding what's underneath our personal difficulties. What are the misconceptions we hold and what were the child experiences that led to them? We must see and accept what is real in ourselves, right now, as well as in others and in life. Honesty will be the best policy, as it will illuminate the many subtle and not-so-subtle ways we are hoping to cheat life.

We will need to face and reform our character defects. We do this by observing them, and not by plunging into despair when we see them and then denying we've ever done anything wrong. Fully acknowledging our faults is an infinitely more effective way to remove them than any other approach. And note, it's not a question of removing them so then something good can happen. It's really a question of being able to quietly observe ourselves *in* the defect. In that moment, we will perceive the existential conflict between our ego and our Real Self.

Our Real Self, which manifests spontaneously, has nothing to do with some religious concept or with a white-haired God living outside of us. It also has nothing to do with a heavenly life beyond this earthly one. These are misguided interpretations that have come about because we have sensed our Real Self—the universal consciousness or life principle—and groped for an explanation on the level of the ego. Because when the ego is still in conflict with the creative life principle, misinterpretations are bound to occur. As such, these false descriptions alienate us more from our immediate Real Self, and we then don't experience it in our practical daily life.

So we may have a deep sense that there are more possibilities available to us, but we can't seem to reach them. Worse, in our alienation, we've become frightened of our Real Self. Over time, people have come up with vague theories that try to bridge the gap between their yearning and their fear. If we look at any organized religion that removes God from the self and from the daily experience of life, we will find that a compromise exists which splits human nature into the physical being and the spiritual being. As such, total fulfillment gets taken out of the *now* and gets shoved off into life after death. Any views like this, though, are nothing more than an unfortunate compromise between what we sense could exist and what we fear.

This fear goes beyond the individual fears that arise from our mistaken beliefs and our personal childhood traumas. So then what really is going on beneath this pervasive fear we all have of letting go of our ego and allowing our Real Self to unfold and carry us along? It's the misunderstanding that to give up our ego is to give up existence.

The Illusion of Separation

In order to understand this situation better, let's look at how the ego formed itself from the Real Self. For starters, the creation of individuals comes from the inherent nature of the Real Self, or the creative life force. After all, life is always on the go, moving and expanding, reaching out and contracting, finding new ways to extend itself into new terrain. Creativity has to create. So life is forever discovering new possibilities for how it can experience itself.

But after a while, after an individual consciousness has drifted further and further from its original source, it "forgets" its connection and seems to be a totally separate entity. Eventually it loses touch with the laws that govern it and the creative principles that enliven it. This is how we come to have an individual existence that's now only associated with being separate. In this case, giving up the ego may look alarmingly like annihilation of this unique person.

This is where we find ourselves today. We are under the illusion that "I" can only be found in my "separate" existence. This is exactly the illusion that has caused human death to come about. For death, as we know it, is nothing more than the extension of this illusion to its final—and really quite absurd—conclusion.

This is not some theory for us to consider with our mind. No, this is what we can realize, here and now, by looking at ourselves in truth. When we shed the illusions we hold about ourselves, we will see that our individuality is not surrendered when we tap into our Real Self, letting the universal consciousness take over and integrate with our ego functions. For in truth, we then become more of who we really are.

When we are living from our Real Self, we experience a renewal of energy and, paradoxically, we find that the more we give of ourselves, the more energized we feel. For that's the law of the universal life principle. By contrast, when we are operating from our ego and separated from our Real Self, we are locked in a land of duality. On this level, it seems entirely logical that the more we give, the less we will have and the more depleted we will become. This stems from the illusion that our outer ego is all there is to us, which is at the root of our fear of letting go of our tight ego defenses.

To be clear, it's not just energy that we tap into. When we access these universal powers, we will also notice an influx of inspirations and ideas coming from an intelligence that's much more vast than anything we've known before. Our outer intellect is no match for this inner wisdom. *This* is our "best self." And while it may seem foreign to us at first, it is not. It's just that these channels have been clogged for so long. This has been partly due to our ignorance that they even existed, together with all the personal little lies we've been telling ourselves and others.

This vaster intelligence will present itself in the form of guidance, intuition and inspiration. This will come, not as some vague feeling, but through concise words and helpful understandings we can readily grasp and apply to our everyday lives.

By discovering this new inner life, the apparent opposites of being an individual and being an integral part of the whole will be reconciled. Being a unique person as well as one with all that is will no longer appear to be opposites, but interdependent facts. This is the first of many such seemingly mutually exclusive alternatives which cause us so much heartache, and that will resolve when the ego connects with the Real Self.

Finding Real Security

Letting go of the ego should not be misconstrued to mean it is disregarded in its importance, or let fall by the wayside. And most certainly it is not to be annihilated. For the ego has crafted itself as a separate part of the Real Self—which is our greater being that is found deep inside of us. Whenever the ego becomes ready to reconnect itself to its original source, the Real Self can be immediately accessed, if we desire to do so. This means that whenever the ego becomes strong enough to risk trusting the Real Self faculties that are greater than it is—especially given the ego's very limited conscious capabilities—the ego will find a treat in the form of a new security we've never dreamed of.

What stops us from taking this step is the fear that we will be crushed. We're afraid we'll fall into nothingness and disappear. To help calm this fear, we grab onto the petrified, unmoving pieces of our psyche. For if it's not moving, that must be a safe place to anchor ourselves, right? What's moving, we think, must be dangerous. And yet in truth, it's the opposite. Life is in constant motion, and it's the desire to hold on that makes life scary.

If we ever let go, we'll find that movement is what is safe. When movement carries us—when *life* carries us—we'll have found the only real security there is. Any other false security—such as hanging on to anything for dear life—is pure illusion, and breeds nothing but more fear.

If we could peer behind the curtain of our own thoughts, we might discover a voice that says: "If I don't hold on to myself, I am not safe." If we start to notice a feeling like this, we are now holding an important key. For we now can consider the possibility that this is an error. In truth, we have nothing to fear. We are not going to be annihilated or crushed. We will only be carried.

The world we live in is created by our present state of consciousness, and not the other way around. Believe it or not, this is even true for physical laws. But we're all so used to putting the effect first and the cause later. This comes from our dualistic state of thinking in which we are unable to see the whole picture and tend to think in an either/or way.

But truth be told, we are not randomly assigned to come live here. Rather, this dualistic sphere is an expression of where humanity is in its development. Everything contained here is an out-picturing of what's inside us. For example, on planet Earth we have the physical law of gravity. This law is a match for our dualistic consciousness. It expresses, on the physical level, our reaction to and concern about falling and being crushed when we give up our ego as the sole form of our existence. Hence, the law of gravity is in perfect parallel with our inner conditions.

There are other spheres of consciousness that have different physical laws, because the overall conscious of those individuals have transcended the duality that exists here. Our reality is not the last and only one that exists. We can ponder this as a way to widen our horizons in how we think about the boundaries of reality. By sensing that a different inner experience is real, our fear may lessen and our illusion about having an isolated, ego-existence may diminish.

Working Through Layers of Consciousness

How do we apply this information in our search to find our Real Self? Consider that such a search will bring us, unavoidably, to the task of sorting out the various layers of our consciousness. Our work will involve making previously unconscious material conscious so we can reorient our faults and wrong thinking. And the more we do this, the closer we will come to our Real Self.

As our Real Self becomes freer to reveal itself, we will be, more and more, released from our fears, shames and prejudices. And that makes us more available to our Real Self. Anyone who has done so can testify to this truth: The more courage we summon to take a brave look at the truth of what's in us, the easier it becomes to connect with this vast, safe and blissful life within. And the more we connect with the part of ourselves that removes any uncertainty and all conflict, the more secure we will feel in our ability to function in the world. Daily practical living gets easier, not by magic but by increasing our capacity to cope. Best of all, we open up our ability to experience greater pleasure, just as we are meant to. If we've become disconnected from this way of living, of course we are going to yearn for it!

If we break it down, there are three fundamental levels of the human personality. First, there is our Higher Self, which holds the greatest potential in each person. This is the universal life force that rests at the core of every human being. Covering over the Higher Self is the Lower Self which is made up all our faults and illusions, our destructiveness, negativity and cruelty. Layered over all this is a third component that we could call our Mask Self, or our Idealized Self Image. This layer is based on our pretense of being what we want to be, or what we feel we ought to be, in order for everyone to like us and approve of us.

There are many aspects to explore regarding these distinct parts of the self, but there is one particular phenomenon that bears mentioning about this topic of the ego and the Real Self. Strange as it may sound, we are often ashamed of our Higher Self—of the best in ourselves. Particularly for those who are the Will Type, it seems shameful to let others see our best, most loving and generous impulses. Somehow, we find it easier and not so embarrassing to show our worst side.

Let's explore this a bit more deeply, as it is connected with our fear of exposing our Real Self. Returning to the Will Type, such a personality may feel shame primarily about being loving or giving. They believe that if they give in to the demands of society to be good, they will lose their sense of themselves as an individual. They fear submitting to the opinions of others, which might make them somehow dependent on another, and therefore feel ashamed of any impulse they may have to please someone else. As a result, a person who is a Will Type may feel more like "themselves" when they are being mean or aggressive.

In actual fact, many of us have a similar reaction to our Real Self and our real feelings of kindness, goodness and generosity. This strange shame shows up as embarrassment and a feeling of being exposed for being who and how we truly are. This is not the shame we feel about being deceitful or our destructive, or of giving in to someone's demands. This is shame on a whole different level, and it's of a very different quality. It's the feeling that what we are feels shamefully naked, regardless of what we think or feel, or how we behave.

This is important to understand, for it explains the reason we create all these artificial layers. Usually we think of these masks, or defenses, as they arise from our misconceptions about life. In this case, as we begin to reveal the naked core of ourselves and our fear of danger abates, we now start to feel more ashamed. The danger alarms go off when our ego gives over to the involuntary processes of the Real Self. The shame, on the other hand, surfaces acutely when we start being who we truly are in the moment.

When this shame pokes its head up, we start to pretend. This particular pretense is different from our "normal" mask—power mask, love mask or serenity mask—that attempts to cover up our destructiveness, cruelty and general lack of integrity. This different pretense is actually deeper, and it's more subtle. In this case, we'll pretend things we actually feel.

So for example, in a case where we already feel love, we may hide our real love because it makes us feel naked, and instead create a false love. Or we may truly feel anger, as we are today, but since this anger feels so naked, we manufacture a false anger. Same for sadness. We might feel mortified to acknowledge our own sadness, even to ourselves, so we slap on a fake sadness that we can easily display to others. Perhaps we really are experiencing pleasure, but because this feels humiliating to expose, we create false pleasure. We'll also fake things like confusion and being puzzled. Whatever our true emotion, we find a way to intensify and dramatize it, effectively faking it.

Walking around wearing this protective garment of fake feelings, we hide our Real Self and we're the only ones—usually deep in our unconscious—who knows we're doing this. This "protective garment" of ours also acts like an anesthesia, numbing the vibrancy of life. For what we have done is built a screen between us and our Real Self. This effectively separates us from the reality of our own inner being, which we can't stand but feel compelled to imitate. We are counterfeiting our own existence.

In the end, because the moving stream of life seems so dangerous to us, we act in ways that affect our personal dignity. What a tragic illusion! For the stark truth is this: We can only be truly safe when we reunite with the source of all that life is, and then we will find true dignity. For then we will overcome the shame we feel about being real, however that is showing up in this moment.

Often, we'd rather be annihilated than bear this strange sense of shame that comes from exposing our true being. Friends, this is incredibly important to look at and not push away when it arises. This is not a trivial thing, and looking this directly in the face will take us a long way on our path. It holds the key to unlocking our numbness that leads to despair and frustration. And that numbness contributes to self-alienation and feeling a particular kind of unpleasant disconnectedness.

It's difficult to put our finger on this subtle fakery, for it's not easy to identify the true feeling from the false. We won't be able point it out with mere words. Instead, we must notice how the flavor and quality of our experiences is off. And often we've been doing this for so long, it's by now second nature. So we'll need to do some very sensitive letting go, while letting ourselves be and letting ourselves feel, and closely watching what we discover.

Now is not the time to rush ahead. We will need to slow down and become exquisitely aware of what happens when we expose our naked feelings. What we may also notice is that our subtle imitations produce opposite feelings, in addition to the identical ones. And our intensification of things makes the false appear real.

So if our goal is to become more authentic, this is the ground we will have to traverse to get there. We can't get there by going any other way. We will have to make peace with the shame of feeling naked. Then, when we do connect with our momentary Real Self, it won't be "perfect." Far from it. We've all got work to do. Yet what we are now is perfect in the way it contains all the seeds we need to live a deeply vibrant life.

We already are this universal life power, which holds everything good that is possible. And what we are right now is not shameful because we have some faults. In the same way, our naked Real Self is not something to be ashamed of. When we marshal the courage to become our Real Self, we can begin to take a whole new approach to life, letting all our pretenses fall away. This includes the easy-to-spot masks we all walk around wearing—well, easy to see in others and typically harder to identify in ourselves—as well as these more subtle cloaks.

But these are exactly what's standing between our ego and our Real Self. They create a screen that blocks the life force and alienates us from our best self. They form a chasm that seems dangerous to cross. They are the cause of our illusory feelings of fear and shame. This shame originates from some of our fears and leads to the creation of others. This shame is as basic as the fears themselves that are responsible for our misconceptions about life and our splits. These are all threads in the same ball of illusion.

We can see the symbolism of the shame about our nakedness reflected in the story of Adam and Eve. To be naked, in reality, is to be in paradise. For when we stop denying our nakedness, we can begin to live a new blissful life. And this can happen right here, right now, not in another life in the beyond. We won't arrive here in a day, of course. We'll have to acclimate ourselves to this way of walking in the world, naked as it were and free from shame.

As we walk on our spiritual path in the outer world, we will also have to walk another path inside. A path within a path, if you will. This is the way we must go to become aware of our ingrained habit of covering up our inner nakedness. And this won't be an easy habit to break! But once we start paying attention to all this and call on the powers available to us—over and over, we need to ask for help and guidance—we'll begin to notice our shame and our hiding.

Bit by bit, we will learn how to drop our cloak and step out of our protective shell. Every day we do this, we will become more real. Not better. Not worse. And not different from the way we are. Without the counterfeit feelings, we'll just be more real, venturing out into the world as we happen to be right now.

Getting Started

We can start by considering the possibility that our feelings may be put on. We don't need to be frightened by this idea, and yet many people are terrified of this notion that their feelings may be fake. We're afraid that if our feelings aren't real, we have no feelings. We fear our own emptiness. And we are devastated by this fear. This fear will prod us to go on pretending.

If we keep peeling back the layers, we'll eventually come to the place where we say, "No. I don't want to feel." This might come from what we've been discussing here, or it may stem from childhood traumas. Matters not. The point is, there must always be an inner resolve not to feel. Often, we've lost our connection with this resolve, meaning it has slipped down into our unconscious. As a result, our conscious selves are helpless about the result, which is that we have no feelings.

What we do feel is the terror of not being able to feel, and this terror is way worse when our conscious self is ignorant of what's going on in our unconscious where we fear feelings. It may help to realize that no one is really without feelings, and feelings can never permanently die. Life and feelings are one, so if there is life, there are feelings, even if they've been shut down. So knowing this, we can ask inside, "Where have I made the decision not to feel?" Notice the fear come up about feeling feelings? Now we're onto something.

The next step is to reactivate our feelings by using our reasoning mind—here's where the ego comes in and asks for help from our Higher Self—and involving a rational evaluation of the circumstance. This is the work. What surfaces will not kill us, as the parts of us still living in child consciousness may believe. But to not feel…that's what it's like to stop living.

"Be blessed, every one of you. May your endeavors succeed to become real, to find the courage to be nakedly real without any false covers. You cannot help but succeed if you really want to. Those who do not move and grow and liberate themselves do not want to — and it is important to know this — and find in you the inner voice that refuses to move. May all your false layers fall away because this is what you really want and decide. You will then discover the glory of living. Be in peace, be in God!"

–The Pathwork® Guide

Chapter 3

The Ego's Cooperation With or Obstruction of the Real Self

As we make our way along our path of self-realization, these words can act like a spiritual bulldozer for the barriers we encounter in our psyche. For at some point, we will come to a crossroads. What we are now facing is a very old inner landscape that is littered with our fears: fear of death, fear of life, fear of pleasure, fear of feelings, fear of giving up control, fear of being real, and the like. It's already taken some genuine fortitude to come this far and see that this is what we've been covering up. Such fears have been hiding all along in the darkness of our psyche.

To our surprise and dismay, this is where we're at. And now that we're more aware of our many fears, we automatically start to feel the effect they are having on our life: What they make us do and how they make us pull back from life. No wonder we have this vague feeling we're missing out on life. We are. We literally fear the creative process of living and therefore we miss out on it.

It's time we find the common denominator behind all our fears so we can start unwinding the unnecessary cycles of fear, frustration and pain. If we have embarked on a path of self-discovery but haven't yet found our fears, don't worry, it will happen. It must. Then, when we see how we've been hiding from life because of our fears, these words can be applied retroactively to smooth the way. Let them plant a seed now that will bear fruit when the whole of your being is ready to see and resolve the problems in your life. And make no mistake, coping with our fears is the main problem we all face in life.

The nature of all our fears is that we misunderstand the function of our ego and how it relates to our Real Self. The problem we face in sorting out this relationship is that it's extremely subtle and therefore hard to put into words. What's more, as with all truths in life, it's chock full of apparent contradictions. That is, at least as long as we are steeped in duality. Once we get over the hump of thinking and living in a dualistic way, then two opposites can become equally true. And as we'll see, this applies to the ego and its relationship to the Real Self.

For example, it's true to say that the ego's exaggerated strength is the biggest hurdle to living a productive life. It's also true to say that a weak ego can't possibly create a healthy life. These are not opposites, people. They are both true.

Before going on, it's important we stress that humanity's plight of being unhappy is primarily due to our ignorance about our Real Self. Knowing it exists, as many of the more enlightened people do, is not the same as experiencing it—as living from there. If we had been educated to realize that the goal in life is to reach the place deep within—that this is infinitely better than the ego—we might explore and experiment and seek communication with our core. And voilà, we would reach our Real Self.

But alas, this is not the case. Instead, we go through life becoming more and more limited in our understandings and our goals. We ignore the idea that there is more to us than our ego. And even when we do manage to acknowledge that such a thing exists, we forget during ninety-five percent of our daily lives that this being lives and moves in us, and we live and move in it. We completely forget it exists!

In our ignorance, we fail to reach out for its wisdom. Instead, we stake our whole lives on our limited outer ego, never opening to the truths and feelings of our deeper selves. We blithely go about living as though there's nothing but the conscious mind of our ego-self, with its pushy self-will and immediately available thoughts. With such an attitude, we unwittingly shortchange ourselves by a lot.

In this land of cause and effect, there are several consequences for our forgetfulness. First, there's a question of identification. When we only identify with our ego—or outer conscious personality—we become off-balance and our lives lack meaning. Since our ego can't come anywhere near the resourcefulness of our Real Self, it's inevitable that we will feel frightened and insecure. And that describes the majority of human beings.

If we're only living from our ego, life will feel flat and uninspiring. So then where do we frantically turn? To substitute pleasures. But these are hollow, so they leave us exhausted and unsatisfied. The ego simply can't add flavor or deep feelings to life. Nor can it come up with anything profound, creative or wise. So then what can the ego do? It can only learn, collect and memorize other people's creative knowledge. Oh, and it can also copy and repeat. It's also good at remembering, sorting, selecting and making up its mind to go in a certain direction, such as inward or outward.

These are the functions of the ego. But feelings are not a function of the ego. It's also not the ego's function to experience deeply or know deeply, which is what it takes to be creative. Here, the word "creative" encapsulates more than just art. For when we are activated by our Real Self, every simple act involved in living can be creative. When we're cut off from our Real Self, on the other hand, every act will be uncreative, no matter how much effort we make.

In truth, acting from the Real Self is effortless. Wherever it shows up, effort is part of the equation, but it's always effortless effort. If that seems like a contradiction, well, it's not.

Fear of Death

Let's come back to those fears we mentioned. As we said, they come into being when we remain ignorant, living with false ideas and staying separated from our Real Self. Let's look more closely at the fear of death, since this casts such a pall over everyone's life. If we're mostly identified with our ego, our fear of death makes sense. After all, the ego does indeed die. If we haven't yet experienced the truth of our inner being, just making this statement might strike a chord of fear in us.

It's frightening for the very reason that so many people's sense of self stops at the edge of their ego. Yet, for anyone who has activated their Real Self and made it a daily reality, they are no longer afraid of death. Such a person feels and knows their immortal nature. We become filled with a reality that can only be one long continuum. That is, after all, the inherent nature of the Real Self. The limited logic of the ego is not able to explain or even comprehend this.

What happens when we give the ego an undue importance in our sense of being alive? It gets scared and sets up a vicious circle. For if we can't conceive of a reality beyond our limited ego, hearing that our ego-faculties might end will frighten us. It's only when we've experienced the stark reality of the Real Self that we realize how insufficient the ego is. Then we'll know perfectly well that the ego is inferior and fleeting, and we'll be fine with that. Fear of death, then, must only exist when our sense of self is attached exclusively to our ego-self.

At this stage we may not yet be able to experience the truth of our Real Self. And while intellectual understanding is a good start, just knowing of its existence won't do a thing to alleviate our fear. We must go further if we hope to do away with our fear of death. We will need to actualize the Real Self, and this requires passing through certain stages of personal self-development. Lip service will not get the job done.

Fear of Life

The next fear to talk about is fear of life. It's an inescapable truth that fear of death and fear of life are flip sides of the same coin. So whoever fears death must also fear life, and whoever fears life must fear death. It's only the experience of the Real Self that can reconcile these two apparent opposites. Then we'll be able to see that life and death are just the sunny and shadow sides of our particular form of consciousness. Nothing more and nothing less.

If we've attached our sense of identity to our ego, fear of life is justified. For the capacity of the ego to cope with life is dismal. In fact, the ego is downright insufficient in the area of living a productive life, leaving us feeling uncertain, insecure and highly inadequate. The Real Self, on the other hand, always has answers. This universal self is a solution-making machine, no matter the problem we're faced with. Any old experience then, regardless of how futile it may seem at first, can become a meaningful stepping stone that leads to expansion. The Real Self builds on our inherent potentials, making us feel more alive, deeply fulfilled and steadily stronger.

These are things that no one can say about the ego. The ego gets easily tripped up in apparently unsolvable problems and conflicts. It's totally adapted to the level of duality, where everything is this versus that, right versus wrong, black versus white, good versus bad. And this is a really bad way to approach most of life's troubles. Apart from the fact that truth cannot be found by looking at one side as black and the other as white, it leaves out a lot of other considerations.

The ego is stuck at the level of duality and can go no further, so it's not capable of bringing into harmony the truth that lives on both ends of any opposite. As such, the ego is horrible at finding solutions, making it feel perpetually trapped and anxious. All in all, identifying only with the ego will automatically create a pile of fear in our wake.

Fear of Pleasure

Now let's turn to fear of pleasure. If we're just starting out and still taking small steps on our spiritual path, this phrase "fear of pleasure" is going to sound absolutely incredible, the same way "fear of happiness" sounds nuts. At this point, you're likely to say, "Well, thankfully this doesn't apply to me." But here's the real situation: To whatever degree we feel unhappy, unfulfilled or empty, we must fear happiness, fulfillment and pleasure. No matter how much we yearn for these things with our conscious mind, if we don't have them, somewhere hidden in our unconscious, we fear them. It can't be otherwise. This equation always comes out even.

Our lives, in fact, demonstrate that we harbor causes *we ourselves* have set into motion. Our lives are never a product of circumstances beyond our control. What we experience comes from our own inner consciousness. The more self-discoveries we make along our spiritual path, the more we'll experience the truth of this for ourselves: We create whatever is amiss. It's important we never lose sight of this truth.

Now then, if we are human, we have fear of pleasure, happiness and fulfillment. This one applies to everyone. Step one is to become consciously aware that we even have this fear. Once we do so, it won't seem like such a puzzle that our life isn't landing us the goodies the way we want it to.

The more the ego cramps up trying to attain what it consciously wants—having forgotten that it alone can't attain the good stuff—the less fulfillment is possible. It's not so much that the ego obstructs happiness, but rather that it is blindly driven to act the way the fearful, unconscious part tells it to. In a sense, the ego is just being an obedient agent, but it's following destructive drives coming from our unconscious self that aren't aligned with truth. When faced with unfulfillment, instead of working to realign our erroneous, hidden parts with the truth, we spend our time rationalizing our unproductive behavior.

The work of giving up our ego—*from the perspective of the ego*—is going to seem terribly frightening. And right here, on this edge, is where so many get caught. From the ego's vantage point, this is an unsolvable puzzle, and it will continue to create the following conflict as long as we remain stuck here: Our lives can only unfold with delight, pleasure and creativity when we're no longer solely identified with our ego. And so, we must activate the Real Self.

To do this, we will need to let go of direct ego controls. The inner movements of our Real Self will not surrender to our ego and its outer thoughts and will, no matter how hard we try. We must find the courage and trust to surrender to the inner movement.

Think back to a heightened moment in life that felt pleasurable, inspired, effortless, creative. Such an experience was deeply joyful precisely because we had been willing to let go. For a time, we were animated by something other than our ego. Happiness is the natural byproduct in such a moment. We can't be our Real Self without being happy. And we can't be happy unless we are connected with our Real Self and enlivened by it. Such happiness is free from fear that the good times must end. It stimulates and excites us, making us feel vibrantly alive and peaceful.

The concepts of peace and excitement are then no longer split, as happens with the duality-draped ego. From the stance of the ego, peacefulness excludes excitement, making it boring. Excitement excludes peace, creating tension and anxiety. To live from our Real Self is to be free from such unnecessary choices.

And so here we are, trapped in this dilemma: How can I fearlessly embrace a state that asks me to let go of my ego faculties, when my ego is all I know? Unless we start to see our fear of happiness in this light, we will not find our way out of this trap.

Until we do, we will waffle between terror at letting go and hopelessness. We will feel haunted by this feeling that we're missing out on life, lacking something essential. And for as long as we cling to our ego, this will be true. We will miss out on the very essence of who we are.

Fear of Letting Go

Now we've come to the fear of letting go. As we've said many times, if we derive our sense of self exclusively from our ego, letting go will look a lot like annihilation. But once we've made some inroads, here and there, little by little, we'll soon see that letting go doesn't bring danger, it brings life itself.

Slowly, we will adjust to the new vibrations. For there's no conflict between being in a body and living with these new conditions. None at all. The ego is perfectly capable of interacting harmoniously with the Real Self. Plus, the ego still has its functions, as well as its limitations and its own power.

We'll return to this in a moment. First, let's note that when we fear our Real Self, we're not only going to fear life, death, pleasure and a whole host of other things, we're going to fear our feelings. Second, it's clear that feelings cannot be controlled by the ego. If we think it's the other way around, we are deceiving ourselves. Trying to do so kills the freedom and spontaneity of our Real Self.

Feelings don't respond to orders, either from our ego or from someone else. Rather, they have a life of their own, coming about indirectly and independently. They follow their own laws, their own logic, and their own wisdom. We will be much further ahead if we work to understand how they operate than to deny them or superimpose the puny laws and logic of our ego on them.

Feelings are an expression of the creative process emanating from our Real Self. And we can't force this process. That said, we can encourage or discourage feelings in the same way we can encourage or discourage the creative process. They are both inner movements, which could also be called soul movements, that give us messages we would do well to heed. Such signs point us toward self-realization and help us establish contact with our Real Self.

Our Real Self exudes a vital flow of energy that consists of a variety of different streams. We call this a transmission of life force. It's a tremendous power as well as a consciousness. It contains deep wisdom and follows eternal, immutable spiritual laws. Exploring and understanding these laws can enrich our lives immeasurably.

To deny the intense ecstasy of this life force—which manifests on all levels of existence, in some areas more intensely than others—is to court death in various degrees. To embrace this life force is to live deathlessly. So denying the pleasure of life *is* death.

Death came into existence because the ego came into existence. The ego, then, is a split off particle of the greater consciousness that remains in all human beings. Unless the split-off part, the ego, is integrated with its origin, it dies. So splitting off and death go hand-in-hand. In the same way, reconnecting and living are tied together. So ego existence, death and living without pleasure are intimately linked, as are life, pleasure supreme and the Real Self.

Therefore, whoever fears letting go of the ego—who also fears and denies pleasure—is dancing with death. This is actually the true meaning of death: to deny the original, true kernel of life. It's not hard to see why so many spiritual teachings have jumped to the erroneous conclusion that the ego must be done away with. As a result, many people are confused about the ego and what to do with it. Neglect it? Discard it? Crush it? Nothing could be further from the truth. Doing so only sends us over to the opposite extreme, and extremes are always damaging, wrong and dangerous.

Lifetime after lifetime, people have overemphasized the ego, mistakenly believing that this is the only safety net there is. Many believe the ego is safety itself, and so they become very tired. For soul movements based on error are exhausting. People also cramp up in an effort to desperately hang on. Then they turn to a variety of false means, hoping for relief. But false ways weaken the ego.

If, on one hand, the ego is too strong, it will always be weak on the other hand. This is really a very practical teaching to work with: To whatever extent we're afraid to let go of our ego control—because we think letting go will cause us to lose strength—to that extent we'll be afraid to assert ourselves. To whatever extent we are able to surrender—to our feelings, the creative process, the unknown aspects of life, to our partner—the stronger we must become.

When we let go, we won't be afraid of making mistakes, making decisions or meeting difficulties. We will be able to rely on our own resources, and we will be willing to pay the price to have self-autonomy. We will have the integrity of our own perspectives and be able to assert our rights, as we meet our obligations freely and willingly. We will no longer act because we fear authority or because we fear the consequences of someone not approving of us.

When we have a strong, healthy ego and can assert ourselves like this, then self-surrender will be possible. But if we have such a weak ego that we fear self-responsibility, both self-surrender and pleasure will be impossible. If we are someone who habitually overworks and exhausts our ego faculties, then we are a good candidate for finding a false solution. While such escapes may take many forms, one of the more crass forms is insanity, where the ego loses all ability to function.

In less crass forms, we develop neurotic tendencies that prevent us from taking self-responsibility. For others, drugs and alcohol are the artificial means used to get relief from an overly tense ego that's deprived of pleasure and too frightened to surrender to the Real Self.

The Work of the Ego

It's important we comprehend what the ego can and cannot do. We need to know its limits. Most importantly, we need to realize this: the ego is only a servant to the greater being inside. Its primary function is to intentionally seek contact with our greater self. The ego needs to know its place. Its strength lies in deciding to make contact and ask for help from our Higher Self. The goal is for the ego to establish permanent contact.

In addition, the ego is given the task of discovering any obstructions that lie between it and the greater self. Here too, the task is limited. Self-realization always arises from within, from the Real Self, but it comes in response to the ego's wish to uncover errors and destructiveness, and restore falseness to its truthful nature. In other words, the ego has a job to do in the process of self-development: formulate our thoughts, intentions, desires and decisions. But there's a limit to how far it can go.

After the ego has decided for truthfulness, integrity and honesty, making an effort and working with good will, it needs to step aside and allow the Real Self to come forward. This universal life force will bring forward intuition and inspiration to guide a person on their path. But the ego's job is not one-and-done. Over and over, the ego must select, decide and intend, if we want to stay true to our path of personal self-development.

The ego is capable of learning, so it must become willing to learn from within, understanding the deeper language of the unconscious. At first, everything may seem garbled and obscure. As we go along, things will become more and more obvious. Our ego needs to learn how to interpret the destructive messages that come from our unconscious and tell them apart from the messages emanating from the still deeper unconscious Real Self. For this is where wonderful creativity and constructiveness bubble forth from.

To do our inner work, the ego must bring focused effort, a good attitude, and pay wholehearted attention. It must know its limits regarding deep wisdom, and tune into the rhythm and timing of the work. It must gather strength for persevering when the going gets hard, and yet be willing to call on the unlimited resources of the Real Self.

Over time, the ego must develop the finesse to sense when it should be more alert and when it should back off so the Real Self can shine through. It must learn to roll with the subtle interplay between being strong and assertive—to overcome resistance, and ferret out excuses and rationalizations—and stepping aside to listen and learn. The ego, then, is like hands that move toward the source of life, and then, when their function is to receive, open and stop moving.

Paying the Price

These teachings are rich and powerful. It's worth taking the time to study them deeply, sentence by sentence, and meditate on them. We should consider how to make use of this material, not just by understanding it theoretically, but by also seeking out that part of ourselves that is eternal.

To know this wonderful, truly adequate part of ourselves is our birthright. And given how valuable such connection is, it makes sense that it won't come easy or cheap. The price we must pay comes in the form of making the effort to overcome our resistance and laziness, and giving up our artificial means of escape.

The other thing we must do is explore the conditions that make it possible to connect with our Real Self. In short, our ego must become compatible with our Real Self. We'll need to have the courage to find our own truth, for the Real Self is not beholden to outer laws of morality. We must find our own inner compass rather than simply give our allegiance to public opinion, society or an outer authority.

The ego then is not being asked to submit, for submission happens from a cowardly place of fear and greed. And we're also not condemning outer morality. We are only saying that outer morality is not the driver for true inner morality. The Real Self holds exacting standards of real morality that are of a far deeper nature.

We must look for where we are selfish and cruel, self-centered, greedy and dishonest. Even if there is only a small particle in our soul, we must discover it. For every such particle, no matter how it is diluted by kindness or genuine goodness, stands in our way—especially when we attempt to sweep it under a rug.

If we cheat ourselves by trying to cheat life in any way, we are making ourselves incompatible with our Real Self. So our work must be to find where and how we cheat. These areas may be well hidden, but if we are unhappy in any way, they exist. And they are separating us from our Real Self.

"Be in peace, be blessed, be in God!
–The Pathwork® Guide

Chapter 4

How Unconscious Negativity Stops the Ego from Surrendering

We have been looking at the relationship between our ego-consciousness and universal intelligence. When we are primarily functioning from our ego, we are going to be out of balance and mired in problems. We can also turn this around and state that if we have inner problems, we will inevitably be unbalanced and enmeshed in outer conflicts. No matter which direction we come at this from, it always adds up the same: The ego has to learn to let go of itself.

A boatload of intellectual knowledge about the role the limited ego plays relative to the Real Self won't help us much. We must find a new approach inside ourselves that makes it possible to let go in a healthy, harmonious way. Let's shed some new light on this important topic.

When the ego operates in a vacuum, without replenishing itself at the inner source where our life force flows freely, it dries up, starves and withers. Literally, if left to handle the business of living without the benefit of support from the Real Self, the ego dies off. This shines a new light on the process of death, looking at it from this point of view.

This source of life is the universal self that dwells at the heart of every soul. When we incarnate, our spiritual being condenses into the coarse matter that this material world is made up of. Such a condensation into matter happens because a separated part of the overall consciousness—the part we call the ego—is disconnected from the whole, from the universal self. This disconnectedness causes the ego state, which in turn results in this material life. And that is how we come to this experience of the cycles of life and death. If any of us overcomes separation, we are released from the process of dying. When we no longer fear letting go of ourselves—from our ego—a reconnection with the universal forces becomes possible. This is not something to hope for in the hereafter. It can take place at any time, in any place, since it's a question of our state of consciousness.

Three Replenishing States

One of the ways we regularly replenish ourselves is by entering into the state we call sleep. If we are unable to sleep—if we experience insomnia—this is a sign that we are enmeshed in our ego and therefore deeply troubled. Since the ego is too predominant, we can't relinquish ourselves to the involuntary forces of life. We are hindered by the ego that won't let go of the reins.

We may not be conscious that this is what we're doing, but nonetheless, we're doing this. If we fear and reject the forces of the Real Self, the automatic and temporary ways we submerge into it are blocked off. Sleep, then, is a state that lets the ego rest from tensions and chores. There is a particular strength that we gain from this immersion into the divine ocean of being. But if our ego is overactive, sleep can't come and we miss out on this most primitive and universal form of rejuvenation.

Another state that replenishes us is mutual love. When we let go through intense, healthy self-forgetting, we dip into the vast sea of beauty and universal power. This happens when we accept and merge with another "sphere," or person. By melting into another being, we make ourselves compatible with the universal life force, and have an experience that fills every level of our being: mental, physical, emotional and spiritual. Therefore, a loving sexual connection is the most complete spiritual experience we can have.

By partaking of our Real Self, we are nourished by this creative substance in all its splendor. By letting go, the ego becomes temporarily immersed, resulting in a temporary release of its duties. But it reemerges stronger and better than before! The ego actually becomes wiser and more flexible, and filled up with pleasure. Once it has dipped into this heavenly ocean, the ego will be forever changed.

The ego not only is incredibly enriched, but its capacity to surrender and remain submerged in bliss—to be in love and in truth—expands proportionately. This intense melding of the ego with another is the most effective way for us to forget and transcend ourselves.

Another replenishing state is meditation. This is not a mental exercise, but a complete giving up of ourselves to the divine intelligence. We must do this to resolve specific issues, rather than in a general way. Wherever our personal hurdles—which often include fear—bar the door to our Real Self, meditating on them can help. If it is too easy, we are likely deceiving ourselves.

When we are able to overcome these hurdles—because our love of truth is greater than our attachment to our errors—we can surrender into the sea of wisdom that will revive and enliven us. As we drink in the truth, new wisdom can open many other inner doors as well.

In each of these instances, the ego gives itself up and then partakes of something greater inside. In a healthy life, ideally we are able to pursue and enjoy all of these experiences regularly. We create the possibility for this through our readiness, right attitude and engagement with life. When this happens, our whole life will eventually be activated by our greater Real Self, until it and our ego are one.

At that point, this greater intelligence takes over our lives, allowing the ego to flow and become flexible. We can relax, permeated with the knowledge, pleasure and power of our true spiritual being. Everything we do, no matter how mundane, can now be infused with the Real Self which operates freely, on its own. We won't need any effort to contact our Real Self, as there will no longer be fear or resistance to overcome. The more this takes place—we let go and merge with our Real Self—the more we will feel replenished.

What stops all this from happening are the inner obstructions our ego is not willing to remove. To whatever extent this is the case, life dries out and death creeps in. When we become completely dried out, physical death is the natural end result. So the cause of death? The separation of our own ego-self from our deeper, greater self.

Unhealthy Ways to Let Go

Ready to go a step further? Let's look more closely at the reasons we're so frightened of the very thing that gives us life. Why do we react the way we do, believing connection with the source of all life will annihilate us? Why do we insist on believing—either consciously or blindly—the kind of enlivening experiences we're talking about are dangerous? Why do we refuse to abandon control through our ego, and immerse ourselves in a vast sea of eternal consciousness and divine laws? Why do we stop ourselves and hinder all this?

For no matter how frantically we strive on the surface, underneath we are the life blockers. *Perhaps,* we think, *I'm just not made that way.* Not so. Longing for this contact can never be wiped out from the human heart, regardless how much conflict and confusion and fear there is. So what is it that causes us to cling to the attitudes that sink our chance to get replenished at the source, given the way this dries out the psyche and leads to death while making life unpleasant and bleak? Where did we get the idea that an ego-driven life is safe and preferred?

It's puzzling, right? In various other lectures, we've already pried open the lid on this a bit, and discovered some of the reasons—pseudo-reasons, really—we think have to protect ourselves from the exact thing that makes us alive and bright with well-being. We've looked at the shortsighted, wrong conclusions and defeatism that makes people so destructive we'd rather give up our life than "give in," or at least that's how it seems to us.

But now we have come to the place that everyone must eventually arrive at on their spiritual sojourn, where we stand at an extremely important threshold we must get across on our evolutionary journey.

Before we dive in, there's something to re-emphasize along these lines. Our need to let go of our ego is so great that when the fearful, distorted part of our personality faces this natural process, it will go in search of an unnatural way around. That's why so many people seek out the solace of drugs. That's why a person who can't sleep will search for a pill to take instead of doing the more difficult task of removing whatever blocks the ego in order to conquer the real problem.

Fear and inner distortions are also the reason a person whose ego has predominant control—and therefore they are not receiving sufficient replenishment—pursues self-destructive aims. To engage in self-destructive acts is to walk with death. We're courting it, and hastening our pace of reaching it. For when all other avenues for gaining relief fail, death becomes the great release we're looking for. We'd rather die than give up our false idea.

Our stubborn refusal to uncover the truth and all the self-destructive habits we resort to instead are essentially slow forms of suicide. To the same extent we fear death, we must also unconsciously long for it. And that longing stems from how unbearable it is for the isolated ego to be perpetually awake but not fully alive. So we are an ambivalent bunch.

On one hand, we fear letting go of our ego in a healthy way, while on the other hand, we're running headlong into unhealthy ways to let go. This is one of the dualities we must live with if we insist on staying separate.

Now it's time to look at the fundamental reason we fear the healthy state of letting go and allowing our Real Self to "live us," as it were. Why can't we trust this greater wisdom and more well-organized divine inner being? Let's lift the reasons out of the depths of our unconscious where they are resting for most of us. For we must see what's going on in the clear light of day. Otherwise, we'll end up trying to force ourselves to change before we're really clear about what's going on with our destructive attitudes. And nothing real can be accomplished that way. Change can only happen by clearing the obstructions, and never by plowing over the top of them.

The Root Cause of Not Letting Go

Here's the root cause of this condition so many are in, where the ego has primary control: *There is a spiritual law that makes it hazardous for the ego to let go, if the ego is hanging onto attitudes that are incompatible with the laws of the Real Self.* That's the key. So anywhere we insist on our destructive ways, it will be simply impossible to let go of our ego in a safe, healthy way.

And what are the healthy attitudes the ego needs to adopt? It must be loving, generous and open, as well as trusting, realistic and able to assert itself. These are the qualities we find in the greater reality and in the divine laws upon which the universe operates. To violate our Real Self is to hate and be weak, nurturing our separation, illusions and lack of trust. We'll have a tendency to damage ourselves instead of care for ourselves and act in ways that go against our best interests.

To live with such an unhealthy ego is to strive for the opposite of what it means to be divine. We won't be equipped to care for ourselves, so life will be fraught with fear. Insecurity will become our constant companion. Without being supported by anything of real substance, the ego will long to escape from tension and perpetual unpleasantness, and if it gets bad enough, may choose to liberate itself through insanity.

What does it look like to be destructive? We don't wish to be positive, to give our best in the areas where we are unhappy and in conflict. We refuse to see that we are the ones blocking fulfillment. And our lack of awareness makes it impossible to step across the threshold.

So it's imperative we start to see how we are being destructive. To do this, we can adopt the stance of the objective observer, seeing ourselves in a somewhat detached way for a while. Such self-evaluation will require a certain amount of self-acceptance and a determination to give up our illusions. We must also stop with all the self-glorification, pretending to be more than we are.

While much of the ego is conscious—we are aware of our behaviors—the ego also has an unconscious side. If the unconscious part of the ego is attached to a destructive attitude, this part is not compatible with the forces of the Real Self. Therefore, when such an ego lets go, there's no net. It's unsupported. It can find nothing to hold onto and becomes completely disorganized.

So an ego that is not guided and inspired by the Real Self can't cope with anything. It becomes completely disassociated from any intelligence. One could even say such an ego was "right" to not let go. For that's no way to live.

For as long as we refuse to give up our destructiveness, the ego must hold on if we want to retain some modicum of sanity. It's better, after all, to have an exaggerated sense of self, caused by an inflated ego, than it is to disintegrate. If the Real Self is not to be trusted, the ego that gives itself up has nothing to rely on. So if we don't trust the greater intelligence, we're left with the limited intelligence, logic and lawfulness of the ego realm. And that's not nothing. No matter how limited the separated ego mind is compared with the greater self, it still has some reasoning ability and limited grasp of reality. And let's face it, without the will of the ego, the divine will —even though it's greater— can't function either.

So there you have it, the reason we have so much fear about letting go. With this understanding, we can look at our lives from a different perspective. Namely, if we feel like we can't let go, that means we have some destructive forces running wild inside. Somewhere within, we have a will that wants to be destructive. This will means serious business. There is not some random force making us be destructive against our own will. No, we ourselves are the destroyer.

It will only seem like we're a victim as long as we refuse to admit to our destructive tendencies, which fly in the face of our tidy self-image. It's actually this destructiveness that's making us fearful and insecure, since we don't want to see it, let alone part with it. Seeing the situation from this perspective will help us eliminate self-delusion. And that alone will go a long way in lessening our destructiveness. Admittedly, we will still want to be destructive in certain areas, but it's good to be able to claim a little progress where we can.

The Truth about Destructiveness

What does it look like to be destructive? It may not be as bold and obvious as we might think. Often, it happens in the subtle way the ego clings to staying separate. Maybe we don't want to expand and be loving or kind. Perhaps we're vindictive, punishing others with our own suffering. Sickness can be one way to do this. Such vague, fleeting attitudes can be hard to catch. They can be so elusive, they almost seem non-existent. Until one day we get a glimpse, and then it becomes hard to "unsee" them. Then they become quite distinct, like a relief map that rises up and shows us the real lay of the land.

Perhaps we think, in the destructive corners of our mind, that no one really knows what we think and feel. Therefore, it doesn't really count. Right? This is a widespread attitude to our less desirable tendencies. We like to gloss over them, believing that by keeping them secret, they become invalid.

To go one further, we feel it is a gross injustice if our little pet destructive attitudes hidden in our inner closets produce any outer effect. "No one knew what I felt, only what I pretended to feel! And if I felt as I pretended to feel, it would be unjust for others to react the way they do." Buried in this thinking lies the illusion that life can be cheated.

This reflects the attitude so many have about life. It tells the story of how we often don't give ourselves honestly to this business of living, but make pretend appearances by which we hope to be judged and accordingly reap the fine rewards. Under these circumstances, kidding ourselves that life really could work this way, it becomes impossible for us to trust in life.

We must catch ourselves in action and see how we don't take life seriously, how we don't lend our best to life and whatever we do. To catch ourselves in action like this—to reveal our little hidden dishonesties—is a constructive activity that is compatible with our Real Self. It can start the minute we begin to say inside: "I want to give my best to this process of living. I want to contribute the very best forces within me. Wherever I don't do this and I'm too blind to see what I'm up to, I want my Real Self to guide me—to help me become aware. I wish to pay attention to what I am really doing." With a sincere attitude like this, we set something new into motion, right at the very instant we utter such positive thoughts.

The places to look are in the problem areas of our lives. Our daily difficulties hold our work and this approach holds the key to unlock our troubles. The more we cultivate an attitude like this, the more our ego becomes compatible with our Real Self. This reduces the fear of letting go of the ego in direct proportion to our sincerity. For it gives us something larger and more reliable to trust.

By calling upon the will of the divine, we will convince ourselves that the divine really exists, because we will personally experience its wisdom and utter goodness. If we access our Real Self, we can't help but discover its warm embrace of loving kindness that knows no conflict. Divine will works towards the good of all, creating fulfillment for everyone. This undivided intelligence is deeply safe and profoundly trustworthy.

But as long as the aims of our ego are diametrically opposed to divine will and spiritual laws, how can we trust it? How can we align with what we oppose? So when we feel shaky and insecure, scared and anxious inside—when we believe we don't matter—we must harbor a destructive attitude. There is a negativity in us that we aren't yet willing to give up.

Any time we feel anxious we can ask ourselves: "Where is my destructiveness? Where is my negativity? Where do I refuse to give of the divinity inside myself?

Loving Isn't the Answer?

In the final analysis, the basic virtues taught in so many religions should amount to happiness. For truly, if everything is boiled down to the very last, central point, it's always a question of love. But by preaching this for thousands of years, few people have gotten anywhere. Knowing that love is the key to the universe has never really helped anyone. Often, it's just made people more hypocritical.

Instead of doing the transformative work of unraveling their destructiveness, people have deluded themselves into believing they are loving, while underneath the surface they are not. They have covered over any feelings that are the opposite of love, and adorned themselves with a superficial veneer that gives the appearance of love. Such cover-ups are nothing more than self-deception, and most of the time others are not fooled.

How often do we claim that our biggest weakness is that we love so much? Meanwhile, we inwardly seethe with resentment and spite. We claim that the reason we're so possessive and dominating is that we love. But inwardly, we want full control so we can win and have our own way. We claim that our arrogant, unhealthy pride is self-love, but really we just want to be better than everyone else and not have to give them an inch.

These are the self-deceptions we must unmask. Even after we've made significant progress on our spiritual path, we can still be blind to such areas in ourselves. Any time we blindly hold onto such self-deceptions, it's a sign we don't want to give of ourselves. And that's a flagrant violation of the law of love. It's this violation that ultimately ails anyone who is troubled. This is what we must sniff out if we are suffering from unhappiness. "Where do I violate the law of love? Where do I hold myself back and remain separated? Where do I lack integrity, either with out-and-out lies or more subtle lies of omission? Where am I deluding myself? Where do I refuse to give, and refuse to budge?" These are important questions that we must ask, and we must answer. And the answer may lie in another direction from what we expect. What's true may be different from what we thought.

To live from our ego is to be trapped in insecurity, creating an insufficient life that is painfully limited. What a frightening reality. No one really wants their life to end. But alas, the separated ego must end. Only by struggling to find our way back to our Real Self, where we are once again in alignment with the law of love and also the law of truth, can our ego safely give itself up, and become one with the divine.

How to Become Unstuck

It's up to us to make the choice to continue to align with the negative. Do we want to continue to indulge ourselves in our resentments and self-pity, in building cases against others, and in the illusion that we are the injured party? All this gives us a certain a pleasure that we are reluctant to give up. Yet the price we pay for these luxuries is high, indeed.

As long as we choose *this* kind of pleasure—and all the pain, guilt and insecurity that comes with it—we forfeit feeling good. And feeling good is our birthright. But as long as we cherish feeling bad, feeling good will seem frightening. If, however, we give up our claim that we are a victim—which fuels our self-pity, resentments and blame of everyone whom we make responsible for our rotten lot in life—we will no longer fear good feelings.

If we clear away our negativity, then our trust will automatically be restored. It operates just like a see-saw. Let's look at self-dislike, for example. It doesn't work to just say we are done with this. Attempts such as this are sure to fail. But to whatever extent we remove the justified reasons we don't like ourselves, the self-dislike will stop, all by itself.

It's the same with trust. We will automatically begin to trust when we uncover the justified reasons for not trusting ourselves. For the universal life force is continually working to reestablish balance.

The best thing to do is to strengthen ourselves daily in meditation. We can say into ourselves: "I want to give up my destructiveness. If I can't do this yet, I ask my Real Self to help me see where I'm stuck, and help me out of the quagmire. This is what I really and truly want." Now, if we feel that in fact we don't want this, let's not gloss over this. For it is crucial to see and understand this obstacle.

This, then, becomes our new point of departure. From here we can say: "I want to discover why I don't want the good. What is stopping me from wanting good feelings?" In whatever area we find blocks, we can say: "I wish I could want this. What's stopping me? I want to give my best to seeing where and why I am stuck."

This is the way out of our stuckness. The way only becomes hopeless if we look away from the point where we're stuck.

Perhaps we notice that we flat-out dislike everyone. What's the way forward in this situation? First, we must realize that dislike of other people—which inevitably is wound up with a basic dislike for ourselves—is also a question of distrust. One possible area to explore is our tendency toward dramatization and over-exaggeration. We sometimes assume that what's happening to us is so bad, there are no redeeming circumstances possible. But we've exaggerated our bad situation and distorted it a hundredfold.

We now need to look at everything that has hurt us in the past—as far back as we can remember—as well as in the present, and see it with fresh eyes. Perhaps there's another meaning than the one we automatically assume. We see everything as though its locked and unchangeable, with no possible outcome that's not devastating.

It's our attitude that needs changing, along with our desire for seeing a better reality. We think we are seeing the whole situation, but from the purview of our ego, we are looking at a limited slice. We can ask: "Is this the whole truth? Could there be other aspects I am ignoring because I have closed myself off?"

We can also ask ourselves: "Do I want to like people?" Maybe our mind says we *need* to like people, but we resist. Just by becoming aware of such an inner conflict will take us many miles along our spiritual path. And awareness is a required prerequisite for making our way out of our suffering. Awareness then is necessary for seeing the side that says No.

With this realization of our inner No, we can ask: "Why not?" Instead of coming up with a general theory, it will be much more helpful if we can come up with a specific answer that truly applies to us. Consider taking a new approach to understanding *why* we don't wish to like people. Let the childish, illogical, irrational answers come forth. Allow anything that comes forth to have some space. This is the way to discover the real truth about our inner No.

It's the same for anyone: Before we can develop our capacity to love, we must first become willing to love. For if we lack that essential willingness, there is nothing that can be done. Willingness is truly the crux of the matter, and it has to exist on all levels for our loving to be whole. If it only exists on the surface, our relationships will also only go an inch deep.

What we often do instead is ignore the fact that we are unwilling to love— we're unaware of our hidden inner No—and then complain mercilessly about the results. *We're a victim,* we cry! We waste tons of energy on complaining and feeling like a victim, energy that could have been used looking for why we don't want to love. We find ourselves locked in a vicious circle, projecting our ills onto the world and not realizing that we hold the key.

With this key, however, we can start to understand our loneliness and give up our belief that fate is playing a horrible trick on us. What a wonderful relief. But no one can give us the answers from outside. The truth can only come from within. Fortunately, that is entirely possible.

Our destructiveness and misunderstandings about life hang onto us only because we hang onto them. Once they're out in the open, it's relatively easy to overcome them. Such a transition is the most significant thing that could even happen in our lives. There is absolutely nothing that could ever equal this process.

Those of us who lack the courage to look at ourselves in truth—to give up our illusions—can't reach this transition. We can't abandon something we don't know we have. We can't give up a destructiveness we deny exists in us. Truth will bring us to love, and love without truth is not possible. These are indeed one.

There is a tremendous power available to us, and it becomes more and more available the more we tap into it. It's not dependent on anyone else, since it flows from the center of our being. It will flow and nourish us wherever we have freed ourselves from the shackles of ego domination.

"Be blessed, body, soul and mind. Be penetrated, all of you, with the love and the truth of the universe, so that they can help liberate you. Be in peace, be in God!"

–The Pathwork® Guide

Chapter 5

Living with Polar Opposites and Finding the Good in Being Selfish

Unhappiness is an indication of sickness. Usually, though, we interpret unhappiness the wrong way, causing us to fight whatever we think is making us unhappy. In our distorted thinking, we think whatever is manifesting is itself the sickness. Yet if we were living completely in harmony with our Real Self and its universal forces, we would not be sick or unhappy. So disharmony and sickness—really any discontentment—are an indicator of our inner health.

When we are unhappy, it is our Real Self—our spirit being—that's talking to us, sending the ego, or outer personality, the message that something should be changed. We are going about things the wrong way. This message arises from a desire to return to health, where we will be happy and in a state of well-being.

Being truthful in life is the same as feeling good in the deepest and best possible way, without reservation, and with security and self-liking. If we're moving through life in a way that is consistent with such a state, our innermost self will be content. So then, any neurosis—any stress, depression, anxiety, obsessive behavior—or unhappiness is a deeper sign that points to the reestablishment of health.

The more free our Real Self is the more clearly such a message will register with the ego. Some may call such an experience, "having a conscience." For a less developed person, whose Real Self is hidden and crusted over, such signs will register less with them. Such individuals can go for a very long time—perhaps many incarnations—without feeling their inner discontent. Their qualms, anxieties, doubts and pains about how they deviate from the truth at their core don't make it to the surface. When they violate their own integrity, they don't register any unhappiness. They might even feel a certain satisfaction at having given in to their destructiveness.

Neurosis then is not a problem, but a signal coming from a healthy spirit that's rebelling against the person's mismanagement of their soul. In our confusion, we combat the nonverbal language of the healthy spirit, thinking that's what is sick. We then try to adjust to an unhealthy life condition, assuming that to rebel against "reality" is to be immature, unrealistic and neurotic.

People who live in such an unrealistic way also tend to flee from self-responsibility. They deny any kind of frustration, and hope to give nothing but get it all. These are the decisions a person has made, and their choices need to be faced and changed.

The funny thing is, the more people ignore their birthright to be happy, the more they overlook these inner messages trying to set them straight, and the more they want to cheat and get away with giving nothing. There's a logical connection here. The more we believe we have to sacrifice our basic happiness because that's what's "good," "right," or "mature," the more we become deprived. Inevitably, the more this happens, the more ruthlessly selfish we become. Underground, we will develop a secret destructiveness.

At any moment, these pressurized emotions could erupt. The harder they are suppressed, the bigger will be the likelihood of a breakdown since they contrast so greatly with the false version of ourselves we're putting out. We'll return to this momentarily.

For now, let's look at an example of what can happen to a person who neglects personal self-development. No surprise, discontent will follow. But the conscious mind of the ego might misread that message, and make the wrong diagnosis. What's more, professional help might try to make the person accept their condition, believing their frantic struggles are caused by rebellion to authority, or some kind of self-destructive behavior that's sabotaging an otherwise safe and secure life. Our own resistance to looking for the real cause contributes to going astray.

What we're afraid of are the consequences to making a full commitment to our personal growth. It seems easier to just remain an unruly child. All this is hard to unwind because, in fact, there is likely also immature rebellion and self-destructiveness going on. But they are merely an effect and not the cause of the problem.

Hence, it's easy to be confused about what's health and what's not. Neurosis is sign of health—it is pointing us to health—and it's also a sickness. It's a message leading us to feel good again after having lost our way. Once again, we see how duality shows up and must be transcended.

From a dualistic perspective, we are either sick or we are healthy. So we look at our neurotic tendencies as though they are exclusively the sickness. True as that may be, it's equally true that they come from, and lead us toward, health. If we can approach everything we think and feel with this view, it will benefit us far more.

Dealing with Duality

Duality is the cause of all our tensions and confusions, our suffering and our fear. In duality, everything is split in half. One half is then judged as good and desirable, while the other half is seen as bad and unwanted. But this way of seeing and experiencing the world is not right.

Opposites should not be divided in such a fashion. In truth, only by reconciling opposites can we reach the state of unity. To arrive there, we'll need to transcend duality, meaning we'll need to face both sides and accept them both. Fortunately, doing so will relax our inner tension.

There are some dualities that we—as humans on this particular plane of consciousness—have made good progress in transcending. We see the polarity but no longer view one opposite as good and the other as bad. So from an evolutionary perspective, we're making progress. We've existed in prior states of consciousness where we weren't so evolved.

For example, we can look at the feminine and masculine principles. Only a person who is very disturbed will experience one as positive and the other as negative. Although the deep psyche of some people may still harbor obstructions that must be overcome, the average person doesn't see the division as representing opposites. Both are seen to be good and beautiful. They have a wonderful way of complementing each other, forming one unity, or whole. They both contain aspects of the divine creative universe.

Here's another example where, for the halfway healthy mind, opposites are transcended and seen as complementary facets: the forces of activity and passivity, which also relate to the expanding and restricting principles, or initiating and being receptive. So even in this largely dualistic state, more and more dualities are seen as mutually complementary rather than mutually exclusive. For instance, most everyone can agree that night and day each have their own value, function and charm. Only in a highly distorted person would we consider one good and battle against the other as being evil.

Perhaps these examples can help us open to the truth that in reality, it's this way with all opposites, even the ones we find hard to comprehend. But as we discussed, even the apparent opposites of health and sickness do not, in reality, represent something good and something bad. For each contains both.

Case in point, if we remain healthy while violating our spiritual needs for personal growth—to have feelings of love and deep experiences of pleasure and union with others—and we remain healthy while our ego isolates itself and is unable to feel, that is not good. Conversely, if we are sick and we see this as a symptom that can lead us back to health, that is good. As such, good and bad can't be divided down the middle. Both sides of any polarity are all good in their natural and undistorted state. Both sides are bad when error and distortion set in.

Life and Death

We struggle the most in reconciling opposites when it comes to the greatest polarity of all: life and death. But in truth, it can't be different even here. Both can be good, and both can be bad. The more we succeed in overcoming minor dualities, the better we will be able to grasp even this one. Both can be good and neither needs to be feared or fought against.

Once we start to see that any polarity, or duality, can be unified, we can discover the meaning and beauty in everything. But until we reach this stage in our own personal development, we cannot help but experience many opposites as good versus bad. To whatever degree we have evolved and realized our own divine nature, to that degree we will cease to experience life in this divided way. Only then will our soul find peace and our soul movements bring us delight.

For tension breeds unpleasure. It makes bliss impossible. But as long as we suffer under the illusion that there are things to fight against, tension will not stop. If we believe our soul is in danger, our soul currents contract and close up to the good of life. And since we are surrounded by opposites, we end up living in a constant state of tension, assuming only one half is good.

The consequence of continually grasping for the good is pain and frustration. And yet this is so confusing. After all, weren't we doing what's right by fighting against what's bad and only reaching for what's good? Why then are we so unhappy? Why the discontent? Why is our life so empty and lacking in joy?

Usually, our confusions aren't that conscious and cleanly stated. If they were, it would be a whole lot easier to challenge the premise that led to this distorted way of being in the world. Yet our difficulties are an illusion, just like the notion that the world splits into good and bad. They sure do seem real, though, given all the discomfort they create.

God and the Devil

We have been geared for century after century to see the world through the lens of good and bad. It's understandable that we've gotten lost in our confusion. We keep trying to resolve all our personal problems on this basis, and they never go away. We can't find real solutions that bring us peace, for the groundwork we start from is illusion, and so of course we get deeper and deeper entangled in error. Tremendous tension prevails.

Only in truthful perception do we accept both opposites, allowing them to mutually aid one another. In distortion, they short-circuit each other. Yet in the darkness of our confusion, we have to make a choice. How, though, can we do so successfully? What if things have become too lopsided? Then an eruption, such as a crisis, may occur. But if the distribution between the two sides is more balanced, then all power currents become inactivated. When this happens, the two opposite sides annul each other and both options look bad.

From here, we move into a state of numbness. We deaden our feelings and become lifeless. We can often point to a fear of feelings as the underlying cause of our deadness, but really, isn't such a fear based precisely on a dualistic struggle? We are struggling against polar forces in our inner lives.

We can understand this better by looking at the basic Yes and No-currents in our souls. The Yes-current is the principle that affirms life. It expands, opens, embraces and receives life. The No-current represents the principle that negates life. It retreats, denies and shrinks back into itself. We generally assume—perhaps even have a deep conviction—that only the Yes-current is good, while the No-current is sick and bad, and therefore undesirable.

Religion itself has furthered this division, making God good and the Devil bad. This is, at best, a half-truth. To blindly accept this is to bring untold confusion and pain onto ourselves. For the minute we believe this, we are involved in error. And all error can lead only to more error and misinterpretation of life. Eventually, we get incredibly lost in this maze.

Let's try to demonstrate this in the simplest way possible. Isn't it true that it's just as undesirable to say Yes to being destructive, as it is to say No to something positive? If we've got ourselves believing it is only and always good to say Yes, anytime we say No we'll have pangs of doubt and hesitation, uncertainty and guilt. This will happen even if it's in our best interest to say No.

These pangs may be quite subtle, filtering up from our unconscious or semi-conscious mind. The next link in this chain reaction is that we'll have trouble asserting ourselves. We will find it hard to claim our inherent rights, and it will be difficult to express healthy aggression.

Such a person is always going to feel compelled to submit. They can never say No to any demand, no matter how such a demand might exploit them. This is not true goodness.

Real goodness is based on freely giving love from a generous spirit that wants to give. Instead, there is a subtle fear that we can't claim anything good for ourselves. This is a lack of freedom that reduces our capacity to love. Below the surface, there is an increased sense of separateness and selfishness that are both destructive.

So even with the seemingly good versus bad notion of the Yes and No-currents, things aren't so black and white. It's never one against the other. We'd be completely in the wrong if we decided to adopt the affirmative principle for all situations, and give up the No-current across the board as well.

From the vantage point of the ego, which can only see in black and white, such a dualistic world view leads to error and confusion, suffering and tension. None of these things lead to true solutions. The only way to relieve the tension is to search for the good in both sides of all opposites. This alone leads to truth, to health and to the expansion of consciousness.

Every teaching from the Guide builds on this underlying theme. As we go further and further on our spiritual path, traveling deeper and deeper within ourselves, we need to keep gradually reorienting ourselves to align with the principle of unity. First, this applies to our thinking process; later we can apply it to our subtle emotional reactions. Slowly, our perceptions will shift.

Over time, we'll reach the point when we can easily embrace opposites. We'll see how both sides can be in truth, and both can be distorted. More and more, we will be able to recognize which is which. We will be able to feel, rather than judge, the difference.

Selfishness

Let's turn now to the topic of selfishness, which is incredibly important for everyone because it applies to every human psyche. As a result, it shows up in every person's life. It's a tricky subject, though, as it can easily be misunderstood by childish, self-centered people who want to proclaim their separated lives and destructive selfishness to be a sign of self-assertiveness and health.

Hopefully, if we've read this far, we've progressed far enough in our self-development that we can distinguish between healthy selfishness and the destructive kind. Try to avoid the trap of pretending that one is actually the other. If we stay out of that trap, we can find tremendous liberation in these words.

Generally speaking, people universally accept that it is wrong to be selfish—it's bad and undesirable—while any and all sorts of unselfishness are good and right, and therefore to be lauded. Rarely do we make the distinction that some kinds of selfishness are right and intrinsically healthy. These kinds guard our inalienable right to be happy, and they protect our ability to prosper and grow.

At the same time, we rarely notice that being unselfish has the potential to be self-destructive, exploiting others by the way we enslave ourselves. When we do this, we aren't genuinely concerned about other's rights. For only when we can be selfish in the healthy way are we capable of having genuine concern for the rights of others.

The origin of being selfish is actually healthy. It says: "I matter. I am an aspect of God and, as such, in my healthy and free state, I am happy. For only a happy person can spread happiness. Only a person growing according to their potential and their life plan is happy. So being happy and fulfilling my destiny is the same thing. I can't have one without the other.

"I am responsible for my own life and the shape it takes. No one can determine my growth for me, so no one else is in charge of my happiness. I won't pretend that I am unselfish so that I can 'buy them,' and subtly hitch my own responsibility onto them. I won't give up my rights, effectively enslaving myself, and fake how unselfish I am."

It's important we take this in as deeply as we can. It's not possible to assimilate it too much. Meditate on these words. We need to look for ways in which we inadvertently drift from this attitude. For the more we live in a self-responsible and healthy way, the more secure we will feel. Because security is what we feel when we are anchored in ourselves. When we are in truth, the divine kernel can sprout within and these roots become our anchor.

When our selfishness is fake, we lose our center. Then we are anchored in someone else for whom we sacrifice. This kind of sacrifice, though, is not made in genuine love. There is no free, spontaneous giving going on. In fact, when there is genuine love present, the idea of sacrifice is not there. Then the act of giving is so pleasing, it's as selfish as it is unselfish. Being unselfish *is* selfish, and the other way around.

In contrast, there is an inner bargaining taking place in sacrificial unselfishness. There is a sentimentality on the outside, and a secret desire to get away with something on the inside. On the outside, we pretend we are being good. But this goodness is loveless and in no way helps us grow.

When our security gets anchored in the approval of others, rather than in our Real Self, we are counting on it bringing self-respect and happiness to us. But we can't understand the messages being sent up from our soul. We're disconnected from our vital life center, so we flounder, flopping back and forth between contradictory alternatives. We get confused about what is right and what is wrong, for ourselves and for the people in our lives.

In this decentralized way of being, we head down a path in which being unselfish is correlated with unhappiness, which is correlated with being good. And we've only just gotten started. This error compounds, picking up speed as it goes. Many chain reactions spin off that have destructive emotions attached. Here are just a few of our errors: We deceive ourselves about what "being good" means. We mistake dependency for concern for the person we are dependent upon. Our helplessness and false humility turn into anger, rage and rebellion. The more we work to keep *these* under wraps—so as to not disturb the house of cards we have built—the greater discrepancy there is between our surface emotions and those that smolder underground.

The more we assume an outer unselfishness that's false, the more the ensuing hostility builds up a hidden selfishness that is wholly destructive. Now, emotionally, we don't care at all about others whom we would gladly elbow out of the way and out of all their rights. The other has no reality for us, for we have given no reality to our own self.

Where does our hidden desire to be selfish come from? Our fear and our guilt—which forms a seemingly insurmountable obstruction inside us—caused by how different the picture is on top from what's happening below.

If we don't know how to be selfish in a proper, healthy way, we have no sense of ourselves in reality. Then all of life becomes a game to see who can skate by the most easily, gaining the most while making the least amount of investment. For if we don't take ourselves seriously, as though our growth and happiness are something to be reckoned with, then how can we experience other people as real? And if others aren't real to us, how can we care about them and their true being?

When we are lost in the illusion that it is always bad to be selfish, and always good to be unselfish, duality and error are running amok. Inevitably there will be conflict between what's best for us and what's best for others. This will seem, indeed, like a real conflict. And on this either/or level, it is.

But once we transcend duality, such conflicts disappear. For what's good for our Real Self must—absolutely and inevitably—be good the other person's Real Self. Ultimate happiness and growth will be served for all. In the realm of universal truth, which is found in the depths of inner reality, there can never be any conflict between what's best for people. Conflicts only exist when we superimpose falseness, destructive selfishness and demands that exploit other people. Only those things that block the unfoldment of truth and happiness stand in our way.

When duality parses selfishness in such a way that it becomes destructive, that which destroys growth and happiness looks to be the right way to go. For the one who sacrifices, this lends a false humility, and therefore a false pride. The one who accepts the sacrifice then becomes an exploiter, although they do so under the guise of being righteous. Neither the one who falsely sacrifices nor the one who accepts and exploits are doing themselves any favors in terms of unfolding truth and beauty.

Even if, on the surface, it looks like this arrangement is righteous, can it be, really? What is happening in the psyches of the people involved? The one who accepts the sacrifice must have a mounting pile of guilt. But they can't allow themselves to look at it because then this flimsy structure that's been built might collapse. And they don't want to part with it. As already mentioned, anger and rebellion begin to simmer in the self-sacrificing person, covered over by a false sense of goodness and a sense in their psyche that they are a victim.

Why We Need Courage

When we reconcile the polarity between selfishness and unselfishness, we accept ourselves as the center of existence. We don't do this by crediting ourselves with being more important than anyone else, but by knowing that our ego is responsible for our life. It's the carrier, the captain who determines which way we should go.

Only then can we grasp that we are one with others *on the inside*. We'll have the experience and perception that our self-interest never interferes with the interest of another, not where it truly counts, on the deepest levels. But our healthy self-interest almost always interferes with someone else's egotistical self-interests. It is for this reason that it often takes a lot of courage and much struggle to follow one's true self-interest.

Ironically, we're surrounded by a world that fights this, deluding itself into claiming that when we follow our true self-interest, we are being egotistical and destructively selfish. This is why it is necessary for us to be strong enough to stand up to the disapproval of the world when we determine to follow our own spiritual path. If we are truly following our own spiritual path, it can't be anything but blissful. But since the world is geared to believe that anything blissful must be selfish and wrong, we're going to need a dose of independence to not be influenced by that, or feel falsely guilty doing something that deserves no guilt.

Of course, bliss will not be the first thing we experience. Sorry to say, we'll need to overcome quite a few obstructions and resistances before we come to feel that walking a path of growth is anything but drudgery, let alone blissful. And yet, it truly can be the most blissful experience imaginable. Before this truth can unfold for us, however, we'll need to eliminate all our self-deceptions.

If we understand this, and are ready to proceed from here doing the work of self-discovery, we are bound to experience a wonderful new awakening. We might begin by asking: "What makes me the most happy?" If we go deeply into answering this question, we'll find that what makes us truly happy must be constructive and bring growth. Whatever it is, it will connect us more with life, and therefore also with God.

Further, if we keep going with our inquiry, not hesitating, we'll find that what is in our best interest cannot go against the true interests of anyone else. Indeed, it supports further unfoldment for those whose egotistical, unhealthy interests play into our dependent and fearful self. This is the part of us that doesn't want to take self-responsibility. It's also possible that what's best for us goes against the interest of stagnation for ourselves and others.

Once we see this with clear eyes, and without sentimentality, we'll find the courage to be ourselves. It will arise from our truthful vision. Falsities will fall away, and with this, much suffering and tension will vanish. The simple kernel is all that will remain. This is the seed of growth and unfoldment in the soul. It bears the fruits of happiness, pleasure and vibrant stimulation. For this is the stuff the goodness of God's world is made of. It's a distortion of God's world to make something commendable that does not further the evolution of one's soul.

"Be blessed, all of you, my friends, be deeply in the truth of your divine being. Let yourself become more and more what you truly are—God."
    –The Pathwork® Guide

Chapter 6

Self-Identification Through the Stages of Awakening Consciousness

Now let's look at consciousness from a different angle. We humans have a hard time understanding that consciousness is something that permeates all of creation. Our human minds are geared to think of it as being exclusively related to the human form, associated with the brain and a byproduct of our personality. This is not so.

Consciousness does not need to be attached to a fixed form, so it's everywhere. It's also in everything, including of course every particle of matter. In inanimate matter, consciousness is solidified, the same way energy is petrified in an inanimate object. These two things—consciousness and energy—are not the same thing, but rather related aspects of manifestations of life.

As evolution follows its course, energy and consciousness become more and more mobile and vibrant, so things move faster. In the case of consciousness, it gains in awareness. For energy, it gains greater creativity to make forms and move about.

Over much time, consciousness has gone through separation. The process by which this has happened is impossible to spell out with words. The result though is that aspects of consciousness now float around, so to speak, in the universe. Every trait we can think of, every attitude known to mankind, every personality trait we can imagine is a manifestation of consciousness. And each particle of consciousness that is not yet integrated in the whole needs to be synthesized and unified with all that is, to create one harmonious whole.

We'll need to use our imaginations here to be able to follow along. For example, can we imagine that some familiar personality trait could exist separate from a person? That a trait is not the person *per se*, but a free-floating particle of overall consciousness?

It doesn't matter if the trait is good or evil. It could be any of these: love, perseverance, laziness, impatience, sloth, stubbornness, kindness or malice. Each must be incorporated into manifesting personalities. For that's the only

45

way for each to be harmonized and purified, enriching the consciousness that's manifesting and creating the conditions for the unification of consciousness as evolution unfolds.

About unification. It's important to realize that if an aspect of consciousness is destructive or disharmonious, it must remain separate. Any person who has done their own personal work can verify this. Positive traits, which are the constructive parts of consciousness, are a harmonious piece of the pie. They enrich the whole and expand the entire unified field. Human language is too limited to go further in trying to explain this, and at any rate, this teaching will benefit us most if the information is practical and not abstract.

Each aspect of consciousness has its own unique characteristics, such as vibrating at a certain rate, according to its nature. This is true for those we can detect with our five senses, as well as for many other sensory expressions we aren't able to perceive. For there are infinitely more colors, scents and tones than we know anything about.

Humans are a conglomeration of many, many aspects of consciousness. Some have always been pure, others have already been purified, and still other aspects are negative and destructive, and therefore separate, like appendages. Our task, when we incarnate, is to transform these isolated aspects and merge them into various aspects of consciousness. What a novel way to explain human existence!

This applies to humanity and also to other higher levels of consciousness where the struggle is not so painful or severe. Becoming aware that there *are* higher states can aid us in the work we need to do here. Our predicament is that we generally lack an understanding of what's going on *here*. We're blind about the struggles we get locked into, and this causes us to only make matters worse.

To whatever degree there is tension and struggle within a person, to that degree the various aspects of consciousness are at odds with each other. We flail about, trying to identify with one aspect or another, unaware of what this struggle is about. Going blindly through this maze, we're also unaware what our Real Self is, where it's located and how to find it in the midst of this muddle.

We're unsure if we are our best qualities, or if perhaps we're the strict conscience that berates us for our negative traits. Or are we maybe the destructive demon that's hiding inside? Which part is our best self? Is it our rage at this demon? Or the part that pretends the demon doesn't exist? Whether we know it or not, this kind of search is going on inside us, and it's better if we can become more conscious that this struggle exists. Any path of self-knowing is going to sooner or later need to grapple with these questions, for fundamentally, it's a problem of self-identity. Who are we, really?

Who Am I?

It's a problem that humans identify with any of the aspects we've mentioned at all. For we are not our negative traits, and we are also not the conscience that punishes us for them. We're not even our positive traits. Despite the fact that we've managed to integrate the positive parts into the whole of our being, that's not the same thing as identifying with them. It would be more correct to say this: I am the part which managed this integration by sorting, deciding, thinking, acting and willing. This is what allowed me to absorb into myself the aspects that were previously an appendage.

Each aspect of consciousness that we work to heal and absorb has a will of its own. If we have gotten started on a path of self-healing, we're probably aware of this by now. If we are blindly struggling and getting lost, we will be controlled by each of these various aspects because we haven't yet found our Real Self. Once we identify differently with our Real Self, we will find our power. Our blind involvement ensnarls us and pulls the plug on our creative energy. Our missing sense of self leads us to feelings of despair.

If, in our blindness, we mistakenly believe that we are only our destructive parts, we become tangled up in a special kind of inner battle. On one hand, we'll react with violent self-hate, self-punishment and self-annihilation. On the other hand, since we believe we are these negative traits, how can we ever want to give them up? Why even face them and try to figure them out?

Back and forth we are tossed between "I must remain as I am, unchanging and unimproved, for this is who I am and I don't want to stop existing," and "I am so terrible, I have no right to exist; I should punish myself right out of existence." If we believe this conflict to be real, how can we bear to face it? So we put the whole mess to sleep.

Then we go about life, living "as if." By pretending, we shift our identify to our mask. Now our struggle is to not expose the false pretense we're living under. And give up the pretense? Never. For the alternative is to dive back into that painful struggle. No wonder we have so much resistance! And yet, this is all such a waste. For none of it is even the true reality. There actually *is* a Real Self that is neither our worst aspects, nor our fear about existing, nor the cloak that attempts to cover all this up. Our main concern: We must find that Real Self.

Work with What We Can

Before our Real Self can manifest fully, there is already a part of it that is readily available to us right now: our conscious self at its best, as it is in this moment. It may only be a limited part of our greater being, but it is us. This is the "I" that needs to start making order out of all our confusion. It actually already shows up in many areas of our life, but we take it for granted. And to-date, we haven't yet brought it to bear on this situation where we're blindly controlled by a false identity and the consequences that result from this.

It is safe to identify with the "I" that is able to make a decision to truly face this conflict. This is the part of us that is able to observe what's going on. And to the degree we wake up and gain a higher degree of self-consciousness, it is possible for us to make decisions and choose our attitude. We can also turn this around and say that to the degree we make certain decisions and choose particular attitudes, our consciousness will awaken and expand.

Most people fail to put this part of consciousness that's immediately available to them to good use, using it where they experience the greatest suffering and conflict. We don't realize how much power this part of us has to help us sort out this problem of identity. But once we start to systematically do this, a major change is going to take place in our lives, and we'll reach a new stage in our development.

We can lean on our already existing knowledge of truth. We can rely on our ability to act with good will. We can call upon our capacity to be positive, courageous and committed in this struggle to find our identity. And we can choose how to proceed in dealing with this problem. To the exact degree we do these things, our consciousness will expand and become increasingly infused by spiritual consciousness.

If we aren't putting the consciousness we already can access to use in the way we conduct our lives, then spiritual consciousness is not going to manifest through us. But if we apply our existing consciousness, then new inspirations and understandings of profound wisdom will well up from the depths of our being.

But if we keep following the line of least resistance, giving in to blind involvement and giving up on discovering our true identity, we will settle for a sorry existence and remain stuck in the old rut of reacting out of habit and then justifying our bad behavior. If we keep indulging in compulsive behaviors and get lost in hopeless, negative thinking, we'll keep spinning in our unhappiness and our present consciousness can't be put to use.

As a result, our consciousness won't expand one iota, nor will it transmute and synthesize those negative traits it now falsely identifies with. From here, we can't bring in any deeper values, not if we won't work with the values already available to us. This is a spiritual law of life that applies on every level of our beings. We should not take this lightly.

What Area Do We Identify With?

Many of these teachings talk about the Higher Self, the Lower Self and the Mask Self. These three abbreviated terms actually cover a lot of ground, as each comprises many variations and subdivisions. For our convenience, we can classify certain aspects of consciousness according to which category it belongs in. Therefore, when we identify with a particular aspect or cluster of aspects, we will become submerged in that area of the self.

For example, one expression of the Higher Self is good will. But we have another will for good that is not an aspect of the Higher self, and we can easily confuse the two. They are, however, by no means the same. The second version is our will to be good for the sake of appearances. Here, our goodness is used to serve denying our badness, or Lower Self. We do this when the conscious part of us that decides and chooses doesn't want to take on the challenge of confronting our negative aspects.

Our destructive aspects—the demoniacal parts of us—are obviously at home in our Lower Self. So then how about the enormous guilt we feel about our destructive aspects that threatens to punish and even annihilate us over our Lower Self aspects—surely that's an expression of our Higher Self, right? No, it's not, although it easily poses for it. In fact, our guilt is more destructive than our destructiveness itself.

Our guilt arises entirely from our false self-identification. If we believe we actually are our demon, then the choice seems clear: we must annihilate ourselves. But we dread annihilation, which leaves us holding on to our demon. But if we will observe the demon, now we've taken a tiny little step that's just far enough for us to start identifying with the part of us that observes.

Don't forget, none of us are completely swallowed up by this struggle. If that were the case, we'd have no hope of ever getting out of it. So our negative aspects aren't all of us. We can find many aspects of our beings where we use the power of our creative thinking, expanding our mind and as a result, build something productive. But let's stay focused on those areas that aren't so shiny, where we aren't being productive or expansive.

As long as we are unable—or more aptly, unwilling—to notice our destructive bits, we'll be lost in them. From there, it's not possible to achieve proper self-identification. And although our desire to hide our destructiveness is worse than what we're hiding, it at least shows that we desire to be done with our destructiveness. As such, our desire to hide the destructiveness of our Lower Self is a misplaced, misread and misunderstood message coming from our Higher Self, which longs for freedom. So it's a wrong way of interpreting the longing of our Real Self and a wrong way of applying a solution.

Our Task

Let's return to the part of us that observes and see how we can better activate and utilize our conscious self. For we want to expand this aspect of ourselves, making room for universal consciousness to infiltrate it.

When we are first starting out on our spiritual path, our work is to disassemble our mask by giving up our defenses and overcoming our resistance to exposing our shameful faults. Oddly, what we experience is that acknowledging our negative traits brings a new freedom. Why is this so? The obvious answer is that by merely having the courage and honesty to see ourselves in truth is liberating and creates much-desired relief. But it's also more than that.

When we acknowledge a part of ourselves that is destructive, a very subtle yet distinct shift occurs in our identification. Before this, we were blindly acting out our destructiveness so we were helplessly controlled by these aspects. This is an indication that we believed them to be who we are.

Because we identified with them, we couldn't afford to acknowledge them. After all, they are unacceptable. But the moment we see what was previously unacceptable, we stop being unacceptable. Now we've become identified with the part of us that can and does decide to take a look.

Then, another part of us takes over that can actually do something about them. Starting out, this may only be to observe them and grope for an understanding of why they are here. But we are now in a totally different situation than before when we identified *with* the ugly traits.

The instant we identify them, we stop being identified with them. This is why it frees us just to acknowledge the worst parts of our personality after eons of battling with our resistance to see our current selves in truth. Once we make this clear distinction, it will become easier and easier to become more and more aware of ourselves, as we are right now.

When we do this—spot, watch and clearly describe what our destructive aspects are up to now—we will have found our Real Self with which we can safely identify. From here, we have lots of options, the most important right now being this ability to identify, observe and articulate. Doing so will dismantle our self-hate. But as long as we neglect this all-important process of identifying with our Real Self, there seems to be no way to avoid hating ourselves.

The power that we have now tapped into has additional capabilities. It can recognize and adopt new attitudes that are free from the self-judgment that feels so devastating. This part has the ability to judge negativity in a truthful way. But there's a world of difference between this kind of helpful critique and believing that what we judge is the truth of who we are. It's helpful to realize that this part of ourselves—the part that acknowledges our destructiveness—has other options available to it, making it much closer to our ultimate reality.

Notice how different it feels to realize that the task of being human is to carry negative aspects with us for the purpose of transforming them and re-integrating them with the whole. This perspective makes space for truthfulness without feeling hopeless. Notice how dignifying it feels to consider that we are undertaking this important task for the sake of evolution!

So when we arrive into this world, we bring negative aspects along with us. There are meaningful laws that determine which aspects we will bring, but every person fulfills an immense task by doing this work. Someone who doesn't offer to do this kind of work may, indeed, be quite purified already, and therefore relatively harmonious and evolved. But they are not contributing to universal evolution the way we are when we do this work of self-realization. Our task gives us a reason to feel great dignity, which outweighs the momentary suffering that accumulates from the fact that we've lost sight of who we truly are.

When we deal with the realms beyond duality, we routinely bump into apparent contradictions. This is just what happens when we approach ultimate reality. One of these is this: We must acknowledge our ugly aspects as being part of who we are, and take responsibility for them, before we can truly understand that this is not who we are. It's entirely possible to be responsible for them and not believe they are our only reality.

Only when we take responsibility for them do we come to this wonderful realization that we are not them. Rather, we are carrying something in us which we are willing to take responsibility of, for the purpose of evolution. Once we've taken this important step, we are ready for the next step: integration.

So to recap the steps we've taken so far:

1) We are half-asleep, living in a climate of not knowing who we are and blindly battling against everything we hate about ourselves, consciously, semi-consciously and unconsciously.

2) We start to wake up, observing and speaking clearly about what we don't like. We can feel now that this is just an aspect of us, and not the secret ultimate truth about who we are.

3) More and more, we are the "I" that observes, and we become aware that we can make new choices. We will discover options and possibilities we never dreamed of before, not by magic but by trying out ways of being we ignored before. Such new attitudes might include: self-acceptance that doesn't blow things out of proportion; learning from our missteps; perseverance to keep going, even when we don't have instant success; begin to have faith in the unknown potentials that will surface only when we adopt such winning attitudes.

After we have begun adopting such new ways of perceiving ourselves, we will be able to move on to the fourth and final step:

4) We will comprehend the reason for our negative, destructive aspects, and this will dissolve them so they can be re-integrated.

As our consciousness expands and merges with universal consciousness, spiritual reality can unfold even more. This is what it means to purify ourselves. To the extent we do this, leading our lives in such a way, the overall consciousness of the universe becomes less split off into separate particles. This is how we all work together to reach unification.

Taking the Next Step

When we consider everything just said, we will understand several important things. For starters, we will see how important it is that we recognize our demonic traits which are based on a distortion of truth. We will take responsibility for these destructive aspects of ourselves which, paradoxically, will free us from identifying with them. We will fully know who we are and see that the negative parts are just appendages, which we can re-incorporate into ourselves as we dissolve them. In doing so, their basic nature and energy can become part of the consciousness we are, walking freely in this world.

No matter how unpleasant our current reality may be, we can deal with it. By accepting and exploring it, we will no longer be frightened by it. The true power of our real selves—as they exist right in this moment—is that we have the ability to notice what's going on and make different choices. The steps toward realizing the greater divine consciousness that we are involve discovering and knowing the self in a new way.

Until we start taking these steps, our deepest, truest self will remain a theory and a potential. It will not be part of our current reality. We may know about it, even believe it exists. But we won't be able to access it until we apply the consciousness available to us right now to address our everyday problems.

As we work through these four stages, our conscious mind will open up to new wisdom and truth. Along with this will come energy, strong feelings, love, and a capacity to overcome painful opposites. Our lives will become enriched as we reorient ourselves toward creating more pleasure and joy.

When we start identifying with our Real Self, a deep shift takes place in which the seemingly bottomless terror we feel in our soul goes away. Many of us may not experience this terror consciously. But when we stand on the edge of our work, ready to cross the threshold from one state to another—as we prepare to change from being lost, blind and confused to becoming our Real Self—this terror will rise up. More correctly, we will become aware of our terror.

For some, this transitional period may last for weeks. For others, it may go on for many incarnations. It's our choice. We can hide our terror or face it. If we opt to face it head on, we'll move through this transitional phase more quickly. Hiding it gains us nothing. Either way, it will leave indelible marks on our life.

But our hidden fears aren't any less painful and life-limiting than this experience of terror. In fact, as these things go, just the opposite is true. The terror only exists because we don't yet know there is a Real Self beyond the negative aspects we hate. If we don't have enough courage to explore whether this fear is justified or not, we can't find out that it is not. We'll never learn the truth that we are much, much more than what we fear we are.

Much of humanity stands on the brink, wanting to make this step. But there we hesitate. For this brink feels like a cliff. So we settle for a half-baked existence. We don't cross over to the next state and the terror simmers in our souls. Then we deny this terror, pushing it down out of our awareness, where this repressed terror wreaks havoc on our personality. We become more and more lost, as we become more and more alienated from the nucleus of our being.

When we finally commit to facing our fears, the terror disappears. We discover that we can find out who we truly are. Life doesn't have to be awful. It can be full and rich, open and infinite. As soon as we start to observe ourselves, we change our identity and no longer feel a desire to annihilate ourselves. Nor do we need to hide our identity behind a mask, since our true identity is not the hateful demon or the petty, selfish ego. In short, by identifying with our Real Self, we remove the terror of annihilation. This is not just a fear of death, but a terror of being annihilated, which is not the same.

Making Choices

Let's go back to the conscious mind we have access to right now. It has the ability to observe the self—or a split off aspect of the self—and it has choices. And the attitude we choose towards our undesirable, undeveloped traits will make a difference. It's key to our expansion.

Awakening, or expanding our consciousness, is often believed to be a magical process that happens suddenly. It is not. The only way to wake up—to attain true spiritual consciousness—is to pay attention to the material in us that is currently not being fully realized. Every moment we are depressed or anxious, every time we feel hopeless or any other negative attitude about a situation, we have options.

But it will require an inner act of will on our part to awaken the sleeping forces and get them moving. When we use the available potential we have available to us to do this, a much greater power unfolds. This happens gradually and organically. Too often, people sit on a cushion or go through some other spiritual practice, waiting for a miracle to happen. Meanwhile, their mind is all tangled up in negativity. We'll either feel disappointed or disillusioned. But here's the truth: No exercise, effort or hope for grace will ever bring us genuine awareness, or make our Real Self manifest.

There is tremendous power in our thoughts. Most of us underestimate what we can do with this creative energy. As such, we neglect the power we hold to recreate a better life for ourselves. To make use of this power is challenging, but it is also a fascinating adventure. Right now, we can begin to explore the far recesses of our conscious mind, searching for new and better ways to meet our difficulties. What would be a more constructive way of reacting? We are not required to react the way we do. We have many thoughts and therefore many possibilities at our disposal. We can aim toward a new goal.

If we resist observing ourselves and shifting our identification, we will remain identified with what we hate most in ourselves. To the degree this is the case, we won't be able to access new options. But if we can pose this question to ourselves, "What attitude do I want to take towards what I observe in me that I don't like?" we will have made great strides.

Actually, knowing we can change our attitude is one of the most significant discoveries we can make at this phase of our spiritual journey. And it doesn't require a grand revelation from our Real Self. It simply means we're using what we've got to work with that, incidentally, we have made available to ourselves over the course of all the millennia we have been evolving.

What are our choices regarding our stance about what we observe? We can continue to be completely dismayed and hopeless, thinking it's impossible to change and ever be different—that this really is all there is to us. By the way, this is what we've been doing up until now, only without awareness. Or we could go in the equally wrong but opposite direction, imagining we have the power to make drastic changes overnight. This is no better or positive since it will inevitably also lead to disappointment, but with an added kick of justified negativity. Both unrealistic hopelessness and unrealistic magical hope are extremes, and each leads to a vicious circle that can never land us in our Real Self.

So are those the only options? Can't our mind come up with anything else? How about something like this: "Chances are good that as I go along, I will forget and get lost in blindness again. It's a conditioned reflex, but that doesn't mean this has to derail me. I am going to need to struggle again and again to find my way, groping for the key. I can do this, and I will do this. Gradually, I will get stronger and I will discover new energy and resources I didn't have before.

"I won't be deterred by the fact that it takes time to build something beautiful. I will have patience with myself. I will not childishly expect all my work to be done at once. I want to use all my powers to do this work, but I will also be realistic. I would like my Real Self to guide me. But if I can't yet hear what it is telling me—because starting out my energies may be too dense and my consciousness too dulled—I will trust and I will wait, and I won't give up.

"I want to give my best to this thing we call life. Over and over, I will try to observe what I don't like, and spell it out so I can identify it more easily in the future and not be identified with it. I will search for ways to understand everything I uncover, so eventually I will be able to grow out of it."

We have the option to choose an attitude like this. This isn't magic. It's a choice, and we can make it, starting now. In every dilemma, the option to observe and identify exists, instead of being submerged and lost. Knowledge already exists in us which we can bring to bear on whatever we find. Using the knowledge we have access to now will broaden the scope of what we can know and feel.

The more we do this, the more expanded we become. We will integrate our split-off aspects into the universal life force and we will become it. This happens best by opening up a three-way inner dialogue. The conscious self, or ego, must speak with the demonic aspects, or Lower Self, as well as with the divine self, or Higher Self. This allows the Higher Self to communicate directly with the Lower Self. Like any meaningful conversation, both sides can speak along any of these three pathways.

It may take some time on our spiritual path before we are ready to enter into such a dialog. But by observing ourselves, we set the wheels in motion for this to take place, as our Real Self—currently made up of both our Lower Self and our Higher Self—emerges. When we can hear these inner voices working together to uncover the truth, then we will know that this is who we really are. This is where our true power lies. In this place, there is nothing to fear.

"My friends, this lecture also requires diligent attention. Much of the material cannot be taken in at first because it is difficult. It requires you to concentrate your mind and use your good will, and also contact through meditation higher realms of spiritual reality and power to help you absorb and put to use what I have said."

–The Pathwork® Guide

Chapter 7
Inner and Outer Experience

Many spiritual philosophies agree that experience is all-important. We could even say the true meaning of life is to experience it, in all its many facets—to breathe in the full depth and breadth of it. But when a spirit being is called to this dualistic sphere—to this material plane—we are drawn here because it's a match for where we are in our development. Our consciousness is limited, so true reality is blurred out to a great extent.

The only way we can experience more of life is if we expand. Doing so requires us to come here, again and again, until all our blocks against life are gone, and we have tasted, savored and assimilated all of it. Then we can experience the totality of life, in all its splendor.

Usually when we hear the word "experience," we think of an outer experience. This, however, is not really the meaning of the word. The real meaning is inner experience. To wit, we can have outer experiences of all varieties, but if our inner experience is inhibited, the outer won't mean much.

We can travel far and wide. We can experience all kinds of situations, experimenting with every "experience" under the sun. We can look at life from every angle, experiencing art, science and nature. We can do all these things, learning everything our brains are able to master, but if our inner experience is dead, all these experiences will add little, if anything, to our life.

Actually, it is possible that such full outer experiences will add to our despair. For it's very disquieting to not understand the cause of what is happening. A person can have everything they ever wanted, and still, a nagging dissatisfaction remains. They can try to grab for more goodies, or run for more accomplishments, but living a fruitful life becomes ever more elusive. For the inner capacity to fully experience life has not been cultivated. The inner soil has not been prepared. Worse, it has been practically plowed under altogether.

The Importance of Feelings

For inner experience to be possible, we must be able to feel. If all our feelings have been blocked, then no inner experience can happen. When we deaden our feelings, we deaden all of life. As a result, we can't feel our lives. And so it is that we must return to the material existence again and again, until we learn to savor the experience, as best we can, given where we are on our spiritual journey.

To fully savor life, we will need to eliminate the defenses we have built against feeling our feelings. This means we will have to walk through our fear of painful feelings. We're going to need to accept what we fear, experiencing it as it shows up in this moment. Chances are good, the way we feel right now is the result of feelings from long ago that we never fully experienced. All this time they have been stagnating, and thereby creating a block in our system.

Whenever we fear a feeling, we block the experience. We go numb. Denial and this kind of emotional anesthesia often seem like the only protection we have against feeling awful pain and suffering. And yet, as we do our personal healing work, what we discover is this: What is really causing our suffering is our fight against what we fear.

Regardless what has been inflicted on us from the outside when we were helpless and defenseless, it won't cripple us if we learn to receive it in the right way—in a healthy way. This, friends, is the only way to rid ourselves of what is undesirable. When we dare to experience—inside ourselves—whatever comes to us, it will no longer be a threat.

Facing Our Worst Feeling

Now we'll look more deeply into the significance of our inner emotional experience. In particular, we'll explore what happens when we block our feelings, and therefore cut off our inner experience.

Of all our emotions, which is the most destructive? That would be fear. When we don't meet and transcend our fear, it becomes toxic. Fear is a poisonous energy that, when unconscious, will show up indirectly, making it even more debilitating. And the most insidious fear is fear of feelings. These are more destructive than a fear of something outside ourselves. For if we fear a real danger, we can overcome it. In some cases, we'll exaggerate a fear of some outer occurrence, which wouldn't be all that harmful, except that such a phobia must be an expression of a feeling we haven't recognized or felt.

We can deal with anything that is outside us through outer action. Feelings, though, can only be dealt with by experiencing them. And they can't be experienced when they are denied. When we are afraid of being rejected, not getting our way, or having our pride hurt, or when we're frightened of pain or loneliness, in all these cases, our primary feeling is fear.

Only by experiencing what we fear—let's say, rejection—will we experience the pain of it. So what we are basically dealing with is fear of pain. When we allow ourselves to go into the fear, we can experience the pain. Then the pain will release and go away, and we will have mastered a slice of life we won't need to avoid any more.

What we usually do is blindly avoid our fear of pain until we lose track of the fact that we fear a specific pain. We are no longer aware of why we feel numb and dead inside. When we do this, we create a magnetic block of energy in our psyche, which is a powerful force. And this magnetic block is going to draw to us the very experience we wanted to avoid.

Now the pain we were avoiding comes to us from the outside. This will happen time and again, until we can no longer run away from it. This is a spiritual law of life.

If we arrive into the world with such a fear, our life circumstances are going to bring forth the conditions we ran away from in a previous life. In other words, if the circumstances of our early life were hard—filled with pain and deprivation—and we once again protect ourselves by denying the pain, instead of fully experiencing it, later in life we will find those circumstances showing up that replicate those earlier conditions.

This will keep happening until we open up to what we fear and allow the experience to *be* in us. This is the only way to dissolve the associated pain. By fully savoring the painful experience, we truly overcome it. This dissolves the energy of the magnetic block, returning it to the general flow of life inside us. After that, the experience we feared will stop coming to us.

It's possible we have temporarily avoided the experience we fear by successfully using our inner defenses to so completely shut off life that nothing can touch us. And using our willpower, we may have built an eventful outer life that manages to fill our inner void, at least to some degree. This works, as long as we don't hold still. This, however, is nothing but a temporary peace before the storm.

Eventually, crisis will come, giving us another chance to overcome our fear. For the more we run, the more energy we invest in blocking off the feared feeling, the more potent the magnetic energy block becomes, the more certainly we will attract a crisis that could be just what we need to heal—if we choose to change our focus, and pay attention to our inner life.

The Value of Being Vulnerable

If we want to experience pleasure, joy and peace, we must become fearless and relaxed. This is the only way to fulfill our potential and expand our Real Self. If no part of our inner self had anything to cover up—if we had no inner territory we felt we needed to defend and protect—then we would enjoy our full potential for creativity and pleasure. But if we guard against any particle of imperfection—against any one kind of inner experience—then all types of experiences will be equally flattened. This is not hard to see.

If we go through life defended, protecting ourselves against our fear of pain—or really against any undesirable experience—we will tense up. For being guarded is the same as being tense. But pleasure and creativity require a state of relaxation. When we're holding tight against movement in our inner life, we can't express ourselves. We've separated ourselves from a vital part of ourselves. It's not a surprise then that we've lost touch with ourselves and no longer know who we are and what we're doing!

We live in a perpetually guarded state, although we don't consciously think of it this way. So the first step on our spiritual path will be to take a good, hard look at our defenses. Once we've done that, we can move on to the next question: What exactly am I guarding against? What we will always find is that we are defending against feeling a pain we have suffered.

We are not able to see, of course, what went on prior to this lifetime. But that's fine. This lifetime is all we need to see. Whatever pains we experienced early in this life are essentially the same ones we suffered last time. The accumulated energy blocks still reside in our system, attracting the same events over and over. They also make it impossible to meet new experiences cleanly, as though we were a fresh slate. The new difficult feelings are just added to the pool. On the other hand, once we empty this residual reservoir, having fully experienced everything we have accumulated in the past, we'll flow with new pains in a very different way.

First off, we will stay open and vulnerable through the experience, allow the pain to pass through us softly and gently. We won't fight the pain and we will fully know why we are in pain. By integrating a painful experience this way, the wave of pain will pass according to its nature—sometimes it will pass quickly, and sometimes it will go more slowly—on its way to dissolving into our inner stream of life.

Because we will be in an open and relaxed state, we will be able to access the inspiration and resources that would otherwise be blocked off. Guidance will come from within, helping us find new actions that will make a difference in our lives and the lives of those around us. We will be filled with a new and continually growing vibrancy when we live like this. What a joy it will be to know that all is well, everywhere.

But when we avoid the painful feelings we fear, and instead try to produce joy through the forceful use of our self-will—joy we can't have unless we live in an unguarded way—then our will must be smashed by life, again and again. For life—the life force that emanates from our core—cannot be manipulated by our small, fear-filled, controlling mind.

Any time we try to use a forcing current—"I refuse to experience this and I demand to experience that"—in place of the relaxed stream of consciousness, which is soul substance that flows like water, we unavoidably bring crisis onto our heads, creating more pain.

The Cause of an Identity Crisis

The duality we are familiar with as humans comes primarily from fear we haven't lived through and therefore haven't dissolved. In effect, we are saying, "I must not experience this." And that's what creates duality. Our fear generates both a Yes-current and a No-current and this split current is the whole basis upon which the painful state of duality sits. Such duality thrives in our state of avoiding. In avoidance, we close off to one thing, and that in turn creates an urgent, tense grabbing movement that goes in the opposite direction that stops the flow of life.

What follows from our strong inner denial are rage and violence. Our rage will dissolve when we give up our fear of pain by fully experiencing our old pain. The pain itself will dissolve back into its original nature, which is to be a peaceful, vibrant river of life flowing through our veins. We are each a vital part of this stream.

So our fear of feelings doesn't only block what wants to flow through us, but it also splits us into a fragmented state. The only way to achieve a higher, more unified state of consciousness is by going through what we fear. Unity can never happen by avoiding fear.

If fear of our feelings causes us to block off our capacity to feel, we will become impoverished—poor in spirit—and this creates the need to come up with a substitution. And what better substitution is there than the limited ego mind. In an effort to not feel how dead and spiritually poor we have become, and in order to feel like we exist, we use our outer mind way more than is natural.

In other words, if we aren't able to exist through our free-flowing, feeling selves, our will and our intellect will take over, putting themselves exclusively in charge of the part of us with deadened feelings. This will give us the temporary illusion that we are alive. But this aliveness is precarious, and in the long run, it's not even all that convincing. Because consciousness that lacks feeling lacks spark. Our life, in short, will have no sparkle.

Such an incomplete life will feel sterile and dried out. So then even if we arrive at the most brilliant formulations with our mind—a mind that is not unified with our deeper feeling experience—we will have secret moments when we doubt that we are real. We will doubt our own aliveness.

This is where we are at today in our present stage of evolution. We often have a highly developed mind, but we aren't able to fully live. We sometimes call this condition—being split off from our feeling selves—an identity crisis, which is what happens when we avoid and repress our feelings. We can't ever know who we truly are when our mind substitutes its so-called "life" for the real thing, which is the greater inner self that can feel.

Mental Traps Lead to Displacement

What happens to our feelings when we deny them? Like, sadness. Where does it go? When we tell ourselves, "I must not be sad. I should not be sad," we are essentially rebelling against the feeling of sadness. From this, we develop a misconception that being sad is a catastrophe. If we are sad, we will perish. We never fully articulate this—to ourselves, or to anyone else—but nonetheless, it kicks up fear.

What we assume to be true becomes exaggerated, turning the fear into terror. Now we have a terror of being sad, and this creates a compulsive urge to avoid being sad. If the circumstances of our lives force us to feel sad—and they will, as we inevitably attract what we fear—this terror may produce so much inner turmoil that we will, indeed, break down.

It's quite possible that we have no conscious awareness of how much re-bellious anger in us is fueling our terror, or of the misunderstanding we now hold about sadness, causing us to struggle so hard against it. Now when we experience sadness, in our current cut-off emotional state, it doesn't seem so bad. Now we think we can bear it. But the problem was not that the straight sadness couldn't be born.

The truth of the matter is this: We can easily bear any clean, straight feeling, no matter what it is or why we have it. What is unbearable—painful, hopeless and frightening—is this inner struggle created by our misconception. When it says in the Bible, "According to thy belief it shall be done unto thee," this is exactly what's being talked about. What is not meant is that there will be magic coming from heaven with rewards for the faithful and punishment for those who doubt. It is simply describing the dynamics we're talking about here.

It's the overactive mind that comes up with the image, "I will perish if I have to be sad," even if we're not conscious we're thinking this. With the mental concepts we build sustaining the belief that we can't bear to be sad—and that it is dangerous—we justify our refusing to feel sad. One way we do this is by building cases against anyone who makes us feel sad.

Our mind scrambles to justify why we shouldn't have to feel this terrible feeling. In this way, we build illusions. And it always seems incredibly hard to let go of our cherished illusions.

Whenever we deny an original experience—like feeling the pain of sadness—this feeling becomes displaced. Then we will experience it elsewhere, in other situations, where it will turn into things like self-pity, depression, hopelessness. These emotions actually *are* destructive, so indeed, they can take us down. By contrast, the original feeling of sadness—if we had experienced it fully and connected it with what made us sad—would have gone away. It would have run its natural course, assuming we didn't manipulate it by denying it or exaggerating it.

As one can imagine, it's extremely important for us to remember this and put it into practice. Otherwise our distortion of a feeling will create part of a vicious circle, and those are always most difficult to get out of. Another aspect of a vicious circle caused by denying sadness is denied anger and rage at life for making us sad.

Anger

Let's talk about anger. Anger, if we experience it cleanly when someone hurts us or damages us, will resolve itself. Pain is inflicted on us by other people when they deny their inner truth—their real inner feelings—just as much as we inflict pain on other people when we don't allow ourselves to experience what is. It doesn't matter if this is what any of us intended to do or not. And we can inflict pain on others by both what we do and what we don't do.

The climate of omission—of not receiving what we need—in the life of a child is actually more difficult to cope with because nothing actually occurred. There is nothing we can connect our pain to, making it harder to acknowledge and feel, which would eliminate it from our psyche. It's totally normal and healthy that we initially react to such with anger. But we need to understand that it could be possible to have such a reaction and not act destructively toward other people. Then we can accept our anger without judging or justifying ourselves to anyone.

By allowing ourselves to feel, and by following it through to the pain that caused it, we dissolve it. We become free. If we deny it instead, it turns into hostility and cruelty. This, of course, we'll need to cover up if we want to conform to the standards of our society. This is how we become further and further alienated from what we truly feel, while distorting the original feeling into something else that's harder to manage.

Loneliness and Despair

Let's look at what happens when we deny the original feelings of loneliness and despair, when we say inside ourselves, "I shouldn't ever have to feel this. I should be spared this experience of feeling despair." In this case, our denial causes our feeling of despair to turn into bitterness, faithlessness and isolation, which all contain an angst about there being no way out for us.

Were we to experience the original despair head on, without adding layers of mental concepts or conclusions, such a feeling would disappear fairly quickly. By feeling it, without making more of it than there is, we are tuning in to what is really happening in us. This will carry us through the tunnel of darkness and back into the light of life.

To experience momentary despair cleanly does not mean to subtly force a feeling of hopelessness, which is what results from a forcing current. A forcing current is what we use to manipulate life and the people we are now substituting for the ones who caused us the original hurt when we were a child. It says, "I demand you give me everything I ask for. You have to protect me from any and all unpleasant feelings. I will feel hopeless as a way to convince you to do this for me."

If we are able to decipher and admit to such an irrational message coming from our hidden inner selves, the artificial hopelessness—which is always unbearable—that we're using to manipulate others will give way to new insight. And this will lead us back to the original feeling we have been avoiding.

If we can make sense of our hidden messages this way, we will take a giant leap forward in self-awareness. We will go through the tunnel of original feelings, and on the other end we will land in the truth and good tidings of spiritual reality: Ultimately, life is safe.

The word "ultimately" does not refer to a faraway beyond. It refers to the ultimate moment when we have the faith and courage to truly explore what's inside us and feel what's there to feel. We arrive here whenever we let happen whatever is in us.

We arrive at the ultimate goal when we loosen up the hard, armor plating we have created to defend ourselves against uncomfortable feelings. When we let go of our defenses, we will feel and we will cry. We will tremble and we will writhe. This is how we cleanly and directly feel the original feeling. Then all residual feelings will slip away.

We will then have a new experience every day as the wave of life washes over us. We will no longer live behind an impenetrable wall that nothing can pass through—a wall through which nothing comes in and nothing gets out. Such a state is true isolation of a fearful being that is no longer in unity. Such a person sends a forcing current out into the world saying, "No, I will not feel this!" in a defended stance held up by tight denial.

Fear

Now let's turn to fear. When we deny fear, it morphs into a vague anxiety that is far more disturbing, for now we have nothing to focus on and so no way to cope with it. But if we face our fear directly, we cascade on to other feelings, including pain, anger, despair and the like. Then there is a way out. So anxiety has displaced fear and, as such, offers no way out.

If we are disturbed or feel vaguely irritated, and can't put our finger on what happened to us, we shouldn't just gloss over this. Doing so will only create more fragmented layers and disorientation. Our work is to focus on the sensations we feel, trusting in the fact that there is something tangible for us to find and deal with. We just need to take it out of hiding. This is the path that leads to a more full experience of both present and past feelings.

When we empty the well of old feelings, we will truly live in the present reality, and stop living in the illusion we are reacting to the present, when really we are reacting to a past we keep running to avoid.

Transforming Pain into Pleasure

Anyone who truly decides to travel into the center of their being can do so at any time. We only need to make the decision to look, feel and experience, and stop projecting onto the outside world what is inside us. We can let feelings happen to us, even feelings of disappointment, fear and pain. We can allow them to go to their resolution, transforming them back into the original flow of life. The good news is that when we do this, we will no longer fear our feelings and then those difficult feelings will gradually stop coming to us.

We need to understand that anything undesirable that happens to us comes only because we say No to it. "No, I must not have that experience. What can I do to avoid it?" Many of us start walking a spiritual path such as this, precisely because we're seeking a better way to avoid undesirable feelings. When it finally dawns on us that the exact opposite is true—that we must turn and go headlong into them—we turn and run away. We are unable, or unwilling, to accept the truth that avoidance is futile. Instead, we insist on our illusion.

It's of utmost importance then that we ask ourselves: "How afraid am I of a feeling in me? What feeling is it?" In truth, nothing happening outside us can be that frightening by itself. We are only scared of what it will do to us—what it will make us feel. But by going into the feeling we want to avoid, a miracle happens: the acceptance of pain transforms the pain into pleasure. Indeed, this can become a stark reality for us, not some principle we've heard about.

The less we block our painful feelings, the more—and more quickly—our pain will turn into pleasure. In this way, we can personally witness the process of unifying a duality.

Construction and Deconstruction

From here, we can go further on our path of self-transformation by alternating our present feeling with a deep, direct experience of residual feelings. We can learn to stop fighting against any of it, and in that way, we will—for the first time—lose fear. We can start right now. What are the feelings you fear? Really and truly face them. Now try to open up to feeling the feared feeling. Let happen what you thought you couldn't bear.

None of what we are talking about here is faraway philosophy. All of these concepts can be applied concretely, immediately. We can each verify them for ourselves, if we truly follow through and don't stop at half-measures. All those who have already done this will attest that what appears, at first, to be a frightening, black abyss turns out to be a tunnel, and on the other end, we come into light. Every single person can experience this. The abyss can never be bottomless, for the true nature of life is not darkness, but light. The true nature of life is not destruction, but construction.

The forces of life that are evil, destructive and demonic are rooted in our fear of experiencing what is in us: our feelings. Based on that fear, we build all our destructive defenses. That's the only reason destructiveness exists. It sets in because of our fear of feelings—of painful experiences. This causes us to become isolated and arrogant, greedy and cruel, selfish and denying of life.

Our denial makes us untruthful on the most vital level of our being: the inner level. Because if we deny what we feel, we aren't in truth with ourselves. And that is the definition of evil, if we are willing to use that word. Destructiveness is what lies behind the inner walls we all build against experiencing the truth of what is in us.

We are the ones converting constructive energy into destructive energy. We are lying to ourselves when we deny the experience of what we feel, falsifying our Real Self. We become so false that we stop knowing who we really are. In our denial, we create the false hope that we can eliminate any undesirable feeling by avoiding it. Our denial is also responsible for the creation of false hopelessness that the tunnel we must go through is really a bottomless pit of horror and annihilation. This is how we waste the life force available to us, by stemming against the truth. This is how we create our own unnecessary pain.

The Cleansing Process

Our unwillingness to face our original pain leads to the formation of insatiable, greedy demands. We believe these will spare us from all frustration and prevent us from being criticized. We demand to always be loved—and loved *our way*. Until we let go of these unreasonable demands and go through our original pain, we will be caught on the see-saw of submitting and rebelling, which is a very unpleasant vicious circle.

We will submit to the equally insatiable and unreasonable demands of others, joining in a power struggle with them for control. Our goal is to get them to finally do *our* bidding. We are ashamed of our submission—we hate ourselves for it—and so we rebel, believing we have to prove our "independence." In either instance, we are violating the interests of our Real Self. In neither case are we aware of what is blindly driving us into submission and rebellion.

To be truly independent, we have to stop making demands. And this will only happen when we are willing to experience whatever comes to us, knowing we are the ones who have produced it, and the place it really exists is inside us.

There are some who purport that children are not capable of reacting any other way to pain than by building defenses that make them go numb. This is only true when, in a previous life, the person did not fully experience residual pain and thereby do away with it. To whatever degree a person has done this— eliminated residual pain—then even in childhood, they will be able to experience severe circumstances in an undefended way.

Such a child will endure the pain and go all the way through it until it ceases on its own, and it will not leave a mark. This is what can happen when pain is fully felt. Feeling pain directly also makes us more resilient, giving us the ability to live a fruitful, productive life. And most definitely, it increases our capacity for experiencing deep feelings of pleasure.

This is the living principle behind "Do not resist evil." We'd have to be blind to not see that children have a great capacity for this. They can cry bitter tears one minute, then turn around and laugh with gusto the next, all because they let the pain take its natural course. It's only when we don't experience the pain that we instead become numb. We become deadened and destructive, and develop any number of neurotic tendencies. So no, we can't say it's true that children can't help but react the way they do—in this self-numbing way—to traumatic situations.

The full experience of feelings is hygiene for the soul. It keeps our spiritual selves from stagnating, when we allow the power within us to fill our whole organism—our spiritual, mental, emotional and physical being. This is the metabolism of our total self.

In the same way physical waste that is not eliminated creates disease in the body, so does unexpelled feeling material cause our souls to become diseased. The healing process that will unify our entire being involves: Committing to feel everything we are able to feel; observing the feelings we fear and the events that evoke those feelings; become willing to at least try to face our fears and experience our feelings.

This is the path to making our lives as full as possible, permeating us with the realization that we are now living our best life, and filling it with deep meaning.

"A lot of love is pouring forth for all of you. May you be able to feel it!"
–The Pathwork® Guide

Chapter 8
Commitment: Cause and Effect

Doing the hard work of deep personal self-development requires equal measures of courage, honesty and humility. The rewards we will receive—in proportion to our investment—are peace and fulfillment. Our problems will begin to unravel, which we may have long doubted in our hearts was even possible. We will start to form closer relationships that are more authentic.

The presence of intimate friends—people with whom we experience peace, light, hope, fulfillment and trusting closeness—or the lack thereof is a good gauge telling us whether something is amiss within. For this gauge is so exact! Our life circumstances reflect with great precision how well we are advancing on our spiritual path. No truer measurement exists.

We can never measure ourselves against anyone else. Wherever we are right now, might be just right for us. It may be the exact place we need to be. Knowing this can brighten our perspective and provide us with a shot of hope. Someone else, on the other hand, might find themselves at an identical inner crossroads, and yet that person may be lagging behind on their personal path.

It's entirely possible this other person won't accomplish the plan they had hoped to fulfill during this particular incarnation. That person, then, will be in strife—with others and/or themselves. The only reliable gauge for how we are doing on the plan for our lives is this: How do I feel about myself, my relationships and how my life is going?

Now let's turn our attention to how we should proceed once we've uncovered an intention to remain mired in negativity. We will need to keep exploring our negative intentionality, owning up to it in a spirit of honesty and openness. Then what comes next—after we are truly ready to let it go—will be to exchange it for positive intentionality.

The key is that we must have a complete understanding of what commitment means, on the one hand, and cause and effect on the other. At first glance, these two things may appear to be unrelated to our negative intentionality, but they are all intrinsically linked, and we're about to learn why.

The Cause: Commitment

We'll look at commitment first, starting with what it means to commit. We tend to throw this word around like we already know what it means, but often without having a true understanding. Above all, it means having single-pointed attention, giving ourselves wholeheartedly to whatever we are committing to. When we are committed, we give our best to whatever we're doing, allowing ourselves to focus on all aspects of the subject in front of us.

Commitment means we don't shy away from giving our all—all of our energy and our attention—using our finest thinking faculties as well as intuition, which we can open up to in meditation. The whole effort consists of using the following: physical energy, mental capacity, feelings and will. With each of these at our disposal, we will be able to activate dormant spiritual powers in service of any constructive new venture.

Such a holistic approach can only come about when we have full use of a will that's not broken apart by negative counterforces. In other words, if we want to be fully committed, we cannot have any negative intentionality.

Commitment is an aspect of anything we can imagine doing. It doesn't only apply to grand and significant undertakings, such as our spiritual path of self-evolution, which is the most important venture we can embark on in life. All the little mundane tasks of life also require commitment. To the degree we commit to something, to that degree it will give us pleasure and be free from conflict; it will be rewarding and focused in scope; it will have meaning and depth; it will succeed; and it will feel blessed.

Any time we give an undertaking our all—and not a drop less—it can only be satisfying and rewarding. But how often is this actually the case? It's relatively rare, indeed. Usually we give half an effort and call it good, then are confused and disappointed when we don't get the results we were hoping for.

This is where cause and effect comes into the equation. When we don't realize that the effect is the result of a cause we set into motion with our half-hearted commitment, a split happens in our consciousness that sets numerous negative chain reactions rolling. In our confusion, we feel helpless and steeped in a sense of injustice. Further, we are not even aware that we commit only part of ourselves while another part still says No. And since we disregard that this has anything to do with the outcome, we can't help but feel bitter.

The world, we believe, is a haphazard place, and there's no rhyme or reason to anything. This frightens us, causing us to become defensive and ruthless, distrusting, grabbing and anxious. Instead of working to fix the true problem—the negative counterforce that cripples our full commitment—we apply our life force to pushing others away, withdrawing into failure and giving up on making an effort.

When we can't find the link between cause and effect—in this case, between our lack of commitment and the frustration that results—we seek to make an adjustment, but go about it in the wrong way. The real culprit, whenever there is flagging commitment, is our negative intention.

Looking for Trouble

To find our negative intention, we must find the inner voice that says something like, "I don't want to give the best of my efforts, my attention, my feelings, my honesty, my anything. Whatever I do, it will be because I have to, or because of an ulterior motive like wanting to get a certain result without having to pay the price." It is monumentally important to be able to have an awareness of an inner attitude like this. It is the key to understanding other connections that also cannot be dispensed with along our path.

Just having the awareness is not enough, by itself. We have to establish the link between cause and effect. For it's entirely possible to become aware of our negative intentionality, yet fail to establish this link. In our work on our spiritual path, we must search for where we deliberately hold back with a spiteful attitude, at least to a certain extent. We must become aware of this fundamental truth: If there is some aspect of our lives we deplore and that causes us serious suffering, this is direct effect of causes we ourselves have set into motion with our negative intentionality.

Most often, though, we blame other people and their wrongdoings for our suffering, or chalk it up to bad luck, coincidence or some unfathomable "problem" with us that we simply can't figure out.

So here is the most important point of all this: We need to explore whatever makes us most unhappy in life. What do we suffer from? Is it something overt, like a problem with our partner, or maybe the lack of the proper partner? If so, we can ask ourselves: What is my intention here? Then, when we can find the voice saying, "No, I don't want to give love or this relationship my best," we will see the link to our suffering. Then we will have hooked up cause with effect.

If our problem is financial security, we can cast around inside until we find the negative intent that says, "I don't want to be able to take care of myself. Because if I do that, I will be letting my parents off the hook. Or I might be expected to give something I simply don't want to give." It's critical we see how our negative intent brings the result. And be aware, this happens regardless of how sneaky and subtle it is. Often, we'll find it hiding underneath a tense striving for some kind of fulfillment.

We can easily deceive ourselves with such overactivity, thinking this should do the trick to bring about the positive result we want. All the while, we continue to ignore the power of the hidden negative cause that is sure to extract an effect. Even after we become aware of our negative intention, it's entirely possible to discount how important it is. But if we're not even aware of it, now is as good a time as any to begin the excavation process by peeling back the layers of the inner regions of our mind and searching for clues about what's leading to the undesirable effect.

Where do we feel frightened or insecure? Where do we feel inadequate? Do we notice a tension or anxiety we can't explain? Do we feel guilty but don't know why, so we try to talk ourselves out of it since it seems so unjustified? Do we hate our weaknesses, or our lack of self-assertion? Friends, all these are effects of some negative intention that, on a certain level, is deliberate. We must find it and bring it out into the open.

For example, let's say we harbor a negative trait—something like spite, malice, rebelliousness, stubbornness, hate, pride—and it makes us feel guilty. Such guilt may find an outlet in guilt that is artificial and unjustified. After all, guilt is not a positive trait so it must lead to self-destructive acts. There's a good chance it can cause all the ills we'd like to be free from, like anxiety or lack of assertiveness. But the only way to be genuinely free from these things is if we make the connection between them and what's causing them—the negative intention. Then we can give up the negative intention.

If we don't become aware of this connection, we will feel like a persecuted victim. The more we're inclined to not admit to our negative intention, the more we'll try to capitalize on that position, hoping to "convince" life, fate and other people to give us what we want. We will lean all our weight on blaming self-pity, resentments and helplessness to get what can only come through a positive intention.

Positive intention requires a lot of commitment—totally and unequivocally. If we are not willing to invest ourselves like that, then we are wanting to use illegitimate means to get the results we want. This, of course, fires up guilt. And guilt ramps up our fear of meeting ourselves in honesty. Hence, we convince ourselves all the more that the trouble must be an outside factor. Or maybe, just maybe, it's something harmless within us. And so we go through life, with a vicious circle well underway.

Making the Mature Connection

Some people, after making some good headway on their spiritual path, get a glimpse of their negative intentionality. This is truly nice progress. But then we tend to forget it. We disregard that it is really having an effect. We fail to connect the dots. Then off we go on our merry way.

Others of us admit that we have a desire to hang onto our destructiveness.

We like our hateful, vengeful, vindictive selves, for example. And yet we miss the connection between our intent and our misery. But how could this not bring unwelcome effects from others? No matter how good we think we are at hiding our negative intention, and no matter how strongly we express our positive attitudes—which are also present—the negative component will color our actions and behaviors more than we realize. Plus, quite apart from that, our negative intent will invariably affect other people's soul substance, triggering unconscious reactions.

For the average person, a lot of perception is happening on the unconscious level, so we are ping ponging unconscious interactions with others under the table, all the time. While our conscious interactions may be civil enough, it's the unconscious one filled with rifts and troubles that both parties find mysterious. In our confusion, we respond with self-blame and deadness of feelings, which call forth the negativities in the other that they have not yet explored.

This is how negative interactions go, on and on and on. The only way to break the cycle is for a spiritually mature person to surface their unconscious perceptions of negative intent. And what a blessing this is. Such a person will be able to avoid the deadly confusion that otherwise arises, and to deal with the situation.

By seeing the relationship between cause and effect in our lives, we will be motivated to give up our negative attitudes and cultivate positive ones. This is how we gain spiritual and emotional maturity. After all, what is maturity but the ability, to a large extent, to put together cause and effect. Such an ability reflects a significant amount of awareness, typically gained by doing personal self-development work.

Consider an infant. When an infant hurts physically, it has no ability to connect cause and effect. An infant simply doesn't have the mental faculties yet to do this. Whatever is causing the pain is totally blotted from its conscious mind. The infant merely experiences the effect, which is the pain.

After the infant grows a bit and becomes a young child, it can start to infer cause and effect when they happen close together. So let's say a small child touches fire and gets burned. It will understand that fire is the cause and that the burning sensation is the effect. In this way, it learns a life lesson: to avoid the burning sensation, it must avoid touching fire. In this example, cause and effect are very close together in time. With this lesson, the child has obtained its first degree of maturity on the road of human development.

But this same child cannot yet correlate the relationship between cause and effect when there is a distance between the two things. A little further down the road, however, when the child is a little older, it will be able to realize that, say, a tummy-ache is connected with overeating a few hours earlier. So now a further degree of maturity has been reached.

The more mature we become, the greater will be our ability to connect cause and effect when the link is less obvious and occurs over a longer range of time. But if we remain emotionally and spiritually immature, we won't have sufficient awareness to trace cause and effect realistically. Such people can't see how their experiences—along with their state of mind—are directly linked to a certain set of causes.

They can't see that their past actions have brought effects, or that underhanded, inner attitudes will not go unnoticed. They may search high and low for the cause, hoping to find answers, and may even turn to look inside themselves. But if they can't close the gap between cause and effect, they'll go around and around in circles, instead of moving along a spiral, which is the true movement of a spiritual path.

Cause and Effect Over Lifetimes

From our human perspective, it does not appear that the relationship between cause and effect remains intact from one lifetime to the next. Only as we increase our level of awareness—by doing the healing work as outlined here— does a person mature enough, spiritually, to realize that causes from former lives are having effects here and now. At first we may sense this, and later, we will inwardly know that this so.

A deeply meaningful, inner knowing that explains key points about our life is a revelation we must earn through our personal work of self-healing. This is not the same as receiving a piece of information from a psychic regarding previous incarnations. Inner knowledge is something that comes about organically.

A psychic or clairvoyant person's ability to predict the future relies on their ability to perceive causes within someone's soul. And the lawful effects of those causes cannot fail to materialize. Many people do not understand what is really happening here, and so end up believing that some mysterious or supernatural thing is manifesting. Many wrong philosophies then spring from this misconception. One such off-base theory is the idea that our fates are predetermined.

Doing the work of self-healing is a maturing process that allows us to increasingly link up cause and effect. The growth in our awareness that's involved in this process ushers in so much peace and light! At first we might find it very uncomfortable to see how we are the ones who have created what we deplore. It can be hard to see that if we wish to have different experiences in life, we'll have to give up what we are fiercely hanging on to.

But once we perceive the beauty of these laws and accept them, a sense of safety and freedom will arise in us that is indescribable. The knowledge will convey to us, like nothing else ever could, just how safe, loving and just this universe is.

Things that seem like a fate beyond anyone's control—where we are born, as which sex, how we look, what our talents are—will be seen for what they are: self-caused and self-wanted, sometimes wisely and sometimes destructively. For everything is established based on cause and effect relationships that carry from one lifetime to the next.

This is the mechanism determining what seems to be our current fate, in this lifetime. For we each have both positive intentionality and negative intentionality in us. And each of these things creates entirely unique experiences and states of mind. Why would this principle change when an entity transitions from one body to another? There is nothing at all wrong with this principle. No exceptions, interruptions or changes are needed.

The Stages of a Spiritual Path
Purification

This path, and others like it, can be broken down into the following stages: First we struggle mightily to excavate deep inner layers. These are filled with 1) misconceptions, 2) negative intentionality and 3) residual pain. The approach varies somewhat for each person, but eventually, one and then another of these aspects must be explored.

Movement on an inner path is never a straight line. There will always be a considerable amount of movement back and forth. As we go along, we will explore more aspects, but the work of purification primarily focuses on these three areas: When we are 1) able to exchange deep misconceptions for the truth, and when we 2) are able to convert our negative intentionality into positive intentionality, and when 3) we no longer defend ourselves against the experience of pain, then a substantial step will have been made. The bulk of our initial purification will be complete.

What, essentially, is negative intentionality? It is a defense against experiencing pain. And misconceptions? They are a result of both our defending and our reacting to pain. So these three aspects are integrally connected. It is a sign of maturity to be able to experience what we ourselves have produced, and not fight it. A soul that is mature makes itself light, receiving its own innate feelings and savoring them fully. This is the only way to erase evil from this world. For all our defenses harbor evil, which is not hard to spot in any form of negativity. Evil then is born from our misconceptions.

On this evolutionary road we are on, it is the task of each human being to eliminate evil by changing it back into its original state of truthful, loving consciousness and pure, clean energy. It takes many lifetimes to get through this phase of the work—the purification phase.

Evil produces pain. Our fear of this pain and the defenses we build against pain produce more pain—which is actually a worse pain—as well as more evil. So our defenses are nothing but illusions that don't work. We can experience the truth of this the moment we fully open ourselves to the experience of pain. Note, we're not speaking here about false pain. That's the pain that is itself a defense. It's a twisted, unbearable, bitter pain that is derived from a forcing current that says, "Life, don't do this to me!"

This kind of pain lacks the mature willingness to let go and just let the real pain be what it is. When we experience real pain, we stop trying to control it, manipulate it or hide it. The pain simply is. In this way, we approach the state of being, with all its associated peace and bliss. We will be able to taste this more and more as we shed all our defenses, which will free us up to adopt a positive intention to give our best in life.

The false form of pain, which is still a defense, is filled with bitterness, self-pity and resentments. As such, it is a peace-destroyer. Real pain, on the other hand, is peaceful because we assume complete self-responsibility—without self-manipulation. We're not saying, "Poor me, this is what life is doing to me," nor are we saying, "I am so bad and hopeless that I can never be free." Neither of these attitudes is in truth, which makes them part and parcel of evil.

To experience real, undefended pain is to open the door to our soul and let in light. This is the way to expose the core of ourselves, with its vast stores of creativity, resiliency, and deep feeling and knowing. When we have learned to make ourselves available for whatever life offers—even if life occasionally offers us pain—we don't need to resort to negative intentionality.

After we have worked off our residual pain, should a new, current pain come along, we'll be able to experience it for what it is. We won't need to deny it or exaggerate it, and we won't need to layer on a bunch of artificial interpretations about what happened. And on that day, no misconceptions, no negative intentionality, no evil and no suffering can exist.

This is the state that brings an end to fear: no more fear of death, fear of life, fear of being, fear of feeling, or fear of loving. And don't forget, fear of experiencing the grand heights of universal life is the greatest fear in the world.

Transcendence through Transformation

To whatever degree evil exists—which we have just identified as our misconceptions, defenses, negative intentionality and refusal to experience the pain we ourselves have caused—bliss will be unbearable. So in the second major phase on a spiritual path, our soul must acclimatize itself to universal bliss. But we will need to evolve to this gradually. For even though our soul is now largely free from evil, we will need to develop the strength to withstand the enormous power that emanates from the Real Self.

The blissful, pure energy of the spirit is so strong that only the strongest and purest individuals can live comfortably in it. We'll taste the truth of this to some extent as we purify ourselves spiritually, only to discover how hard it is to be with pleasure, ecstasy and happiness. We feel more comfortable in the greyness we've gotten accustomed to.

The power of the universal spirit is not compatible with the slow moving energy of unexperienced pain, defenses and evil. This explains why people who were present during the transmission of these teachings would break into tears in response to the pure influx of spiritual power. The grip of strong feelings would cause people to cry, as it elicited old residual feelings of sadness, longing and pain. For whatever has not been experienced always slumbers within.

But even as people were experiencing the welling up of difficult feelings, they could also feel the spiritual nourishment, joyfulness and freedom that accompanied the love pouring forth. As we go forward, more joy will manifest, as it bubbles up from within. For it is our tears that open the channels of joy.

When we stay tightly defended, we make ourselves hard and "safe." Our willingness to expose the temporary truth of the evil that lives in us will give us the strength we need to let go, so that we can be able to feel and become more real. By no means does it serve us to justify our defensive hardness by doubting and judging. This, ultimately, is the way we defend ourselves against the truth of who we are. What folly! For we deal ourselves out of life and then complain bitterly about it.

When we are ready to commit, 100%, to feeling whatever is in us, then we can become free. Then we can wake up. As we let go of our defenses, then we can transition from bitter, hard false pain to the real pain that is soft, melting and joyous—yes, joyous. For real pain carries the germ of life embedded in it. This seed will soon take root in our consciousness and bloom, as we commit to our feelings and to experiencing life—with no holding back.

A joyful life is possible, if we will only give up our stubbornness; our ties with others can be enriching and warm. Each of us has taken on a great responsibility as part of our participation in the great plan. This responsibility is not a burden; it is a privilege. In fact, it is the greatest privilege a person can experience. Nothing could make any of us more happy, joyous and free than to come here and have the chance to heal ourselves.

To consider this responsibility an unwelcome burden or an undesirable constriction is the hallmark of immaturity. As we mature, we will discover the truth, which is that freedom and self-responsibility cannot be separated. If we are not willing to feel responsible, we can never be free.

Painful or Positive Interactions

Our negative intentionality is not ours alone, in that it breeds unhappiness which we then exude, spreading it to others. Whether we are aware we are doing this or not, it must leave a shadow of guilt in our soul. When we are unloving and withholding, we hurt others. We may not do this with our actions, but our invisible interactions with others are just as damaging, especially when the other person does not yet have enough awareness to grasp what is happening.

What happens on the physical level is the result, not the cause. What occurs in our inner reality is always the cause. This explains how a seemingly good outward action can end up with disastrous results, because covert negativity spoiled the day. On the other hand, an apparently bad situation may turn out to be blessing, if underlying motives were positive and in truth.

What happens on the unmanifest level is actually more real than what we perceive with our five senses. As such, negative intentionality can pack a stronger punch than the physical body can. If someone has already done considerable work to free themselves of their defenses, they will not be unaffected if someone hurts them, for they are aware. But since they will experience the hurt cleanly, they will be unscathed in the long run. The momentary hurt will not pile up in a residual pool of pain.

But as long as we're still doing battle with our masks and defenses, and also have not yet resolved our negative intentionality, we will feel a bitter pain. We'll feel rejected all over again, although we may not be conscious of our emotional reaction. It's our choice to make our pain conscious, embarking on a path of self-development. Or we can continue to justify, fortify and shore up our defensive walls.

The more good spiritual work we do, the more our responsibility grows. As we mature, the impact of what we put out into the world grows along with us. The bigger our light, the greater the shadow we cast with our negativity. This is an unalterable spiritual law.

At the same time, as we progress as individuals and collectively as groups, we generate positive energy that eclipses the work itself. Yes, the results of our efforts can be seen in the world, but the invisible benefits are greater, far surpassing what we can comprehend at this point.

When we reach out to brothers and sisters, leaning into our commitment to heal at all levels, we are doing a beautiful thing. This is how we fulfill our spiritual responsibility. Our way of being in the world—both with our positive and negative actions—ripples out and has strong effects. We need to realize that this is true and let this be an incentive to do this work of healing.

We have now come full circle, talking about the importance of committing ourselves wholeheartedly to our truth and to giving our best, and also to letting go of spiteful withholding. Seeing all this is an important step in wanting to give up our negativity, allowing God to help us create the opposite: a positive life.

"When you are troubled, seek the truth and all will be well. Be blessed, my dear ones. The love of the universe envelops you."
–The Pathwork® Guide

Chapter 9

Moving the Mind to Push the Divine Light Spark Into the Outer Regions

When a spiritual group forms, or really any kind of group, there will be difficulties that must be overcome. These are an expression of the sum total of beings making up this "body." For any created entity has its own spiritual body, and this body will consist of many different aspects, the same way an individual person consists of many different aspects.

We are all aspects, then, of the greater consciousness, which is all one. These are nice sounding words, but they are not just words. If we open to them inwardly, we may be able to sense the truth that, in consciousness, we are one. We will start to get a glimpse of this as we make our way along our spiritual path, learning to recognize various aspects of our personality and dealing with them.

Some parts of us, we will find, are out of step with our conscious good-will, while other parts are working in harmony. At the deepest level, there is an aspect of our consciousness that surpasses in many ways—in beauty, wisdom, love and strength—even the very best of our intentions and abilities to bring all our parts back into harmony.

One by one, we learn to identify each part of the self and to see when we are identifying with each of them. In this way, we get a glimpse of who we are. When we spot parts we don't like, we can work to accept them and thereby transform their energy. This is how we restore negative qualities back to their positive form, rather than separating ourselves from them, which causes them to manifest out there in the world where we can see their destructiveness.

What we are talking about applies to all of creation. Just as we have parts that make up our total personality, we are part of the make-up of the universal consciousness. Yet we all fear bridging the gap between our separated ego—our own little consciousness—and the big all-encompassing consciousness, out of the misguided notion that if we do so, we will lose ourselves. But this is completely untrue. It can't be true. For the more we come to realize all that we are—

the more we become our Real Self—the more complete we will be, not less.

What is the aim of creation? Why are we here? Exactly to bridge this gap, establishing the all-in-one consciousness everywhere. "But why does this gap exist?" is a question we repeatedly ask ourselves. There are many explanations, including the story of the Fall which, in religious terms, refers to the fall of the angels from grace. Now let's explore another version of this same process without any religious overtones.

A View of Creation

What we are about to learn regarding cosmology is not theoretical knowledge, but rather has practical value that we can use immediately for our own personal development. This information can open us to profound cosmic truths outside us, and if we wish to see them, it will also help us realize these truths inside ourselves, as they exist right now. For it will help us understand why we identify with our ego—a split off aspect of consciousness—and why we are so afraid to let go and merge with the greater consciousness.

With this information, we will be able to see how our fear is an illusion, and that our suffering is not necessary, as it exists only because of our resistance. If we let them, these words can help us open inner doors to knowing and experiencing the immutable, unending truth about all that is.

It's not easy to talk about the truth of all reality using words that humans can understand. For our language is fashioned to fit a very narrow slice of reality. The terms we use in this three-dimensional space are not well-equipped for talking about dimensions we can't comprehend. As a result, it can be easy to distort or misunderstand what is being conveyed. Many may find this teaching to be confusing, contradictory and difficult to comprehend.

Rather than only tuning in using our ego mind, it will help if we can open up our inner listening ears, deliberately allowing our heart and soul to hear this message. If we engage our deepest intuition, these words will penetrate more deeply into us, and there will be an echo of inner understanding that goes beyond words.

So now let's jump in and talk about creation. First we will talk about how creation "started." Notice how we are already challenged to find the right words to use, as creation never really started. But we must squeeze this concept into human language where there is no other word to use. Try to feel the truth of this!

What "started" creation was the divine spark. This spark may have been very tiny within an enormous vacuum, yet this itty-bitty spark was comprised of the utmost reality, and it was divine. It contained everything that is conscious as well as the most powerful creative energy. It held the most incredible love and wisdom.

The aim of the divine creator—which is infinitely good—was to fill this vacuum of nothingness with the spark that contained it all. Gradually, this spark began to spread, and it slowly penetrated the darkness. For the spark had incredible light. It filled the nothingness of the vacuum with glowing aliveness—with all that it contained.

This vacuum formed an infinity in the "outer" regions, and the spark formed an infinity in the "inner" regions. Here, from the perspective of our dualistic mind, we bump into a contradiction: How could there be two infinities? It's literally impossible to convey the truth of this to human consciousness, that there could be an infinity, but it is both a vacuum and an inner spark of light, with the spark filling the vacuum.

This eternal spark spreads into the infinite inner regions. Perhaps we can visualize this in the form of a picture. Imagine a thick, golden, sparkling liquid that is teeming with energy and creative potential. This liquid contains the seeds for everything. It bubbles with aliveness. It is intensely conscious, endowed with every conceivable power—as well as powers we can't even conceive of—to create worlds and beings.

As it slowly spreads, its goal is to fill the apparent nothingness that goes on forever. The infinite all—the All That Is—fills the vacuum until there is no more vacuum. It can't help but penetrate the entire void, since the All is made up of vibrant consciousness and powerful energy. As such, the outer regions will be entirely filled with the inner world of light and life.

During the process of spreading, the divine spark—the particles of this All—get lost, and "forget" where they came from. They forget their original wholeness and connectedness. These particles start believing they are dots—isolated bits of consciousness—that have been hurled into darkness. Now they struggle against being swallowed up by the darkness.

But the struggle is an illusion. The fear is an illusion. For each apparently isolated dot is not really isolated. The connection still exists, but in the process of advancing and spreading, the All is partly diminished in each dot. In this diminished state, there are "times" when the outer darkness seems more real than the inner life of light.

The outer vacuum is not evil, for evil is not nothing. Evil is what comes into existence when the dots—the particles of divine spark—lose their memory, and haven't yet remembered that they are connected and struggling against the vacuum.

This ferocious struggle in which the dots fight against existing and being fully alive distorts energy—what's positive becomes negative—and divine reality—truth turns to untruth. This transition forms a state we might call evil, but it is a temporary state.

This temporary dot—the apparently separate aspect of divine reality— must inevitably be drawn back into the All that is continually spreading. Although it is not really drawn back. It's more that the fullness of the spreading spark catches up with the dot that has moved ahead in a diminished form. The fullness of nature, with all its various forms, is included in this ever-growing wave that keeps moving further into the outer regions.

We can look at our lives and our struggles in this light. Through our personal development, we can feel how we are bringing truth and divinity to our whole being. This is the spark within that is pushing us to penetrate the outer regions—the outside world. The more we all do this, growing into truth, love and justice—into oneness—the more we fulfill this creative process.

As individual dots, we have lost sight of our connection with this whole scheme and our purpose in it. We can no longer identify with the All we are part of, which explains our resistance to giving up our struggle against it. This is our evil. If we give up our negative attitudes—which is how we express our struggle against the dark vacuum—we feel threatened with extinction.

To give up our evil—our struggle—is like volunteering to go into the dark nothingness, and we confuse that with physical death. But this is where we must eventually go, since divine reality must eventually fill everything that is. All the particles must reunite themselves, and then they'll rediscover they were always united with the All. The connection was never really lost.

When we—as individual dots—meet our innermost terror, we are coming face to face with our fear that the vacuum will consume us. So while as remote, metaphysical and philosophical as all this may sound, is not unrelated to what's happening in our day-to-day lives. When we go deep inside ourselves, we find this fear running our lives. We will also find the terror of this vacuum. Ultimately, we will also find the all-consciousness which is actually us and which can never die. We are the divine spark that must slowly continue to unfold and push further into the vacuum.

The sooner we make room for these truths, opening up to them and making room for all that wants to unfold inside us, the sooner we will figure out who we truly are. But when our conscious self—our ego mind—is convinced our separateness is the only "reality," mistaking this temporary state for the permanent reality, our mind blocks off the experience of the true state of our being.

This is why we are here. This is the plan of creation and what evolution is all about. This is where all this is heading. The question is: Can we see how we are each part of this? We are each a particle of God—in this sense, we are God— and we each have a task. The All in each of us—the ultimate in us—is sending us forth. It is sending an aspect of itself forward, which then shows up here as an aspect of apparently separate ego-consciousness.

The task for each separated aspect is to search its own depths to find its potential for power, wisdom, love and beauty that are eternal and infinite. For just as the part is contained in the whole, the whole is contained in the part. Our work is to make our whole being aware of this, so we can consciously choose to spread ourselves into the vacuum, filling it with our real nature.

When we meditate deeply on these concepts, we will see how we can use them to understand our lives. We will intuitively connect with the truth nestled in these words. Once we know their truth, something vital will change inside us. We will be motivated to accept both the positive in us and the negative. As we start to unify ourselves, we will begin to see our surroundings in the same way. We will now know that all people—whether we like them or not, whether we approve of them or not, whether they are developed or not—are aspects of the whole, just as we are.

We will now also realize that whatever is negative—both in ourselves and in others—is merely a distorted aspect of a positive thing. So we will stop feeling alienated and frightened by it. But what really matters most is that we stop feeling alienated and frightened by ourselves. For the more we fear parts of ourselves, the more we will project this fear onto other people and life. The only way we can stop this is to meet what we are most afraid of in ourselves. This is the path. *This* is that path!

Movement on Every Level

Let's explore some specific exercises that can help us move forward on our path. We'll start with a very important one that involves the level of feeling. But first, a short explanation.

We all harbor a misconception about feelings, which is that we can somehow "get rid of" negative feelings. So first, we need to make a clear distinction between residual feelings that have become stagnant and which we don't realize we are holding back, and our innate capacity to experience any feeling, as long as our soul is in a free-flowing state.

Let's take anger. The less we fear our repressed anger and learn to accept it, the more we will assume responsibility for it and express it appropriately, rather than project it on others. This will free us to produce anger when anger is appropriate. But if we think we must "get rid" of our anger, we will become confused and think that when we transform the energy of a destructive feeling, we are wiping it out.

Many people have a false idea of what a highly developed state looks like. We think it comes complete without anger, rage, fear, pain or sadness. This is a distorted idea that leads to a rigid, unrealistic image, or misconception. For in truth, the more we are capable of experiencing any feeling, the less we will be enslaved by it. We can become conscious of such a free-flowing state—which is currently only a possibility—in which we are flexible and so in command of ourselves that all feelings can be moved along. The potential always exists in everyone.

But the less we can summon our feelings, the more frightened of them we will be. As such, we will be at their mercy. When that's the case, we may act out destructively and in an uncontrolled way. Either that or we will repress our capacity to feel at all, causing our creative energies and potentials to stagnate. This is the kind of double bind that all dualities must eventually lead to.

The unitive state is fully alive, so movement is one of its key attributes. Whereas the vacuum is fixed, the spark of the All is constantly in motion. As humans, we constantly battle between these two states. We have a hankering for nonmovement which results in a fear of the vacuum. The illusion is that movement will carry us into the vacuum, where consciousness will cease to exist. No wonder we want to hold back and not move. Yet the divine spark in our core is constantly urging us forward, into motion.

This is why, when we walk on a spiritual path, we must learn to move our bodies, just as we must learn to move our feelings and move our mind. We need to do this so that our spirit can move through us. We must allow the moving spirit to move us so it can manifest. All the levels of our personality—spiritual, mental, emotional and physical—must align with spirit's inherent nature, which is to move.

When we move our bodies, energy is able to flow and penetrate into our entire physical system. So then we have more physical energy. We also need to move our feelings by learning to let them out. We need to let ourselves feel moved by life. We can move our minds by opening them up to new ways of looking at things. And it is essential we do this.

Our fixed ideas stop our spirit from moving our mind, inspiring it with higher truths. Our task is to allow this. We're not talking about opening up to general concepts, but to truths about our current personal situations. But what often happens is that we have a judgment or opinion we invest so much energy into, we actually start to believe these are our real feelings. Then negative energy is generated by these rigid thoughts which are unavoidably false. For truth is always fluid and free-flowing. We mistake this limited truth for the whole truth, and this error becomes the tool for self-deception.

So what we now believe to be our emotions are really just fixed opinions. Where our feelings should unfold, we are frozen. It is the task of this spiritual path—of really any genuine path—to bring the whole system into harmonious movement. But this requires a lot of finely attuned timing to know what is the right move when, so as to not do any harm.

We need a different approach for each level of our personalities. Also, we will need a certain amount of agility in our body, mind and feelings before we can even use certain exercises, otherwise distortions are apt to set in. For example, if we attempt to deliberately move stuck feelings, we will likely produce dramatization, fakery and exaggeration. Essentially we will use our will to put on a good show, hoping to foster the illusion that our soul is flexible.

The mind can learn to exercise itself by trying out alternative ways of seeing a situation. But if we jump ahead, seeing things differently because we have an ulterior motive of escaping blame, we will end up justifying why we are a victim. Then we may escape this by layering on a false serenity that attempts to cover over our negative feelings. So it's easy to see how timing can play an important role in our work of self-knowing.

Remembering what we said about negative feelings, namely that it's a distortion to think we can get rid of them, let's look at feelings. We can cultivate our ability to experience any feeling we want. Once this is the case, undesirable feelings won't have any power over us. But we can never put our feelings behind us, once and for all.

There is no future state we can reach where we have accomplished all our goals and no longer need to move. Such a concept comes from our fear of movement and hence our rejection of movement. It is based on the illusion that movement is undesirable. But if we are living in a state of truth, we will desire movement and avoid non-movement.

Looking at movement on the physical level, suppose we have worked on ourselves sufficiently enough to have removed all our muscular blocks, which of course are related to our emotional blocks. Does this mean we can now stop moving our bodies? Obviously not. For if we did that, new blocks would immediately start forming all over again. Any choice to remain static and unmoving is built on a wrong idea about how life works. From our misunderstanding, negative feelings develop which in this case would be fear. If we don't look at this fear to see what it is about, we will give in to the fear and it will prevent us from moving on any level.

The Joy of Movement

A healthy person is going to want to keep moving, not for therapeutic reasons but out of sheer joy. When this is the situation, movement becomes a pleasure, not a chore. But if we choose to think of movement as a chore, we'll stagnate, for it's very tempting to give in to the vacuum.

But we can overcome this. The way to get started is by moving our mind in a new direction. We must make the decision to move on all levels so our spirit can reach and enliven every part of us. Our spirit is ready and willing to carry light into the darkness. It wants to bring movement to where we have become stagnant. For if we stop moving, we are starting to die.

The same holds true on the level of our feelings. It's possible for a person to be very far along in their development, and they may still hate. Yes, they may have worked through their residual pain and their residual anger may have dissipated. But that doesn't mean we won't ever experience these feelings again. It's actually the reverse. The more work we have done to accept old residual feeling—so we no longer fear and reject them—the greater will be our ability to allow soul movements to move. These currents can then go in any direction at any time.

Such a person can now experience any feeling at will. But this is not the tight self-will we're talking about. The experience of feelings has to come from our healthy inner will, which is smooth-flowing. When we are in full possession of ourselves, we can be moved from within. This means we can, at will, produce violent anger and hate; at will produce sadness and pain; at will produce fear and terror; at will produce peace and harmony; at will produce joy and pleasure; at will produce love and compassion.

If we are still at a place in our development where we tend to overdramatize—we use our will to create counterfeit feelings—we are not yet ready to do these exercises regarding our feelings. Because we must first shed our mask that is hiding our shame of our real feelings. Also, if we have a tendency to use certain limited emotions as a way to defend against other emotions, we are not yet ready to practice with superimposed feelings. For example, say we use fear as a defense against hate, spite, malice or violence. We will need to work through all of these feelings before we are ready to attempt any feeling exercises.

It's not hard to see that people who are very contracted and alienated from their core can't produce any feelings, or at least a very limited amount. They are still numb and paralyzed on that level. By contrast, people who have already freed themselves from their inner shackles—by letting go of their defenses—have dealt with their residual feelings. As such, they are much more flexible and so can easily decide whether to be angry, sad or whatever emotion they wish to feel.

We each need to evaluate where we are in this respect and gradually build up to doing the appropriate exercises. For doing the right kind of movement exercises for each level will help us immensely in our development. We can also call upon our inner guidance to help us know how to use them. It's important we understand the principles that are at work here.

Practicing Soul Movements

When we are able—more and more, over time—to produce feelings, we will be able to bring out any last vestiges of feelings we have overlooked. Even after we are empty of old feelings, we should practice keeping our emotions fluid so our soul substance remains vibrant and flexible.

The movements of our soul are very important. In fact, there are cosmic movements that are constantly streaming within us, and we can only become conscious of them when we have the ability to emote easily. If we are ready, we can practice expressing various feelings. It works best to do this with a room full of people, as it is more difficult to do such exercises alone. But eventually we will be able to do that as well.

A good way to start is by listening inside and determining the predominant feeling we are aware of right now. At first, it may only be faint, so we will need to build it up. Now we can allow ourselves to experience and express it intensely. Then other feelings will begin to surface, and we can explore them.

At times, the person who is helping us—a therapist, counselor, coach or helper of some sort—may suggest a certain feeling to focus on. At other times, our own inspiration can direct us. We always want to be taking our work into our meditations, asking to be guided and inspired.

Ultimately, if we want to become aligned with our center, we must become fluid and flexible. Here is an exercise we can do to loosen up our mind. We can take any situation we are now in that bothers us. Any disturbance or disharmony will do. Now we can look at the mental construct we have built. What are the tightly held, fixed conclusions we use to convince ourselves we are right? How are we using them to eliminate self-doubt?

Using our active mind, we probe into the situation and see what position we have chosen. Now we can decide to think of other alternative choices that could be made. Play with the alternatives. Again, we can let our spirit inspire us, guiding us into new channels. We can see that we don't get annihilated if we abandon our original fixed view, which we previously pinned in place with a single interpretation. This fixed view is, to a large extent, the reason we are facing this conflict to begin with. We need to see this.

Our first move is to unearth what we actually believe in this moment. Once we have done this, our beliefs are a bit more flexible already. But this is not the only belief. We can become aware of other beliefs. We need to broaden our outlook about the particular subject we are doggedly protecting with our ironclad opinions.

We like to think that our judgments and opinions are a result of a specific situation that is disturbing us. We really wish this were true. But it's actually the other way around. We are faced with disturbing situations in our life due to our tendency to harbor particular ideas, opinions and judgments. Underneath these lie a particular intention or motivation.

By allowing our mind to become more flexible, we can try on a fresh perspective. Doing this might help us face our current position with less resistance. For any tendency we have toward a certain cluster of opinions and judgments waits, ready to pounce on the next set of circumstances that can activate them. In other words, with our fixed, inflexible mind, we're poised to see the world a certain way. This is the root cause of various psychological problems.

As we do our work of healing, year after year, we will get better and better at having mental agility. By becoming more fluid and flexible on every level, we will restore our well-being. We will bring all of ourselves—our mental, emotion, physical and spiritual beings—into alignment with the truth of who we are in our divine center. This should be our motto for our work, as we seek to find and become our Real Self.

Working with Our Faults

For people who are familiar with the Guide's teachings about the primary faults of self-will, pride and fear, here is an additional exercise we can take into meditation that will help us in dealing with this difficult triad.

Taking the same bothersome situation that came to mind earlier, let's now look at it from the point of view of pride. In what way are we acting from pride? Now we can try to visualize this situation, focusing our attention on how it would feel to give up our pride. If it seems the only alternative is to feel humiliated, it's time to start probing around for other possible options.

We can call on our inner guidance to help us see ourselves in this situation with dignity, instead of humiliation. We will need to make a voluntary step into new territory if we want to see ourselves walking in a way that harmonizes dignity with humility, leaving out both pride and the humiliation of submission. If we are ready to walk this way in the world, our divine spirit will begin to produce it from within. But for this to happen, we must first make ourselves receptive to it.

Now we can follow the same process with self-will. We start by envisioning ourselves having a new kind of reaction in which we are neither spineless and taken advantage of, nor are we self-willed. We are able to assert ourselves, but we can also let go and give in. For any given situation, we can find the proper balance coming from our core. But for it to surface, our mind will need to be flexible and open enough for the new possibilities to get in. We will also need to cultivate our connection with our spiritual center so we can come to trust it and the inner guidance that it sends forth. Note too that it will require a certain amount of courage to get through the anxiety that will surface when we first attempt to let go of our pride and self-will.

And now, last but certainly not least, we need to address our fear. The fear is not going to go anywhere unless we abandon our pride and self-will. For as we may know, at least in theory, fear is the product of pride and self-will. Fear also comes from our inability to trust the universe. For it's evident we have come to believe that the only things that can protect us from danger are our pride and our self-will.

The implication is that the universe is not safe, and we are stuck using this puny protection—our pride and self-will—as our only safeguard. It's time to question this premise by asking, inside: "Is this true?" We can experiment with a new alternative, and open ourselves to another possible way to be in the world, which is by allowing the divine reality to flow through us.

Eventually, maybe today or maybe a long time from now, it will come. It must. And it will penetrate us with a state of consciousness in which there is no pride, no self-will, and then also no fear. When that day comes, we will have transcended all our conflicts—inside and outside of ourselves.

Now let's try doing an exercise in truth, by opening ourselves to the possibility that the universe will gladly give us whatever we need. For just a moment, sit with this thought: "Who and how would I be if I trusted the universe? What might happen if, in this particular instance that is disturbing me, I gave up my fear—which is rooted in distrust—and also let go of my pride and self-will?" We can actively do this exercise, allowing our central core to give us a taste of the state we could reach if we were to react to life without pride, self-will and fear. What do we have to lose?

"The universe is good and beautiful, and there is nothing to fear, neither inside nor outside, no matter how much it may appear otherwise, due to your present distortions. Let love flow into you so that it can come out of you. Be blessed, be in peace."
–The Pathwork® Guide

Chapter 10

The Three States of Consciousness

In this dualistic dimension, we speak of consciousness and energy as though they are two distinct things. But this is not correct. To start with, it's important to realize that everything in all of creation is permeated with consciousness. So all energy contains some variety and degree of consciousness. That said, consciousness is what creates energy. In fact, the energy of direct consciousness—the energy of our thoughts, feelings, intentions, attitudes and beliefs—eclipses, by far, any other kind of energy, whether electrical, physical, biological or atomic.

Each thought then is energy, and our experience of this energy is what we call a feeling. So there can be no thought—not even the most sterile, cut-off thought—that doesn't also contain a feeling. We can imagine that a very pure, abstract thought might be completely divorced from any feeling content, but this is not the case. In reality, it's just the opposite. The more pure and abstract a thought is, the more feeling must be attached to it.

Actually, we need to parse the difference between an abstract thought and one that is cut off. We need to not confuse the two. An abstract thought comes from a spiritual state that is highly integrated. A cut-off thought is a defense against feelings and parts of the self we think are undesirable.

But even the most cut off thought can never be totally devoid of feeling, or energetic content. Beneath the surface there may be a feeling of fear or apprehension—some sort of anxiety about something the person hopes to avoid. And when such feelings are present, self-hate is usually also part of the package.

Below the surface of a purely abstract thought there will be an energy current—a feeling—of utter peace. This comes from the inherent understanding of spiritual laws that are bound to the thought, and therefore bound to produce joy. A more subjective thought is less pure. So the more subjective a thought is, the more it will be tinged with negative feelings.

What exactly is a subjective thought? It is a thought derived from our personal desires and personal fears. It comes from our ego, the separated state that believes it is me versus the other. Such a thought, then, is not in truth.

Let's examine, for example, desires. In this land of duality, desire—like everything—plays two roles. To use a paradox, we could say that from a spiritual point of view, desire is "undesirable." After all, a desire that is too intense—a desire emanating from our ego and its distortions—alienates us from our core. This kind of desire is filled with pride, self-will and fear, and lacks trust in the universe. Too much desire, in this sense, contracts our energy system, creating tension and preventing the flow of the life force.

This is why spiritual teachings often advise desirelessness as the necessary condition for connecting with divine self. This state is then cherished for realizing our spiritual self.

It is, however, equally true that if we have no desire, we cannot expand. It's not possible to venture into new spiritual lands—into new states of awareness—without desire. If there is no desire, there can be no purification. For what would motivate us to persevere and muster the courage needed to grope in the dark long enough to find our way out of our suffering? Only desire can do this. This kind of desire holds faith in the possibility we can attain the courage, patience and commitment needed to reach a better state.

This is an example of the kind of dualistic confusion we create by saying it's either right or wrong to have desire. For it really depends on which kind of desire we are speaking of. If we hope to transcend the limited dualistic state of consciousness that is trapped in painful, confusing thinking, we will need to see beyond this kind of either/or situation. We will need to train our eyes to see both the truth and the distortion that exists on both sides.

The moment we can see this, opposites will no longer exist. And in that instant, we pass into a deeper and wider state of consciousness. From there, we will be able to see beyond the limitations of duality. This applies to so many areas of our lives. Rarely, if ever, is something good or bad, in itself. What matters is how it manifests and what the true underlying motivations are.

In order for people to overcome hurdles, we must have a desire to do so in our heart. We must want to do away with the temptation to deceive ourselves, for this is what blocks us from discovering abstract knowledge which is aligned with truth. Again, be careful to understand the words used here. We are not speaking now of abstract thinking that is mechanical, dead, cut-off, unfeeling, superficial or defensive.

How could it ever be possible for consciousness—which is our inner knowing—to ever be unfeeling? Even intellectual knowledge—which is how we might refer to unfeeling knowing—must have feelings connected with it. And although people may use such knowledge to escape from the feeling aspect of living, it still contains feeling, even we if don't recognize these feelings.

So even if we have no awareness of it, consciousness is also always a feeling. A mechanical, cut-off, fragmented thought, then, can set off a series of energetic chain reactions in our psyche. The very choice regarding which thought to think stems from such strong movements of energy, and creates an affect. So as we started out saying, consciousness and energy must be one.

If we look at the average human being, we may find it hard to believe this is always true. But when we dig a little deeper, we see that whatever thoughts we are holding, they connect with a feeling. It bears repeating, because it is so critical we get this: cut-off, dry knowledge must always also contain feelings.

Often, fear will be the underlying feeling, while the energetic state on the surface may be boredom. Boredom is a negative energetic state. If we look more closely into the deep corners of our soul, boredom is always accompanied somewhere by fear—perhaps fear of the self and how we fit into the cosmos. But over time, as we become more honest with ourselves and stop acting out, we will start to better understand the relationship between ourselves and the universe.

First State: Lack of Awareness

We can organize the states of consciousness into three different groups. We start out in the least developed state, which is the state of slumber. In this state, a being does not know it exists. There is no self-awareness. Animals, plants, minerals and inanimate matter are at this stage. The being may be able to move and feel and grow, and to some extent it can even think. But still, it is below the threshold of being self-aware. There are, nonetheless, built-in patterns this being must follow for creation and self-creation.

An organism beneath the state of self-awareness follows meaningful, purposeful ways that align with particular laws. So while there is a state of consciousness here, there is no self-consciousness. Let's consider the life of a plant, which follows its own built-in plan. It's consciousness is now slumbering, yet it has a plan that imprints it with lawful cycles by which it lives, grows, dies, reincorporates itself, rebirths itself, expresses itself, and on it goes in this same lifecycle. This does not happen by accident or by "itself." It requires an incredibly intelligent plan that can only come about from consciousness. This can't happen through a dead or disconnected process.

When we look at minerals, it may appear that such inanimate matter must be completely disconnected. But in fact, the consciousness of this being is just temporarily frozen. This happens when consciousness creates in a particular direction that slows the life spark down until it becomes petrified. The energy becomes condensed into such a thick crust that the underlying energy looks to be invisible to the human eye. There are some people, though, whose consciousness is so expanded they can perceive the highly potent energy that still lurks within, even when there appears to be no consciousness. They can also pick up on the consciousness contained in the apparently "dead" inanimate matter.

What is a being in this slumbering state essentially "saying?" It may say, "I don't want to know who I am. I don't want to know how I relate to the world around me." A statement like this is a creative agent, and it has been deliberately made by a consciousness that has such an attitude. This statement results in a chain of events, that surely but gradually leads to a slowed-down, condensed state. This finally hardens and forms a "crust," making it appear dead. This, friends, is what matter is made of. It stems from a sequence of events that creates inanimate matter based on a negative statement that goes against truth.

Nevertheless, after the hardening process has gotten rolling, consciousness is able to use matter for a positive purpose that affirms life. So a free consciousness can then "communicate" with the consciousness that is nestled within the hardened matter.

This brief explanation gives us some idea of how it could be possible that consciousness can exist even in an inanimate object. From a scientific perspective, we have figured out that energy exists within matter, so that part is not news to us. What we haven't yet uncovered is this piece about how consciousness is also contained in matter.

We are aware that we can reach the consciousness of plants, animals and other people with our own consciousness. It's to a lesser degree that can we reach the consciousness within inanimate objects using the more active and strong consciousness of our human mind. But matter is still malleable, and we can impress it with our human consciousness.

Since consciousness has the ability to create and invent, we can mold and shape the substances that are inside of matter. So if we need an object—like a plate, or glass, or piece of furniture, or piece of jewelry—we have a desire to have that object. Our desire molds the inanimate matter—with its energy and consciousness—which receives the direction of the stronger, more connected consciousness, and fuses with it in a certain way. This is the process that creates an object.

So each object we use and enjoy is fulfilling its task. Even in this "deadened" state, the nucleus of this consciousness is seeking to express its divinity through its loving, truthful service. Even in this separated state, it is moving toward being by "replying" to the creative consciousness. As such, it is fulfilling its purpose in the great plan of evolution.

In the end, even the deadest of all dead material isn't really dead. For such an object contains energy, so it has an energy field. This is its antenna—its receiving station. This is what it uses to react, since its consciousness is still too limited for it to be more than a reactor. It can't initiate anything at this stage, so it can't create the way a human can. But it is most definitely a reactor.

Perhaps we find that we have a certain close relationship with certain objects. We cherish them, need them, and enjoy them. They do well for us. We might even think we love them because they perform so well for us. They give us good service, or joy, or beauty. This is a harmless, benign circle at work in which it's hard to say who even got the thing going.

Think of a car we like, for example, or an instrument we use. Whatever it is, we love this thing! We may even use it in support of our spiritual growth somehow. So then a purely utilitarian object isn't really so utilitarian after all. We care for this machine or item. And our appreciation makes it respond, even though that is all it can do. With its small, limited consciousness, it is only geared to react and respond, to be molded and impressed. But our appreciation affects its energy field.

There are other objects where it's the other way around—they never work out well. We are annoyed by them and therefore hate them, and they respond accordingly. Although we experience a separation of consciousness from them, this is debatable. The whole universe, after all, is permeated with consciousness. The separation then between objects and entities is only true on the surface. Below the surface, there is constant interaction happening.

In summary, the first state is consciousness without self-awareness, which includes animals, plants, minerals and inanimate matter. All contain consciousness and have processes for growth and change, although it happens more slowly at this stage of the game.

Second State: Self-Awareness

In the second state, there is self-awareness. This is where humans are at. What do we mean by self-awareness? It means we are capable of thoughts such as, "I am," "I think," "I am able to make a decision," "What I think has an effect," and "I can reach other beings with my feelings." This second state is the starting point for self-responsibility.

Being aware that we can affect the world around ourselves makes us accountable for our attitudes and the way we think, act and respond. We can choose these things, and we must take this responsibility seriously. Due to the fact that our level of awareness is now more expanded, there are more options available to us than before. In this state of consciousness—being above the threshold of self-awareness—we can make choices. Beings in the prior state have a pattern implanted in their soul substance they blindly follow. In the human state, we can re-create the plan. In doing so, we avail ourselves of wider possibilities for expressing ourselves that are in line with our level of development.

It's clear that within this state, there are widely-varying degrees of self-awareness. There are humans who aren't yet aware of themselves and their power to make changes, create new things and affect others. They have a limited ability to differentiate, and an equally limited power to act on their own and to think. The concepts presented here wouldn't make much more sense to them than to an animal. These teachings would essentially be meaningless to them.

There are other people whose consciousness is already a lot more developed. They are well aware they have the power to choose, to create, and to create an effect. They take responsibility for their choice to think one way or another, and are accountable for their decisions. To such people, these words will make sense, and they will be inspired and encouraged by them. In between these two categories are people of varying degrees of consciousness.

But even those in the first group, whose consciousness is least developed, are aware they exist. They realize they have needs and, up to a point, can figure out how to fill them. They are aware they can take action. Perhaps their scope is rather limited, so their power to affect others is more diminished than it would be for someone who is more well developed, but nonetheless, they are leaps and bounds ahead of an animal. And while animals may be awake enough to think, they completely lack any sort of self-consciousness.

Being a human and having some level of self-awareness lands us in a self-created dimension that includes time. So for us, a sense of past, present and future has awakened that doesn't exist in the lower states of consciousness. As in so many areas of development, there are similarities between the highest and lowest points on the curve. In this case, most people have some sense of time.

By contrast, animals, plants, minerals and objects don't have a sense of time. They don't have awareness of themselves and their ability to advance themselves, and so exist in a timeless state of being. Humans, on the other hand, exist within a framework of time. So rather than existing in a state of being, we exist in a state of becoming. This is the case, even though we already possess self-awareness. As we rise up on the curve of development, we will come back to a timeless state of being, but now our consciousness will be awake.

Third State: Universal Consciousness

This third and final state is the highest level of consciousness of the three states. We could call this universal consciousness, or maybe even cosmic consciousness. Such a state is beyond the state of being human. In this state, all is one. There is no more separation. In this state of consciousness, all is known: the Godself is known and the innermost self is known.

The Godself of other entities is also known in this state, as well as the truth of being. In this state, an entity lives in a state of being, but now, at this level of development, the state of being goes beyond self-awareness. It has come to a universal awareness. Another way to say this is that the self is seen as being a part of all that is.

Transitioning through States

If we ponder the deeper meaning of all this, taking it into meditation, we will understand significantly more about the greater scheme of life of which we are a part. The "innocent" state of being only exists in a purity. But this purity can exist in a being who is as yet blind, unconscious, powerless and unaware, just as it exists in one who has recaptured the state of innocence through their hard work of descending and at the same time ascending to self-purification. At that point, power reunites with the eternal now in a timeless state.

As long as a soul is not yet purified, the untapped potency of their consciousness is protected by their lack of awareness. As we proceed along our path of self-development, this power increases according to our ability to be in truth—with ourselves and with others. For if we could be aware of our power to create while we still have evil intentions, we could do harm to a greater degree than we would heal. As it stands, healing is what happens when we allow negative results to become our medicine.

When we allow evil to manifest through us, it causes results that appear unjust to us. It only looks that way to us because of our limited state that is bound in time, causing us to lose track of the connections. Were we to become aware of how all the dots connect together, we would see how all negativity—which can appear to us to be very cruel and unjust—is the self-created medicine for the ultimate healing purpose of achieving purification and therefore reaching a state of bliss.

Ultimately, evil does not destroy, although it can temporarily do so within the framework just mentioned. If it was possible for consciousness to expand without the simultaneous progress of self-purification, then evil would be able to destroy the divine. So, as a built-in way to protect this from happening, negativity closes off our perceptive organs. As a result, blindness, deafness, dumbness and numbness set in. So when we are steeped in negativity, we will unavoidably have lower awareness.

The only way we can come out of this ignorant, limited state in which we are quite powerless—cut off from the center where all of life is connected—is through our consistent efforts to know ourselves, where we are right now. This must be our goal, rather than having a goal to know the universe and what goes on outside of us. That knowing will come later, almost as a freebie. But to pursue that is to pursue illusion.

Waking Up

The process of coming to know ourselves happens slowly, one step at a time. It doesn't ask us to do impossible feats. It only asks for what is possible, which is that we deal with what's right in front of our eyes—if we are willing to make the choice to see it. Using our goodwill and best intentions, we can find out whatever we ought to know about ourselves each step of the way.

There isn't any fraction of time in anyone's lives when this is not possible. Any time we find ourselves in a state of disharmony, we are not as aware as we could be. The process of becoming more aware asks us to grope in the darkness. Intense searching will be required. This is, indeed, part of our task in life.

Too often, we look in the wrong direction to find answers about our current disharmony. And too often, we also resist looking because we fear something "worse" than what is actually there. If, at all times, we will gather the courage and determination to see things all the way through, we will discover this isn't so.

Whatever disharmonious state we are in right now—a state of anxiousness, unhappiness, depression, unrest, fear, or pain—it is always a reflection that there is something we should know about ourselves, but choose—yes, we literally choose—to not know. That choice results in a potent, negative field of energy.

The steps we are encouraged to take on this spiritual path help us deactivate these negative energy fields by changing the consciousness they contain. Our first step is to transition from "I don't want to know," to an attitude that says, "I want to know." The next step is to follow through. We can embark on this kind of discovery adventure any time we choose.

When we are just getting started on this phase of our evolutionary journey, we will need to eliminate the blind spots we have about ourselves. Otherwise the self can't figure out answers about the self. We can't wake up as long as we won't look at what we are choosing. We must see what we now think, feel, need and desire. Once we have this in hand, we can turn up the power on our ability to change what is currently undesirable and destructive.

As we go along, working in this way, we will reach a period in which we will know ourselves fairly well, but we still aren't fully aware of others. So we get lost in what they create. We are still blind to what they are doing—to the exact nature of their negativity—so we get confused and become disturbed.

If we focus in clearing ourselves further, searching for more and more honesty, we will come to a clear awareness of others and what they are up to. This will bring us peace. It will also show us the way out of tangled up conflicts with them. Along the way, we'll start to see aspects—positive ones—about ourselves we hadn't noticed before. Often, the only thing that can bring forward such previously ignored aspects is a crisis with others.

The first phase of this waking-up process is self-exploration. The second phase will be to expand our knowledge of others. The first and second phases typically overlap. The third phase leads us beyond the human state, into universal awareness. That is the organic path we follow when we are on this spiritual journey.

We can interpret the word knowledge in several ways. We might have gained knowledge on a purely mechanical level, but such knowledge doesn't contain wisdom, insight or true perception. It does not leave us with a sense of wonder and awe, and it also doesn't give us joy or peace. This is dry, cut-off knowledge.

The knowledge we gain through our spiritual growth is a different kind of knowledge. With this kind of knowledge, a sort of comprehension takes place that brings together our fragmented understanding. This deep, feeling knowledge unifies things, and indeed brings us peace and joy, excitement and awe.

A revelation fills us that resolves all disharmony. We experience in a new way, and we relate. But friends, this doesn't happen on our first day of walking a spiritual path. It only comes much later. At first we will only experience inklings of this, and then only occasionally. When we move into a position, for instance, of helping others, it will manifest much more fully.

The more we expand, the more we will be filled with this kind of knowledge. As this happens—more and more, little by little—cosmic knowledge arrives from deep within. This goes beyond the personal. It's timeless and affords us a deep awareness of the stream of life we are flowing in, along with everyone and everything else.

We will be filled with an indescribable peace—imbued with joy and security— and gratitude for all that exists. This is an awareness we must earn through our personal healing work. We cannot aim directly at cosmic consciousness, but it will come if we do this work. This is the last leg of our journey, reaching this state of expanded self-awareness. This is what we are cultivating when we use these spiritual tools.

The Ego's Choice

This teaching is specifically designed to make us aware of how powerful our thoughts are. Given their potency, everything we decide to think, and every attitude we decide to adopt, has great potential. Our thoughts create experiences and reactions, inside and outside of us. Within us, they will either generate a new field of energy, or they will fasten an old one in place, reinforcing it. It just depends on whether it's a new thought, or a recycled version of something old.

This can apply whether the existing energy field is constructive or destructive, real or false. When we become truly conscious of this potency, we will start to behave more responsibly and become more capable of creating. This is how we approach the state in which we know God-consciousness is in everything.

The job of the ego is to decide which way to turn. This means that, right now, in our thinking mind lies the potential to express God's consciousness in whatever way we like. So if our experience in the moment is negative, we need to make sure we find out what and how it got created. What, in us, created it?

We each have the ability to discover the truth about how powerful our consciousness is. We can get started by making the commitment right now—and of course, we will have to commit over and over again—to be in truth. In any daily concern that puzzles, confuses or disturbs us, we can look at our reactions. Our emotional reactions are always giving us a clue about where to look.

When we feel resistance to looking, we can look at the resistance. We can admit our resistance—instead of glossing over it as we're often tempted to do—and in our admission, we let in some new light. In spite of our resistance, we can admit our resistance. We can also have faith in truth.

More and more, we will free ourselves from the shackles that are now keeping us confined in a state that is less than we have a right to. Liberty is our birthright, and so is joy. In every possible situation, we can continue to make the commitment to find and be in truth. In every conceivable situation, there is always a way out.

"With this message and suggestion I bless you all with deep love—the love of the universe—for all of you, my most beloved friends. Be in peace."
–The Pathwork® Guide

Chapter 11

The Era of New Consciousness

"Blessings, love, and greetings to all of you, my dearest ones. With immense joy do we resume our contact for the coming working period. The rejoicing in our world is great. This rejoicing can communicate itself to you if you open yourself to it. It has to do with what many of you have accomplished individually and together. But the rejoicing is also about what is to come. For more growth and liberation, peace, and joy will come to those of you who really devote yourselves to your own innermost path."

–The Pathwork® Guide

Many spiritual sources are delivering messages about an immense cosmic force that is sweeping this planet. A force has been released into this universe with the goal, not of sweeping us out, but to sweep us clean. There is a surge happening in our world, leading us toward spiritual truth. New values are pushing their way through old walls of resistance. Let's look into what this cosmic force means in terms of a spiritual community, our individuality, and our personal healing and growth.

Earth, as a planet, is an entity, and each person who lives here is a cell. It's much the same as the cells of a human body. Each cell, on planet Earth, is an energy center with consciousness, just as the cells of a body are conscious and have energy. Now, the entity we call Earth is growing up. It's at an inner crossroads, in the same way a growing person comes to inner crossroads.

At some point on our path, we each find that one part of us is ready to expand. In this part of ourselves, we are willing to take a risk and expose our secrets. We want to move into a new mode of living, with a new vision of ourselves. In this new modality, we are not going to shed what's old, but transform whatever is not compatible with this pure, new influx. We are going to incorporate the pure substance woven into the old self, into an expanded version of ourselves. This will create a new version of ourselves.

What we come to realize is that another part of ourselves, our Lower Self, is going to attempt to obstruct this movement. This part fears and distrusts—and therefore resists—this kind of growth. It's our ego consciousness that decides which part we will align with.

It's inevitable that in such a conflict there will be crisis, created by the resisting part as it obstructs the evolutionary force that cannot be stopped. The less we are able to recognize what is happening in this struggle, the more we will deny and rationalize the true significance of what's going on. And this will result in an equally great upheaval in our lives that will frighten us.

Conversely, the more we can see the struggle for what it is, the more we will be able to align with Higher-Self principles, and the more quickly the crisis can be resolved. Then the crisis will transform into an experience of previously unimaginable joy.

A crisis then, is both healthy and unavoidable. Without a crisis, growth can't take place, yet to the extent we resist growing, we create crisis. Our Lower Self is not only dishonest, selfish and devious, it is also ignorant. And this ignorance makes us stubborn and unperceptive, in addition to being negative and destructive.

Planet Earth also has a Lower Self. Like a person's, the Earth's Lower Self is not just negative, selfish, dishonest and greedy, it's also ignorant—with a vengeance. It too resists what its soul is ready for, which is to move to a higher level of consciousness. And so there must be crisis on this earth.

The movements of expansion are not always without their exaggerations and distortions, without their misunderstandings and fanaticism. And so we can see Earth go through crisis as it expands into new ways of being. In short, expansive movements sometimes miss the point of how to handle a great new wave of consciousness by avoiding the confrontation of some unpurified matter. When, as individuals, we abuse the growth process this way, it will be particularly costly for the person and highly disappointing as well.

This cosmic force has tried to get the attention of humanity many times, in many ways, but we have largely not understood its meaning. So often, a spiritual movement comes along trying to follow the pressure that builds from within, but the necessary cleaning work doesn't happen within the soul.

For centuries, the spirit world has been preparing us for this expansion, investing a great deal of energy. Many are being called, but not everyone follows. For not everyone is willing to heed the call coming from within. It would be better for us to clearly acknowledge this, leaving the possibility open that the call may come again. But if instead we explain it away, preferring to accept illusions and delusions like they are valid reasons for our decision, then our soul is going to remain in a state of confusion.

Serving and Leading

Right now, earth, as an overall entity, is going through a struggle like this. If we are resisting the light of the new consciousness that is coming in, we have a stake in making ourselves blind and deaf to what is happening. Many people have the mental capacity and spiritual development to follow the movement that is happening, but choose—out of pride, self-will and fear—not to follow the movement, or to realize what is taking place.

Of course there are, at the same time, people who are at such a place in their spiritual development that they aren't ready to know that other levels of reality exist which we can't see with our eyes. Some may follow the movement, however, even though they don't quite grasp what is at stake.

Those who follow the movement will discover deep joy and many blessings, and will have no need to fear anything. They will be able to rejoice. By following the flow of the influx, they remain in harmony with the universe. They move with the process and don't try to obstruct it. These people are needed as physical channels of the Christ consciousness as it penetrates further and further into the planet, pushing us into a new era.

Such individuals who continually renew their decision to devote themselves completely to the process that is unfolding will not only make their lives full and meaningful, they will become useful for the whole cosmic evolution.

In order for this surge to fulfill its purpose, profound purification must happen. We begin by doing our own work. Then we enter a new growth phase in which we become ready to join a cohesive movement that sweeps our whole world. In other words, there is more at stake here than just our individual fulfillment.

By "more," we're not implying that individual fulfillment is not as important. Our individual happiness, wholeness and ability to walk freely in the world, without obstructions, is vitally important. Our personal fulfillment—which we can't enjoy unless we purify ourselves so we are no longer alienated from the truth of who we are—is the most important thing there is. At the same time, there is something else at stake. There is no contradiction here.

Maybe we can put it like this: We can only find total fulfillment for ourselves when we serve a greater cause. Many of us have practically tripped over this truth, as we have moved forward on our spiritual path. The guidance of the events that occur help us realize—sometimes more intuitively, and sometimes more intellectually—that there is a great task we are simultaneously serving while we are fulfilling ourselves.

What we find is that this greater service enhances our own fulfillment, in the same way our service requires that we become happy people. We start to experience that our own fulfillment lies in being of service. And we can be of service only by way of self-fulfillment. Once again, if this appears to be a contradiction, this is only so because we have a faulty perception of things.

For what appear to be opposites can coexist nicely as complementary parts of a whole. They exist in oneness, so an individual person only appears to be opposed to the whole.

As we do our spiritual work, we will learn to more consciously and deliberately perceive how important it is for each of us to work in service of the wave of Christ consciousness that is infiltrating us now. For those of us who are willing to follow this movement, it will drastically change our lives and our consciousness.

We will see, going forward, that there are old values and there are new values. There will be old consciousness and new consciousness. We will come to see that our own personal fulfillment is a tool we can use to serve. For frustrated people cannot serve. Unhappy people cannot undertake the task of enriching the lives of others and themselves. They cannot set a desirable example.

For how can someone who is poor enrich others? Someone who is poor also can't pretend. For followers do know. They do know, in a deep inner place, whether the ones leading are genuinely fulfilling, or just pretending.

Only people who sit firmly in themselves, fully centered in their own God-consciousness, can create lives for themselves that meet their desires, that enliven others, and that teach their consciousness to others. There are many different tasks in this world, but everyone who serves in this cause must also teach and lead. They represent the new consciousness and live the new values, both through instruction and by example, as they transmit joy, love and the capacity for a person to be their best self.

The Grand Dichotomy

Like many people, most of us who are doing this spiritual cleansing work feel a compulsion to be good. We fear being selfish, so we use some kind of mask to cover over our selfishness and our mean little ways. This mask forces us to comply with higher standards so that it will appear we are, in fact, a very good person. Often, there will be a message and a genuine surge coming from our Higher Self that gets woven into the threads of our mask, creating this cloak of false goodness.

What we find, as we go deeply into our work of self-discovery, is that a part of us has been selling out our true self-interest—giving up our real rights—in an effort to please some make-believe authority. We are not doing this in a spirit of pure service, but rather, by design. We are wanting this authority to do something for us that isn't fair to expect, and which is something we should be doing for ourselves in order to fully become ourselves.

Over and over, we must see how we are doing this until we find the strength to give up this secret hope. We have to let go of this false form of give-to-get service, become more self-responsible and, as a result, learn to be more self-assertive. This is the way to find balance. We must stop cheating and then pretending we don't. And the more we do this—while we stop with the false goodness—the more we can expect to receive the best life has to offer.

When we start to live honestly, our guilt will go away. But as long as we remain dependent—and consequently submissive—we will lack selfhood, and we will not yet be ready to serve a greater cause. We will misuse our service and put our energy into keeping our mask shored up. The answer? We must learn to be selfish.

Of course, as we have discussed, there is a right kind of selfishness and a wrong kind. The right kind establishes and preserves our right to unfold in the best way possible, no matter what anyone's opinion of us may be and their possible motivation to exploit us. With this kind of selfishness—which has roots in independence—we will be able to recognize and deflect any exploitative demands, for we will no longer submit out of our own hidden agenda.

When a person has the right kind of selfishness, they feel deserving of being happy, for they never want it at the expense of someone else. It's only the distorted form of selfishness that splits off the interest of the self from that of others. The right kind unifies the self with others.

At first, it's rather complicated to sort out all the misunderstandings. But once we have traveled some distance along the spiral movement of our path, there is no longer any dichotomy between the self and the other. When we free ourselves from the real guilt caused by our pretenses and our hiding—by the hidden agenda we are disguising and the negativity this keeps perpetuating—we won't feel unworthy of becoming our best selves. We won't hesitate to be the happiest and most deeply fulfilled person. Then our service won't be something we do to compensate for our guilt.

This particular spiritual path has been designed to prepare as many people as possible for the great event now sweeping our universe. This requires guilt-free souls who are strong, and who can act for real—not false—reasons. This is why our work on this path begins by bringing out both our false and real selfishness, in an effort to help us become unselfish without sacrificing personal fulfillment.

Our Lower Self, with its lower aims, has to be sacrificed often. But is giving up our Lower Self really a sacrifice? It only seems to be so. What ultimately arises is genuine fulfillment. Then our outer self—our ego consciousness—will no longer go against our Godself.

We can only reach this state, though, when we have learned to let go of our mask of false service. We must expose our short-sighted selfishness that stems from our littler self. Then and only then, after we learn healthy selfishness, do we come into a true selflessness that isn't in any way contradictory.

When people align with spiritual teachings that focus on service too soon in the process, there's a danger that some will use the teachings to escape from their work—from their hidden selfishness. To compensate, they offer service through being a martyr, which is never wholesome for the soul. Any time we refuse to truly become self-responsible and independent, we are not meeting our hidden selfishness, and so whatever service we offer is distorted.

If we look at our personal healing work in this light, we will see more clearly the overall dynamics. We might represent our work using a certain symbolic figure, which is widely used in spiritual expressions because it is a recurring thought form. It consists of three circles in a mandala-shaped design: The Higher Self is represented by the center circle, which is surrounded by the Lower Self, which is surrounded by the Mask Self and our defenses. We can apply this to our individual work, and also to the work of a spiritual community, as well as to humanity as a whole.

Healing Through Community

When a spiritual community forms, there will be people who represent the Higher Self of the group. They will be the ones taking the most responsibility for the community, who have worked the most deeply and exposed themselves. These are the people who are starting to reap the tangible fruits of fulfillment, having traveled through their outer layers.

More and more, they have learned not to fear any part of themselves. They have come to accept themselves—all of themselves, including the good and the bad parts—thereby uniting what was previously divided. Such people will identify, more and more, with their Higher Self, since they can now see the difference between this part and their Mask Self, which is filled with the wishful thinking that one can hide the distortions and untruth of the Lower Self.

In this way, such leaders have learned to hear the true voice of their Higher Self and have increasingly learned to trust it. We will find evidence of this kind of leadership in the growing number of group members. We can see it in the nature of the new people showing up who are ready to listen to, understand and follow the new cosmic force. We'll see it in the deep connections that form among members. The more each member works to remove their blocks and obstructions—resolving conflicts and clearing up problems—the more this deepening will continue on all levels. Growth in such an environment is not a coincidence. It is a natural expression of the development of the group members.

So a number of people will form an inner nucleus, which will function as the Higher Self of the community. Does this mean these people are perfect? Of course not. But they are perfectly capable of establishing a channel to their Higher Self—to their inner light. Such people are increasingly able to commit themselves completely to the will of God, and to sense the importance of the Christ consciousness sweeping the planet. And they will have what it takes to serve it.

By living and working together in this way, these people will be protecting themselves in a remarkably effective way against the onslaught that is sure to come from the countermovement. By immunizing ourselves against the counter-termovement of one's own Lower Self, we are immunized against the Lower Self of the planet.

Then there will be others who will be diligently working on their spiritual path, but who are still struggling. These people are still in the phase of owning up to their own Lower Self. They are laboring to get to know how it works by penetrating the concealment of their Mask Self.

In the midst of this struggle, there is great temptation to hide, and there is also the habit of hiding that one must overcome. These are strong obstacles. Other strong obstacles include guilt and fear of exposing the truth. We can eliminate the illusion of the fear only by gradually testing it until we are able to realize that this process is trustworthy. Some people will struggle to find the channel to their Higher Selves, and therefore they won't want any of this. They will fear it, and they won't trust it. Such people will put all their trust in their old, habitual, destructive defenses.

Then, of course, there will be those who still identify strongly with their Mask Self. These people will have the most difficult time, and they will look for reasons to judge this process and discredit it. This won't make them any happier, but nonetheless, they will proceed in this fashion. They have a stake in not growing that is strong, and a fear of growing that is equally strong. They have no desire to find out just how unjustified their fear is.

These aren't necessarily new friends, people who are just now joining a spiritual group. For development is not always a matter of time. These friends of ours will need to realize that they are identifying with their Mask Self, and must start to do the work of traveling through their inner layers.

It is worth outlining this here so people can figure out, for themselves, where they stand. In the same way some have already learned to take responsibility for their Lower Self—by overcoming the shame of it and admitting to it—so must these people now learn to take responsibility for their Higher Self, and not be ashamed of it. We need to admit, indeed, where we have already arrived.

Then we will be able to give ourselves even more fully to it. Then we will be able to fully commit ourselves to becoming a part of the great movement. We will also be able to feel the beauty and excitement of it, as well as the honor and privilege. To be of service as part of a greater cause will cleanse any little selfishness that still resides in us and makes us fearful.

We believe we can't give all of ourselves to a greater cause because we're afraid to do so. But in truth, it works the other way around. We are afraid because we still cling to a little piece of selfishness here or there. To consciously give ourselves to a greater cause that is sweeping the entire planet is, in itself, a cleansing process.

The New Consciousness

The wave of new consciousness that is arriving is bringing with it new values based on these new truths. They are not actually "new," however, as they have always existed in highly developed people who have incarnated to accomplish a specific task and who have not been widely known. The big difference right now is that the whole planet is growing up, and stepping into its own divine consciousness.

The first thing for us to do, in this respect, is to gain a conscious understanding that our life must reach beyond the bounds of our immediate personality. We also must understand that this expansion will lead us to happiness, even though a prerequisite for experiencing it is also happiness. There is nothing dividing expansion from happiness. We will not be deprived if we choose to follow the will of God. So in the years to come, we must become proficient in trusting—to totally surrendering to the God within—every single day, in all issues, in any venture, in each decision we make, even regarding the opinions we elect to adopt.

With this new consciousness, we won't make superficial decisions using just our head, hoping to get the immediate fulfillment of our desires. With the new consciousness, we will make decisions in a whole new way. The new consciousness is already aware that our outer self doesn't have the answers; that it's full of prejudices and highly colored distortions.

The new consciousness consults the Higher Self in all things, and is willing to wait patiently and quietly to receive an answer. It is not opinionated. It is happy to accept when, as of yet, it doesn't know, and it stays open. It doesn't have a stake in getting a certain answer. It makes room for the possibility that the answer could be just about anything. What comes may be what is desired, or it may be the exact opposite, but either way, it trusts that whatever comes, it will be good.

This is the kind of approach that has no fixed opinion—it makes itself empty. This is a hallmark of this new value system which has already started to sweep the planet. Of course, this is going to clash with the old value system, which functions at merely the surface level. The old values focus on the little immediate emotions, and take the narrow view which has a stake in not even wanting to consider what's possible or to widen one's perceptions.

These old values are going to clash with the new ones as they rise up in each of us. In our communities, the clash will be between those who align with the new consciousness and those who align with the old. As this unfolds, it will become increasingly clear where we stand. It will not be enough to claim, "I belong in the new consciousness," while continuing to act in the old ways. We can say whatever we want, but our actions and the way we approach decisions will be the litmus test revealing in which camp we belong.

Many people walking on a spiritual path have already made the commitment, and they are already being caught up in the remarkable surge of new golden light that is sweeping the earth. This light is only unbearable to those who are refusing it. They are the ones who are only able to perceive the negative countermovement, and they are blind therefore to the light itself. They feel a strong discomfort when the light approaches them and they do not interpret their reaction correctly. The light carries the greatest joy to those who want to receive it, who are willing to give themselves to it, and who fight for the light and serve it.

"Be blessed, my dearest ones."
–The Pathwork® Guide

Chapter 12

Creating from Emptiness

Now is the time for the arrival of a new era. The arrival of this event has required that many people were made ready for it—regardless of whether or not those walking a conscious spiritual path have been aware of this preparation. So we have been filing away at our impurities—and we are still doing this work—making ourselves available for a powerful force that is being released in the universe—in the inner universe.

Many channels and spiritual teachers have been aware of this event, but many have incorrectly interpreted what this event would look like. They've had the idea it would come by way of geological cataclysms that would affect humans on the physical level. But this is not true. The changes, which have been in progress for decades already, are changes in our consciousness. And this is exactly what we are working on here.

As we do our personal self-development work to purify ourselves, we become steadily more ready for inner enlightenment, for the arrival of this awakening force with its self-perpetuating nature. Its arrival is unprecedented, as there has been no other time in the history of humankind when this force has been as available as it is right now.

If we have been doing our own healing work, then what we experience will be a result of this power landing on a receptive channel. But if this power hits a channel that is unreceptive, a crisis will arise. What we're talking about is a tremendous, creative force that is highly beneficial and which could help us thrive in an entirely new way. But if we block it, even if only partly, we put ourselves under great stress—psychically, physically, emotionally and spiritually. This is what we must try to avoid.

Let's now discuss how important it is to be receptive to the energy and new consciousness arriving with this force. This is Christ consciousness and it is spreading throughout human consciousness wherever it can. But in order for us to receive it, we must also understand another important principle: *creative emptiness.*

Preparing the Mind

Human beings are famous for creating an agitated mind, which we do through overactivity, both inside and outside ourselves. We do this because we are afraid we might be empty—that maybe there is nothing inside us that will sustain us. Rarely are we conscious of this thought, but when we're walking a spiritual path such as this one, the time will come when we do become consciously aware of this fearful thought.

Then our first reaction is something along the lines of, "I don't even want to acknowledge that this frightens me. I'd rather keep on busying my mind so I won't have to face the terror of realizing I'm nothing inside—that I'm only a shell that needs sustenance from outside myself."

Obviously, such a self-deception is futile. So it's critically important we face this fear head on and deal with it in an open way. To do this, we must create an inner atmosphere that will allow us to be empty. Otherwise we'll go on deceiving ourselves, which is such a waste since this fear is not justified. But we'll never be able to live in peace with ourselves if we don't know what it is we fear, and our avoidance makes it utterly impossible to figure out: Whatever we fear, we don't need to fear.

Humanity has, for centuries now, been involved in a process of conditioning ourselves to make our mind a very busy place. So when this busyness stops temporarily, we confuse the quiet with emptiness. Our mind does indeed suddenly seem empty. As the noise recedes, what we need to do is welcome and embrace the emptiness, as this is the most important channel for receiving our innermost Godself.

In order for us to nurture this emptiness and turn this process into a creative venture, we need to comprehend a couple of spiritual and psychic laws. And some of these laws will seem like they contradict themselves.

• If we can't let ourselves be empty, we can never be filled.

• From the emptiness, a new fullness will arise. (Yet we can't just pretend our fear doesn't exist; like everything else, we must go through our fear.)

• Our work is to challenge our fears, and at the same time, we need to welcome the emptiness, for this is the doorway that leads to the divine. (It's understandable that this sounds like a contradiction, but really it is not. We need to embrace both attitudes.)

• It's really important we become expectant and receptive, yet we must be without impatience or wishful thinking, and we must not have any preconceived ideas. (It's hard to even explain this one using human words. It's just something we have to try to feel into. What we want is to have a positive expectancy that's free from preconceived notions about what will happen and how it should happen.)

• We must be specific, but our specificity needs to be neutral and light. (So we are challenged to be specific in a certain way, but not in another way. If we are confused by this, now would be a good time to ask our inner being to relay an understanding to our mind. This will be more effective than trying to wrap our ego mind around it.)

Here's the thing: The workings of the greater mind surpass the ego mind's imagination by so much, being more specific would only hinder us. Yet our outer mind must know what it wants. We also need to be prepared for what we want, to reach out for it, to claim it, and to know we deserve what we want and will not misuse it. Plus, our outer mind will need to be able to constantly change, so it can adapt to the larger scope of the God-consciousness within.

Our goal is for our outer mind to become empty and receptive, while at the same time we keep our mind open and poised for anything. In this condition, our mind will be able to connect with the inner stillness—which at first appears to us as emptiness.

As we empty our mind and soul—in a spirit of patience along with positive expectation and perseverance—a new fullness will come into being. Then this inner stillness will start to sing, as it were. Energetically speaking, this stillness will feel warm and light. A strength will rise from within that we've not known before. All the issues in our lives—from the smallest to the biggest—will be seen from this wise viewpoint that is both inspiring and infused with guidance.

We must truly nurture this creative emptiness by gently listening to it with our inner ear. This isn't something to do with urgency, but rather by opening to when and how we will be filled. This is the only way to move ahead in finding our inner sustenance and divinity. We must become a receptacle for receiving this tremendous universal power that is being released and which will show up in our lives even more than we have experienced already.

This moment of evolution is a significant time in history. We all need to comprehend what is happening so we can help perpetuate a profound change in the way we perceive and think about the new values and laws now spreading across the world. We must open the way from without and within, creating as many receptacles for the Christ consciousness as we can.

Our mind can either help this process or hinder it. As we may realize, our mind is only limited by our idea that it is limited. To whatever degree we limit our mind, we can't perceive what's beyond it. In truth, the mind is infinite. Our goal then is to extend the edge of our finiteness until we measure up with the infinite that is beyond the ego mind and that is inside us—right here, right now.

When we do this, our mind merges into the infinite consciousness of our inner universe where we are already one with all that is and yet we are infinitely our personal selves. As things are right now, we carry our mind around with us almost like it's a burden, for it has become a closed circuit.

We give ourselves a little leeway to have particular opinions, ideas and possibilities that we've made room for with our education and by what our society allows. Our limited mental circuit includes the things we have chosen to learn and the knowledge we have picked up through our personal experiences and from being part of the group consciousness.

To whatever extent we have expanded and grown, we have widened the closed circuit of our mind. But it's still a closed circuit. So the limiting ideas we have about ourselves still burden us and restrict our world. It's necessary then— if we want to open to creative emptiness—that we start questioning all the things we think are impossible for us. Then we will find the edges of our mind.

Anywhere we feel hopeless and have fear, we must also have an idea of finiteness that our mind has locked onto. As a result, we are locking out the great power that is here for all who are ready to honestly receive it.

Once again, we are looking into the eyes of an apparent contradiction. On one hand, we need to open up our limited mind, opening ourselves to new possibilities and new ideas. This is what we are learning to do in meditation. What we'll discover is that whenever we make room for some new possibility that we desire, it comes into our life. We'll also find that when it doesn't come, there is some reason that we are denying it.

We must start to puncture this closed circuit. Note, we can't just immediately dissolve our mind, because we need it to live. But by puncturing our mind, the flow of new consciousness and energy can work its way into it. Any place it has not been punctured, we stay locked inside its narrow confines, which our spirit is quickly outgrowing.

On the other hand, our mind must become neutral. It must rest and not hold onto fixed opinions. This is what will allow us to be receptive to the great new force that is now sweeping the inner universe of all consciousness.

Opening the Mind

How do we go about puncturing the mind? We can start by telling ourselves that we are holding onto limiting beliefs. For we need to stop taking these beliefs for granted. Then we need to challenge these limited beliefs. This means we must take the trouble to really think about them, by observing and confronting ourselves. We need to practice doing this and get good at it.

We must start to see, not just that we have a false belief, but that we have a negative intention to hang onto it. This is how we are keeping the closed circuit shut, and thereby depriving ourselves of the inner abundance we are deeply yearning for.

It's important that, as we go about this task of opening ourselves up to the greater universal consciousness, we don't think of this as some kind of magical process that's going to help us bypass the process of learning and growing. Yes, our ultimate goal is to be filled and sustained by this power, but our outer mind will need to go through the steps of acquiring the knowledge needed for this to happen.

We can look at how this process works in the areas of art and science. A person cannot be inspired as a great artist—regardless of how much genius they have—if they don't develop the technical dexterity needed and learn the craft. So if our childish Lower Self hopes to find a shortcut to the greater universe, hoping to avoid the tedium of learning the ropes, then this channel will remain closed for us. For in the end, what this amounts to is cheating, and God will not be cheated.

When we cheat, we are seriously doubting that anything exists beyond our mind. After all, when we try to use "magic" to coddle our lazy, self-indulgent selves, we don't receive any inspiration. None at all. For there is a spiritual law at work here that operates the same way in science, or really in any field, as in art: Effort is always needed at the beginning.

How does this spiritual law work when it comes to inspiration regarding our personal life and the decisions we make? Here again, our ego-self cannot fail to go through the work that's necessary to become a proper channel for the universal consciousness, or God-consciousness. This is what we're doing when we do the work of this spiritual path.

We must come to truly know ourselves. This means we must get to know our Lower Self by seeing our weaknesses and knowing where we tend to be dishonest. We must learn where we are corruptible. This is hard work, but it has to be done. If we keep avoiding it, our channel will never be reliable. We will be filled instead with wishful thinking that stems from our "desire nature," and our channel may reveal "truth" that is completely unreliable because it is based on fear and guilt.

Only by working on our personal development in the way we learn on a spiritual path like this one, will we reach the point where we don't confuse wishful thinking and gullibility with faith, or mix up doubt with discrimination. A great musician can become a channel for higher inspiration—which makes playing effortless—only after going through hours and hours of practice, and doing finger exercises. God-inspired people must go about things the same way as they work on their purification process, uncovering deep self-honesty and self-knowing.

This is the only way to become a receptacle that's a match for higher truths and new values. Then we will be fit to be influenced for use in a higher purpose—one that enriches the world and ourselves. But we also, at the same time, have to cultivate an inner field of neutrality. If we want to devote ourselves to fulfilling God's will, we must have an attitude that says, "Whatever comes from God is OK with me, whether I desire it or not."

Having too much desire, then, can hinder us as much as having no desire at all, which we usually recognize as resignation and hopelessness.

If we refuse to endure frustration of any kind, we will create tension inside ourselves and build inner defensive structures that seal up the vessel of the mind. As such, the circuit stays closed. This is why we, as a receptacle, have to remain neutral. But by giving up our tight, strong, self-willed Yes or No, we will make way for developing flexible trust and being guided by God.

Our goal is to become willing, flexible, pliable, trusting and always ready to make a change we didn't see coming. For when it comes to the divine life that flows from our inner well, there is nothing that is fixed. So what's right for us today may not be right tomorrow.

Our mind has come to believe that security lies in fixed rules. But nothing could be further from that truth. Yet this very idea of a flexible universe makes us feel insecure. This is one of those beliefs we were talking about that needs to be challenged and changed. Just imagine what it could be like to forever keep meeting each new situation with new inspiration. In this lies a new kind of security we haven't yet found.

The right thing to do in one situation may not be right to do in another. This is the law of this new era that opposes the old "stable" laws that say what's fixed and unchangeable is what's secure.

Following Spiritual Laws

We're going to need to study these new laws that pertain to this new venture in creative living. We're going to need to work with them. These aren't just words for us to take in—we must make them our own. And this may not be easy, as spiritual laws are filled with apparent contradictions.

So we need to acquire new knowledge, expand our mind, and allow ourselves to conceive of new truthful possibilities. At the same time, we must empty our mind and become neutral. This only appears to be a contradiction from the perspective of the mind that is stuck in duality, or dualistic consciousness. But from the viewpoint of the new consciousness—which is the golden light spreading through our inner universe—these attitudes aren't contradictions at all.

For when something is in truth, making it a match for life's higher spiritual laws, opposites that are mutually exclusive on lower levels of consciousness are reconciled. It always works this way. Things that produce conflicts on the lower level—the level of duality—will interact and help each other on the higher level, which is the level of unity.

As we go forward, it's important that we discover the truth about unification, where dualities no longer exist and contradictions simply stop contradicting. In this new world, we will experience two things, which we formerly viewed as opposites, as both being valid aspects of the same truth. When we understand what is happening here, and start applying this principle to our lives, to our values, and to our outlook on our lives, then we will indeed become ready to receive the new consciousness that is being released in realms that are far beyond this one.

Continuing with the theme of apparent contradictions, to say we must not approach our divine channel with an attitude of wanting it to save us the effort of growing and healing, does not negate the need to be passively receptive. It's more that we must shift our balance. In places where our mind has been overactive, we now need to quiet our mind and let things happen. In areas of our lives where we insisted on always being in control, now we must let go of the reins, relinquishing control and letting this new inner power take the lead.

On the other hand, in the areas of our lives where we have been self-indulgent and lazy—always seeking the line of least resistance and as such, making ourselves dependent on other people—we are now the ones who need to take over. In these areas, it's time to actively nurture the principles that will help us establish a direct connection with our inner God. We also need to actively express the messages we receive from our Godself, into life. So we need to reverse our relationship with activity and passivity.

This is the way to turn our mind into an instrument. This is how the mind opens up and punctures its limits, acquiring new ideas—not new tight concepts, but light ones—that it can play with for awhile. By donning a new lightness in how we perceive the world we make our mind flexible. And this motility of mind is what makes us as receptive as we can be to what, at first, seemed to be emptiness.

Working with Emptiness

So how do we go about approaching this emptiness? What does it feel like? What's it all about? Once again, we will bump into the limitations of human language, as it's nearly impossible to squeeze an experience of emptiness into words. But let's do our best to talk about it and learn about some tools. Try to also listen with your inner ears.

Notice that as we listen into the "chasm" that is inside us, it will at first seem to be a big, black gulf that is empty. What comes up is the feeling of fear. Notice how this fear seems to fill us up. Let's look at this fear. What is it? It's both a fear of finding out that we are indeed empty, and a fear of finding ourselves to have a new consciousness—a new being that is evolving right here inside us.

Even though we long for this, we are also afraid of it. We have a fear of both of these possibilities. We want the new consciousness so much, we're afraid of the disappointment of not getting it. Yet we fear finding this consciousness, because it might impose obligations and changes on us. We are going to need to hold on to ourselves and travel through both of these fears. On this path, the tool we learn for dealing with this fear is to question it. We need to question our Lower Self.

Eventually, despite the fear, we become ready, because we have connected all the dots. We now know, for instance, what our Lower Self wants, and we have figured out why we have negative intentions. Then, in spite of any remaining fear, we must make a decision to quietly and calmly, wade into the emptiness. So the reason to empty our mind is so we can meet the emptiness deep inside.

If we don't run away, we will discover that, lo and behold, the emptiness will start to feel, not full like we might think, but alive. This is a new aliveness that our old artificially full mind made impossible. As we hang out in this space, we'll also notice that we made ourselves artificially dull. We packed our mind full and tight. We were tight in the mind with noise, and our channel to the divine was tight because, with our defenses, we had contracted our energy into hard knots.

We had killed our aliveness through our artificial fullness. And this, in turn, made us needier. Because without access to our inner light, we could never feel filled, not in a real sense. We created a vicious circle by striving to get fulfillment from outside ourselves, since we refused to take the steps necessary to allow fulfillment to come to us—from within.

We fear the aliveness, in one sense, more than we fear the emptiness. And we would do well to face this. What often happens is that we become empty enough to get this initial taste of aliveness, and then we slam the lid tightly shut again. So we started out by denying our fear, but then we also deny that we are really quite unhappy about how our life lacks aliveness. Yet the fear is what causes the lack of aliveness. And the only way to make the fear give way—to open up our aliveness—is by allowing ourselves to be creatively empty.

What does this aliveness feel like? It's like having our whole inner being—both our energy and body—become an "inner tube" that is vibrantly alive. Energy will go through this tube, and feeling will go through it, as well as something else that is vibrant, which comes to the fore but which we can't name.

If we don't let ourselves shy away from it, whatever this unnameable thing is, it will sooner or later start to continually offer instructions—like encouragement, guidance and truth—from within. The wisdom it carries will be specifically oriented to serve our life, right now, wherever we are needing it the most. So then what actually is this vibrantly alive emptiness? It's God talking to us.

All day long, wherever we need it, God talks to us. At first it will be vague, but over time it will grow stronger. If we really want to hear it and tune into it, we will discern what it is saying. We will need to practice using our inner ear to be able to recognize it. Over time, recognition will dawn on us—we know this voice! This vibrant voice that speaks in tones of wisdom and love—talking specifically to us, not in generalities—is a voice that has always been there, but we have become conditioned to not hearing it. To not listening to it.

And in this conditioning, we have tightened ourselves up, packing up that "inner tube." Now it's time to unpack it and let it fill us with the vibrantly alive music of the angels. What do we mean by "music of the angels?" It's not meant literally, although that too could be possible. But what most of us need to hear more of is direct guidance to help us make decisions about what attitude or opinion we should consider in any particular situation.

And instruction like this is on par, in its glory, with the music of the angels. One can hardly describe the wonder of this kind of fullness. This is a treasure that is far beyond words. This is what we are forever searching for. We long for this, but usually we're unaware that we're searching for this, mistakenly projecting our yearning on substitutes we hope can fill us from the outside.

It's time to turn our attention back to what has always existed inside us. Our mind and our outer will have confused us and complicated our lives for long enough. So making this contact is like finding the way out of the maze—a maze that we ourselves created. Now, we have what we need to rebuild our inner landscape, this time without the maze.

Living in Fullness

Now the question comes up, "What's a person like, in this new era?" The new person will be a receptacle for the divine consciousness. This universal intelligence is the Christ consciousness that permeates all of life, including every single particle of every single being. The new person doesn't function from their habitual thoughts.

For century after century, we humans have been developing our intellect. This had to be cultivated so our ego mind could fulfill its role in becoming an important stepping stone in the evolution of humanity. But by now, through our overemphasis, we've overshot the mark.

This doesn't mean it's now time to revert back to being blind, only following our emotional "desire-nature." What it means instead is that it's time to wake up. It's time to open up to a higher realm of consciousness inside us, and let this light shine. Our true self is ready to unfold.

There was a time in history when it was very hard for people to think. We couldn't sort out situations, weigh ideas, hang onto information, remember what we had been taught—in short, we didn't know how to use our brains. Back then, the use of our mental faculties was as difficult for us as it now seems to be to contact our Higher Self.

In this new era, the new person will have established a new inner balance. And in this new system, we don't want to leave out the intellect. It's an important instrument that must continue to serve us, and now become unified with the greater consciousness. For ages, people have believed that intellectual abilities represent the highest form of development. Many still believe this. Such people don't make any effort, then, to journey deeper or further into their inner nature where, if they looked, they would find a far greater treasure.

That said, many spiritual movements have sprung up that practice completely inactivating and discarding the mind. This is just as undesirable, because rather than unifying us, it creates splits. Although each of these extremes has some validity, each has gotten lost in half-truths.

Let's look at another example. In the past, people were irresponsible and undisciplined, behaving more like beasts to satisfy their immediate desires. They were driven by their desires and their emotions, not by morals or ethics. So during that stage in our development, developing our intellect was helpful and served a function. Our intelligence could then serve as a sharp tool for learning and making choices.

But when it stops there, the whole thing turns into a farce. For this is what happens when a person is not animated by their divinity—they become a farce. By the same token, it's a good idea to practice temporarily inactivating the mind, and doing so is also recommended as part of these teachings. But to treat our mind as though it's the devil—and to therefore try to oust it from our life—is really missing the point.

Any time we are caught in either extreme, we are not full. For we need to have all our faculties functioning in good working order if we want to express our divinity. Without our mind, we turn into a passive amoeba. Conversely, when the mind is credited with being our highest faculty, we turn into a hyperactive robot. The mind is then nothing more than a computerized machine.

We can only be truly alive when we are able to wed the mind with the spirit, allowing the mind to express the feminine principle every once in a while. Up until now, we have linked the mind with the masculine principle, which is all about action, drive and control. In the new era, the mind has to express the feminine principle of receptivity.

Becoming receptive does not mean that we now become passive. In some ways, we will be more active, for we will become more independent than we were before. For when our mind receives inspiration from the God-consciousness within, we must put this into action. But our actions will be harmonious and effortless—rather than like a cramp.

When we allow our mind to be receptive, we are allowing our mind to be filled with the higher spirit that resides within us. From here, we will function completely differently, as life will be forever new and exciting. Our routines will not become ruts. Nothing will become stale. Nothing will be redundant. For our spirits are always alive and forever changing and renewing themselves. This is the kind of energy and experience that can flow more and more from our center, where the new influx is moving so strongly.

The new person, then, will be making decisions from this new consciousness, once this person works through to truly becoming a receptacle—to being receptive to the spiritual being that is arising from within. Such results sound like utopia to a person who hasn't yet begun to experience this. But once we get on this train, we too will start to experience undreamed of joy and expansion. Problems we thought were unsolvable will begin to unravel. And so it will continue.

There is no end to our fulfillment. As we start to serve a greater cause, we will create meaning in our lives that will awaken us to the productivity and creativity of living. Joy, love and happiness are always included in this.

The time has now passed when individuals can live only for their selfish little lives. We cannot continue this way. Anyone who insists on living in that way will lock themselves out from a power they can't be trusted with. For such a power will turn destructive in a mind that is still geared to serve only the selfish immediate self.

This kind of selfishness always comes from the false belief that we are only happy when we are selfish, and if we are unselfish we will be unhappy. In our work, the first misconception we need to face and challenge is this false belief.

If we do this, we will create a life for ourselves and our environment that's of a kind humanity has never known. People all over the world have been silently preparing for this as they have been doing their personal healing work. From the dark and gray matter of untruthful thinking, these are the golden nuclei that will spring up.

Each person has the opportunity now to further their inner channel, to open to this new reality. This is what we have been waiting for. It will bring us the peace and excitement we always wanted. It's time to join this new phase, to enter it gladly, with courage and a Yes in our heart. We need to get out of the attitude we still have, as though we have been beaten down. We are not beaten down, unless that's the role we want play.

But we can rise up and each of us can become who we truly are. Then and only then will we experience life at its very best.

"All of you are blessed, my very dearest ones. The blessings will give you the sustenance you need to go all the way with all of yourself and become enlivened, activated, actualized by the God within. Be in peace."
–The Pathwork® Guide

Chapter 13

Changing From Outer to Inner Laws in this New Era

"Greetings, my very beloved friends. Blessings for every one of you. Divine love reaches out to you, seeps deep into your heart and embraces you. Let it give you the peace of the ultimate reality that you can and will find within your innermost being if you go all the way with yourself."
–The Pathwork® Guide

This planet and the people on it are going through a growth process. Every seed that is contained in this plan of ultimate self-evolution carries its own plan for fulfillment, and each seed will unfold in its own organic way. We experience this phenomenon when we do our work of personal growth and healing as we are guided to do on this path.

Again and again, we watch as an organic process unfolds that operates independently from our conscious mind and our expectations. A plan like this goes in stages, with new energies released each time we transition to a new stage.

Let's take a look at how this phenomenon manifests on the material level, which is the most superficial level. For example, what happens in the outer growth of a person as they go through very distinct growth phases. For a baby, when they are ready to learn to walk and talk, dormant capacities unfold in them. In order for this to take place, new energies must become available to them.

On the physical level, this is the first major change that takes place after we incarnate. The next major phase of expansion happens when a child leaves home and goes to school. This big step is not just a physical one, but also involves an inner expansion. This is a step out into the world that involves unfolding the child's built-in potential to cope with other people who live outside the home. Growth continues in this way throughout the span of a person's entire life.

After a person becomes fully physically grown, it's harder to notice these transitions. Nonetheless, they are just as real and distinct. Each new phase involves changes, growth and the ability to express oneself more creatively so one can better deal with the world—both the outer world and the inner one. Physicians know that there are changes in our cellular system every few years. In fact, the chemical components of the outer structure change completely. And even though we may not notice this happening, it's real.

The changes that happen on the other levels of our being—mental, psychic, emotional and spiritual—are even more dynamic. During each stage, we take an orderly step to fulfill the plan of the seed, and the seed plan releases new energies automatically. When we are following our plan, these energies provide us with just the boost we need. They help us expand and change and grow, so we can reach a new dimension. This motion starts from within and moves outward, reaching to embrace more of reality. After all, the aim of inner reality is to reach out and transform outer reality, following its own unlimited beauty, perfection and infinite possibilities for expression.

But when the outgoing movement is obstructed—such as when the ego-consciousness hinders the process, ignoring its urgings and acting insensitive to them—then the energies can't unfold in their natural, harmonious way. This is when these energies, which are originally constructive, turn destructive according to our human view of things.

Actually, the aim of the destruction is to destroy the obstruction, the untruth it holds and the way it is infringing on the free unfoldment of the divine. Our work is to dissolve the blocks that untruths in our consciousness have caused, which get in the way of the energies being released. What does this look like on the surface level of life? Painful crisis, upheaval and destruction. We need to figure out that these unpleasant events are not haphazard events. We have set them into motion, and it's important we start to see and understand this.

If our consciousness is in accordance with divine laws, meaning we're in truth and our system is open, the energies will move in a harmonious and organic way. But wherever our consciousness is not in truth, the energies become inverted, and then they turn against the self.

We are not being picked on. This process works the same way everywhere, embracing all beings in all of creation. This means it applies to individuals just as it applies to entities. And this planet we call home, Earth, is an entity. So it is subject to the same laws of growth, and it goes through the same stages of growth and unfoldment.

For both a person and a planet, we experience distinct periods of expansion. For both, the energies inherent in the seed plan must be strong, since when they are released they must be able to make expansion possible. As such, it's easy to spot the positive manifestations that accompany these energies: New potentials unfold; changes are made; creativity is renewed; new approaches are made that reveal a higher level of maturity; there is an increased sense of well-being; there is an elevated vision of how we can express ourselves. All this happens in accordance with the seed plan.

But when we resist the new energies because we don't realize they are an influx of divine forces, then crisis and destruction are the result. All radical revolutions as well as all reactions in which we regress to immature behaviors, are nothing but blockages. The first is an outward projection of withheld emotions that are now being emphatically misdirected.

Growing Pains

Earth is now going through a stage of expansion, unfolding a new influx of Christ consciousness energies. So how does all this apply to what's happening now? We can look first at what happens when a person is ready to reach adulthood but blocks it. The adult energies that are released into the systems—physical, emotional and psychic—create a crisis. Generally speaking, most people ignore what is going on.

The same thing is true for our planet. It's ready to move into adulthood and is striving to unfold. At the same time, the planet harbors elements that are resisting and wanting to ignore this process.

So too we can see factions of people who are oblivious to this inner growth movement. And then there are others who are well aware of the inner reality, and they see the outer reality for what it is: just a reflection of the inner. So whether we are speaking of people or planets, there are less evolved parts that are focused only on the outer picture and are caught in a state of separation. Since they can't perceive the oneness of all beings, they proceed to act in ways that split them off further into separation. This turns their mind toward cruelty, ruthlessness, greed, selfishness and lack of concern.

Since all these things are based on illusion, they inevitably must prove to be painful and unworkable. These are what is being destroyed by any new influx of divine energy. It takes considerable maturity for a soul to grasp the inner meaning of such a crisis, and see the true significance of this truth.

The blindness that can't perceive the oneness is distinct. It is based on what seems to be a diversion of interests between people. When a person is blind like this, they neglect—even refuse to see—any points beyond what's right in front of them. They get stuck on a point and can't see past it, so they miss all the connection points that really link us together.

Long, long ago, back when the planet was still in the early stages of adolescent consciousness, people needed to learn to make a crude distinction between good and evil. We had to learn what was social behavior and what was antisocial, between which were constructive acts and which were destructive ones. At that point in our development, it was inevitable that the whole planet was locked in a totally dualistic state, unable to perceive anything beyond duality.

But that was also a necessary stage and it prepared us for the next era, which is the one we have now entered. This is now the time for people to find the strength of character—to not fall for temptation—to sort out that we don't sacrifice anything by growing up. For our real interests can never differ from the real interests of others.

Before now, we weren't able to make this kind of distinction. We couldn't even tell good from evil or tell the difference between constructive and destructive acts, especially if there was something in it for us. During those early periods, people let impulse and desire govern them. If it was immediately gratifying, it seemed "good," and we didn't think past that. Consciousness was, at that point, in its infancy. Not until now, as the previous era is just ending, could we take up the struggle to make certain choices when interests seem to go in different directions.

The undeveloped state creates blindness, and blindness creates pain. This pain then becomes its own medicine and its own lesson. This is a divine spiritual law that few are able to recognize. If we are able to give up—to sacrifice—what we think is in our best interest, because we see that not doing so will harm others, we become prepared to enter the next stage of development where we will have more clear vision. This applies to the entire planet.

But many people still only see the world in a dualistic way. Duality is, after all, embedded very deeply in our consciousness. So then everything appears to require a choice between either me or the other. This way of seeing things, which is not in truth, creates conflicts—with others and in our conscience— and the consequences of this are very hard to live with.

Needless to say, many people are still unable to make an apparent sacrifice in an effort to preserve kindness, constructive behavior and decency. Because deep in their psyche, it would seem like they are acting against themselves. As such, when we attempt to sacrifice but are still steeped in a dualistic consciousness, we will do so to our own detriment. In this case, our sacrifice is done within the framework of illusion, and is not really an expression of kindness, love, decency or honesty.

Further, if it seems to us that these attributes extract a severe sacrifice from us, then it shouldn't be a surprise that a sacrifice must be experienced. For we experience according to what we believe. As we go through our purification process, we will see how deprived and resentful we feel when we don't get to act out our destructive behavior, and yet we feel self-rejecting and guilty when we give in to the temptations of our Lower Self, with its demanding call to always have our immediate desires met.

The Pendulum Swings

In the era that is just ending, the mores of societies hinged on a limited vision of reality: they were based on duality. This was a testing ground for us. Every time we turned around, we were facing conflict over something or other. That era has now come to an end. If we have sacrificed for the good of all—for doing God's work—we'll now find that's not necessary. Now we can reach a deeper level of truth, for now we can see that what harms another, harms us, and what harms us, harms another.

If we've been acting primarily from a selfish, destructive level, we will need to have a change of heart if the new energies being released on the planet's inner plane are to be constructive for us, and creative. Otherwise, these energies are going to create unbearable tensions that will erupt in a crisis.

At this stage in the development of this planet, we can't maintain the old structure any longer. We can't stand the restrictions and tensions of our old limited consciousness. We will need to discover a new vision in which we are able to perceive the truth: We are one with others. We will need to search for this new vision, which lies beneath the limited vision the ego is so used to.

This new vision comes with a tremendous sense of peace and security, self-expression and joy. It's not an illusion filled with wishful thinking; this is stark reality.

As we all know, humanity is not cut from one cloth. The distinction between people who continue to be steeped in old consciousness and those who can share the new perception is not simple or easy to make. Many people are on the brink of change, and they just need some help and guidance to pull them over to the new world.

Even people who already embrace the new Christ consciousness, and who are, by and large, close to letting the new consciousness express through them, have inner areas that maintain the old vision—the limited, narrow dualistic view of life. We typically refer to those areas as our "problems." Perhaps these teachings will shed a new, more comprehensive light on things. For it's too simple to just call these our problems. They are an expression of an obstacle to expansion and growth.

Some people are already prepared for this era of new consciousness. And so, in this sense, we could say this new consciousness is already here. These people are the pioneers, and they will create a new civilization. There have already been beginnings made, in various places around the world.

At the same time, there are a large number of people who aren't quite there yet in this new consciousness, but they are capable of reaching this state, which will require doing some intense inner work. The way to go about this is presented through these teachings. More people need to become involved in this kind of preparation throughout the world. And that will happen.

Those of us doing our spiritual healing work have a very important task. We are called upon to do our own purification work, going through our own growth process, so we will have a larger vision. Then the state of our consciousness—as it manifests currently—will change, according to our seed plan. When this happens, we will be able to help others do the same. It's not necessary, then, to make a strict delineation between who is in the old and who is in the new.

There are others who, at this stage, aren't ready to do the work. They currently lack the necessary discipline. Then there's another camp—more people than we realize—who might be able to do it, but unfortunately won't. That said, there are many who can, and who wish to deepen their consciousness, according to their life plan.

This spiritual work has not yet spread sufficiently on this plane. It needs more emphasis, and this will happen. The work must be done. We must liberate God within ourselves, and we must liberate God within the general consciousness of all humankind. We can't let everyone just stay where they are.

In previous eras, God-consciousness was always projected outwardly. Then the pendulum had to swing the other way, putting an emphasis on the self. People gave up God outside and started to assume responsibility for themselves. To transition from God outside to God inside—to bridge the gap in space and time—a transition period came about in which atheism and agnosticism rose up. This had to come, to prepare people for reaching full selfhood and full autonomy.

At first this had to happen only on the outer levels. Because full selfhood and autonomy can only exist when our oneness with God has been found, and God within has been freed up. When this happens, we are living in true reality.

Following the Plan

On the level of the planet, when the seed plan calls forth powerful energies and they are resisted, development must be affected. Certain aspects of the planet's consciousness will develop differently from the aspects that are ready to embrace the new unfolding. This division is inevitable, organic and even necessary.

People who are blind to the meaning of the event—to the reality it was caused by an obstruction to forward movement—will feel like they are a victim of the crisis, and insist that everything is hopeless. But those who appreciate the truth of the situation won't fear it. They will be aware that a change is happening that may, presently, make it difficult to adjust to the new situation. But because they are in the know, they realize liberation and joy must also come.

The same thing takes place at the level of the individual. What we will find as we do our spiritual healing work—if we are really willing to look at what we find—is that, beyond a shadow of a doubt, any personal crisis stems from our own negation of the truth. We have violated our own divinity. And *that* is why we are having difficulties. *That* is why we are suffering. We are, in fact, blocking the immense stream of powerful energy that is flowing through us and for us, underpinning our spiritual growth.

Now, with this awareness, we hold a wonderful key in our hand. With it, we can find the places in our consciousness where we have blocked the flow of this healing power, inverting it so that it has turned against us. On this path, we learn to harmonize this whole process by surrendering all of ourselves to the Christ that is waking up in us, on the plane of our inner reality. And this is exactly the same process that must happen on the level of the planet.

Many people have visited spiritual centers—retreat centers and the like—and experienced the truth of this process. They have encountered life and growth, as well as joy and pain and authentic peace by doing this. It's tempting to believe that this life—the life we are living during these short stays—is too beautiful, too meaningful, to be real. Reality can't really be this way, we think. This is too much, we feel.

So when we return to our daily lives, we call this our "real" life. Friends, nothing could be further from the truth. What we refer to as "real life" is a most illusory life, where everything has been turned on its head. In this version of life, we only concern ourselves with the outer world, which is the most superficial level of life. That's all we deal with. As a result, life fragments into meaningless patterns.

In the new world, we will learn to make connections between cause and effect—between these fragments of consciousness and how we have created them. We will learn to uncover the deeper, more real life within that is responsible for creating our outer circumstances. By working this way, we will approach reality. Over time, we will live in more harmony, in a more true reality.

Once we connect with our inner reality, we will be better able to deal with the superficial issues that arise out of illusion. Assuming, that is, we don't fall back into the trap of seeing duality as the only reality that counts. For as soon as we do this, we will once again distort truth.

The time has come to start living in this new kind of civilization and culture. The forces working to build this new reality are, at the same time, destroying all that gets in the way of this movement. For it's not possible to grow and create without also destroying what is destructive. Whatever is now obsolete must go. But destructive consciousness clings to its destructiveness, opposing this purifying movement.

When we were in a less developed state of consciousness, these obsolete attitudes may have had their place. But to keep pursing them now does not make sense. We will all find this is true when we do our individual work. The attitudes and reactions we had when we were small children and infants were understandable—appropriate even. But then we held on to them, as though they still have value for us as adults.

To whatever extent we are still doing this, we are creating obstructions that lead to strife and crisis. We will end up frustrated and unhappy, and this leads us to becoming destructive—*so the old can crumble and we can build anew.* If we become willing to give up our obsolete, old attitudes and find new, more appropriate ones, the painful crises and their associated destruction won't be necessary.

When we become willing to change our inner stance, outer change can happen organically and harmoniously. But when we deliberately deny and hold back—when we choose to delude ourselves that all is well inside, or that it probably doesn't matter anyway, or it's too hard so I can't do it—we court crisis and we invite pain.

This applies to all of humanity in exactly the same way it applies to a person. What each person is, relative to all of humanity, is the same as what an attitude or reaction is to our whole personality. Just as we find that our inner strife is due to our conflicting parts—part of us wants to grow, and part of us wants to hold back—so it goes with planet Earth. Parts of the planet want to grow, and other parts want to hold back, denying there is even a conflict. In this global community, of which we are all a part, there are some who want to change, and there are some who resist.

If we are able to understand this teaching, we may be encouraged to commit ourselves to changing on a deeper level of our being. For change is one of the hallmark features of this new era we are in.

Changing to New Rules

Before delving into the importance of change in this new era, let's go back to the concept of good and evil, defined as that which is constructive and in alignment with truth and divine law, and that which is opposed to it. In the past, living in a world steeped in the primitive consciousness of duality, we needed rigid laws; we needed dos and don'ts; we needed commandments and prohibitions.

For a consciousness that is childish and self-indulgent needs rules to be imposed from the outside. Without them, there would be complete chaos. Without rules, people would act on their destructive impulses to a much greater degree. But such severity brought a superficiality to people's live, and also a certain rigidity.

Further, it's tempting to blindly obey such rules and avoid thinking for ourselves, for that would mean we need to struggle with the more complicated matter of inner morality. By blindly obeying rules, we encourage laziness in our thinking. We take the way of avoiding responsibility and not participating in the search-and-find effort needed to uncover true answers—to reach enlightenment.

This is why these teachings stress, over and over, that it's an error to believe one action is right and another is wrong. This is, most of the time, faulty thinking. As we have been painstakingly taught in many other teachings from this source, most of the time, either alternative we follow could be in keeping with either sincere motives, or dishonest ones. It's only by sorting out our dishonest motives on both sides that we open our inner channel to God and get the guidance we need.

We will need to have the courage needed to search for such understanding. And this is hard work. It's easier to just obey outer rules. This kind of inquiry, though, will be exactly what's needed in this new era of new consciousness that is spreading more and more across the planet as humanity grows up and wakes up.

There is another way the dualistic approach to life creates confusion and distortion of truth. There are some who claim it is desirable to adopt a particular attitude toward life, and the opposite attitude is then supposedly undesirable. Another group of people will feel it's the other way around. Each side resorts to fanaticism, exaggeration and distortion to make their point.

Some people say the introspective life is the only way to go. Being outgoing and extroverted then is harmful, and even wrong. Others say the exact opposite is true, believing it's always best to be active. So then anything passive or receptive is rejected. Many other approaches to life are divided down the middle like this. Entire philosophies are based on such divisions. Whole treatises have been written using half-truths to present one side of a matter.

So many issues today meet this fate. Going forward, such rigid divisions based on shortsighted either/or thinking will no longer fly. And yet this kind of polarization was an inevitable byproduct of a system that runs on rules. Again, such rules were necessary in the past to stop people from destroying each other, blindly, willfully and selfishly. For this is what happens as long as we remain in a state of emotional alienation and then don't experience another person's pain as real.

What to Follow

The point here is not that humanity is now developed enough that we don't need outer rules. Obviously that's not true. As we know, even in spite of existing rules, there are those who willfully harm others with their cruel, selfish and irresponsible behavior. But whether we are talking about a person or a planet, this only applies to the darkest, most undeveloped parts—the Lower Self of the entity.

As we increasingly develop, the rules naturally fall away, making way for a new conscience and inner morality. As the Christ consciousness evolves from within, it gradually brings humanity, bit by bit, to a state where rules are superfluous. For our inner God knows the truth. From this place within, we know what love is and we know divine reality. Once we start living from this place, our personality can begin to act from our innermost center.

We can already see this, at least to a small degree. As we walk a psychological inner path to explore our emotions, outer rules don't apply. What we discover on our inner path is the beauty of divine laws working in utter perfection, along with justice and true love. Our childish Lower Self—sometimes called the Little-L Lower Self—in us might blindly rebel against these laws. But once we wake up, we must be overwhelmed by the grandeur of the divine scheme in which all is well. If we choose to see the plan that is playing out—to read the script we have been following—and go along with it, we'll see there is nothing to fear.

We know, deep inside, what our inner truth is. No one can tell us this. On this level, there is no single act that is right or wrong. And yet, at the same time, sometimes our inner plan wants us to go in a certain direction; our divine self is telling us we *need* to go this way, and not that. But this can't come to us from the outside.

Only after we have gone very deeply into ourselves will we find the ultimate truth. Then, and only then, we will be able to transcend the rules. Then we can be done with adherence to public opinion, the self-interest of the Lower Self, the façade that covers the Lower Self, the need for approval, and the need to spite others and rebel.

Outer help and guidance, though, can have great value on our path. It can guide us to go deeply enough into ourselves that we see how invested we are in this false vision of reality—in the dualistic illusion. We can easily get lost in our inner maze, but someone outside of us can often see the maze we can't see, and therefore they can help us find the way out. But our ultimate goal is to realize our own inner law, once we find our own inner God. Our current reality is urging us to go in this direction.

Outer laws run parallel to inner laws. Many outer laws arise directly from divine law, but we've lost the thread to their divine origin. So they are, by now, disconnected structures. Sometimes the connection is obvious. For example, destructive acts like killing, stealing or somehow robbing another of their rights are clearly parallel to inner law. But when situations get more complicated, the inner law may not be so simple to see. This is where using our new approach can help, as it brings forward truth and the reality of divine law as it exists on an inner level.

We may at times find that outer law is completely contrary to God's inner law. Here's a simple example of this: If a person lives in a land where the government is corrupt, people may be required to commit acts that go against humanity—in other words, that go against God. To follow outer law, in this case, is to go against divine law. It takes a lot of courage to stand up for inner truth under such conditions, and defy outer law.

But people can get lost in a maze of confusion and then find refuge in following the outer law. For them, that may be the easier—possibly even the better—way. By the same token, someone could misuse these words to justify a Lower-Self desire to defy an outer law. We must always study our motives carefully to see the true situation. There aren't any rules telling us what to follow, when we should break the rules, or how to go about following them.

The Christ consciousness sweeping the planet is not a revolution. It is not a rebellion. It is not, in itself, about destruction of the old ways. It is about change. It is a reorganization of eternal values that already existed in the old consciousness, but which we must now express in a new way.

The Christ consciousness, with its new inner morality, will slowly but surely wipe away outer commandments, outer regulations, and outer laws—written and unwritten. For sure, laws will still be needed for quite some time, in terms of Earth years, but this is the direction things will be moving. For now, we need these laws to protect each of us from the Lower Self of others. But when we have outgrown the Lower Self, we won't need to be told not to hurt someone else. We will know this, and we will have no desire to do so.

To the extent we allow God to wake up in us, outer laws will go away. The new laws of inner morality are totally flexible. Every case is different. But to uphold them, we will need courage and the honesty of self-knowledge so we can't be corrupted by sneaky, slippery Lower Self motives. We will need to learn to look at every situation individually, and deal with it as though it is completely new. This is what adults can do. And maturity is now humanity's goal. But we are not being mature when we resist change.

We will need a flexible attitude to thrive in the new ever-changing world. For change and freedom are inseparable. What else is inseparable? Rigidity and enslavement. If we want to live in a world that is simple, where we don't have to search or put any energy into unraveling a difficult situation—if we want everything handed to us on a platter—we will need to deal with inflexible rules that enslave and confine us.

We can be free only if we overcome our rebellion against authority—because we have found our own inner authority, and our own self-honesty. This will require that we embrace change. And flexibility. Situations that look the same on the surface may in fact be quite different and require a different approach. Freedom, then, is totally dependent on our ability to change.

"Find that part within that can create an echo now to the words I have given you. Let these words nourish and strengthen you where you need it most. Make room for the ever more emerging new consciousness as it spreads on the inner plane and fully embrace the movement. Go with it! Trust that this can only enhance you and your life. You are all being blessed in truth and in love. Be your God."

–The Pathwork® Guide

Chapter 14

The Pulse of Life on Every Level

A new era has begun. It is, among many things, a time of linking and connecting in many areas, on many levels, in many ways. The primary place to connect is on the inner levels, within the personality. But we must also connect on the outer levels, so that eventually the differences between religions, nations and the like, will disappear. Does this mean that individuality will go away? Absolutely not. Just the opposite will happen.

In a very practical sense, we are now moving out of duality. During the era of duality, there was a lot of diversity on the outer levels, while conformity and unity was more often *within* a person. This had a way of wiping out true individual expression. The age of unity now ushers in a different picture. Outer differences will go away as they lose their importance. We won't attach our personal identity to our nationality or our religion. As such, we won't be blocked from finding our soul's oneness with the All because of a rigid focus on differences.

What will gain importance in the new era will be our diverse divine expressions. From unified groups, a group consciousness will arise that will allow clearly defined individuals to evolve. And these people will be able to bring an even greater unity to the group process. Let's now turn our attention to how the pulsation of life and consciousness works behind the scenes to support such an unfolding.

Everything in the universe is divine pulsation. As the universal spirit pulsates into matter, matter becomes enlivened by the pulse of the divine. The movement of the divine, as it expands and contracts, pushes its way into the void. Eternal life advances with each expanding move, enlivening the void, or vacuum, with spirit. At the "momentary" meeting of the void with divine substance, matter is created.

This pulse we are speaking of is an aspect of life we're well aware of on this physical plane. Our own physical bodies are alive and we have a pulse. The heart, the lungs and the bloodstream all pulsate. We are quite familiar with this phenomena. What we are not so familiar with are the more finely calibrated pulsations that happen in the mind, in our feeling self and in the body. In addition, there is a pulsation of life that is a spiritual push, which reaches out into the void, turning the void into life.

Each manifestation of life—whether it's a person or a different kind of organism—is itself, a pulse beat. For life penetrates everything that is, so it is in all organisms. As long as a being is alive, this pulse of universal life expands into it. It's one single pulse. But the pulse rate is not always the same. According to the rhythm of the entity, there will be a particular pulse beat that follows particular laws.

There are pulse systems in the physical body we have not yet discovered. For every molecule, pore, cell and organ has its own pulse system. In the same way, the layers of consciousness have different pulse beats, pulse systems and pulse laws.

Our very life is a single pulse beat on the universal clock. And each planet has its own system of pulse beats. A star appears, a star disappears, with a pulse beat of maybe billions of years. But of course time is an illusion. We perceive this illusion as we observe different spans of time. So we find it hard to see how a single pulse of blood through our heart is of the same nature as the pulse beat of a planetary system.

Three Movements of Pulsation

There are three movements—universal movements—that comprise every pulse that brings life into manifestation. These are: the expanding, the contracting, and the static movements. Let's look at this in terms of the pulse of a single person's life. During the expanding movement, life penetrates into the body of matter. Then during contraction, life returns to its source as it withdraws into the inner realm. Life then refuels during the static movement, regenerating itself. The potent energies of the nucleus restore the entity so that it once again becomes ready to thrust itself forward. This is how it fulfills its innate plan. And it will do this over and over, billowing further and further into the void, until divinity has completely filled all there is.

In the case of the human body, it has a main pulsatory system—the heart. This cascades throughout all the systems and organs of the body, so that altogether, they form the totality of a person's body. If one of these pulse systems doesn't work correctly, life will be impaired. It's no different on all levels of our being, and each level has a main way the pulse shows up.

Our feeling body, our consciousness, our will—all these systems have a main pulse, which causes it to show up, or appear, in matter. In addition, each pulse has nested pulse systems that must function properly for us to be healthy.

If there is a strong, full pulse, we will be able to see this in a person, for divine aspects are "pumped" into an entity in the same way the heart pumps blood into a body. This shows up as intelligence, talent, beauty, health, goodness. If there are any imperfections—lack of intelligence, lack of talent, unattractiveness, ill health, problems, poverty, and such—this reveals a weak pulse of divine penetration.

What is responsible for a strong pulse beat? Our inner consciousness and inner will, of course. When a being appears in matter, the underlying consciousness may or may not be strongly motivated to fulfill a certain task. This will affect whether the pulse is strong and full, or not. If a particular consciousness is only half willing to fulfill its own destiny—to follow its seed plan—the pulse will be weak.

So the rhythms of every pulse system—of a human being or another kind of being—depend on the will, intention and determination of the entity, on all levels of their being. If the pulse is weak, this will bring about a quicker contracting movement—that is, withdrawal from life. A short life span is a demonstration of this.

We can see then that the prime regulator of life is consciousness, as that can influence the pulse beat. As we do our healing work on a spiritual path such as this one, we will delve deeply into the various intricate levels of our inner consciousness. As we do this, we become aware of an intentionality that is often quite hidden.

In other words, we can see our pulse beat in the way our life unfolds, and this is a direct expression of our inner, often hidden, intentionality. The power level, if you will, of the pulse of our spirit then—which is what enlivens our body, the shell of matter in which we live—determines our well-being, vitality, creativity, fulfillment, perfection and degree of trust, to name a few aspects.

Every pulse is a billowing force. Too often, though, unconscious levels of our personality interfere with the thrust of our spirit. But we do have the power to change this. We can strengthen our pulse beat, and thus extend our life.

When we see a person whose main life pulse is weak, we will observe lack of energy, lack of vitality, lack of creativity, lack of health, lack of any divine attribute, really. As the pulsing movement withdraws, going back into the person's inner reality, the matter that had been enlivened dissolves and returns to particles. These particles won't ever return to the state they were in when life was pulsing through them.

For that life force has now gone back, and it will wait to billow forth when the cosmic pulse beat pushes through again, enlivening other matter, creating new form, and forever working to fill the void. This is the plan of evolution, and it will continue until divine life permeates all existence—until it has pulsated all the way through all that is. This is the process of evolution: constantly thrusting, billowing, expanding, and then withdrawing. It is forever pushing forward and then pulling back.

So the motion of pulling back is a natural part of the pulse. But we have the ability to regulate this. And in doing so—by use of our inner attitude and intention—we can strengthen the pulse. Never lose sight of this fact: everything that exists is consciousness, even the tiniest, invisible particle. And so everything is a pulsating expression: every emotion, every thought, every self-expression, every level of consciousness, every expression of our will. Everything.

Looking around, we can see there is great variety in the level of life pulse among people. When we incarnate in matter—when a person is born—we manifest many aspects of consciousness. Our divine self chooses which aspects to bring in, while other aspects of our consciousness do not manifest. We will choose some "finished" aspects of our eternal being, which we have already purified. But we will also choose some unfinished aspects to incorporate into the person we will become in this lifetime. Altogether, this will create our personality. Therefore, many divergent aspects coexist on this planet.

When we do our personal healing work, we are often surprised to discover some of these divergent aspects in ourselves. On our conscious level, we're convinced we only think one way about certain aspects of ourselves, others or life. But when we peel back the layers and go inside, we find thoughts that are completely the opposite. We also find feelings, attitudes and expressions of our will going in opposite directions on deeper levels of our being.

So it is of utmost importance we allow unconscious elements we're not yet familiar with to come into our conscious awareness. This is the only way to incorporate them into our process of purification and transformation. If we don't do this, our work will remain half done.

Creating a Strong Pulse

In the previous era, it was not only enough, but it was our task as humans to focus on our outer awareness and the level of our volitional will. Our work was to purify and strengthen the outer aspect of our personalities—our ego—as a prerequisite for what would come next. It was absolutely necessary that we strengthen the outer levels of our personality. In those days, all that was expected of us was that our conscious mind and will learned how to be pure and good. Now humanity has reached the end of that old era, and it time's to take the next step into something new.

The development we successfully accomplished on the conscious plane opened certain channels in us that, at least to some extent, reached the inner reality of our divine selves. So those with enough discipline to do the work on the conscious level could—and can—establish connecting channels to God within.

But when a person does not attend to the material that exists on unconscious levels, the pulse weakens.

The pulse can only be strong to whatever degree a person's whole package of consciousness is in harmony with the divine. Disharmony influences how reliable a channel is, as well as its width, depth and scope. It's possible to have a channel that is only reliable in a specific area of our life, while it remains limited in others.

Therefore it is quite correct to predict that in this era of unification, during which self-purification takes place on inner levels, the average age of human beings will become much longer. Because through a person's inner purification work, their life pulse is strengthened. The life span will extend way past what we currently believe is possible.

Simply put, when our whole personality is operating in harmony with itself, when we have no more divergent levels, when we have become totally conscious of our entire selves, then the pulsation can come through very strongly. Our spirit will be able to enliven matter fully, energizing it and vitalizing it.

Currently, in humanity's present stage of development, even in the best circumstances only some levels of our being are conscious. What remains in our unconscious levels stops the divine pulse beat from expanding further. We have each brought certain negative aspects into this incarnation with the specific intention of making them known to ourselves. If we don't become aware of these negative aspects, it's unavoidable they will weaken us and cause either illness or quite possibly—on a level that is unconscious—a will to die. When this happens, our life span becomes shorter than it needed to be.

So in this new era, it is utterly necessary to discover what exists on unconscious levels of our personality. For to complete the process that is unfolding, we need to include what those unconscious levels are holding—currently in distortion and waiting to materialize. We are now past the time when it was enough to only pay attention to what was happening on the conscious level of our being. Now, in order for a community, a group, or an individual to grow harmoniously and completely fulfill its task, we need to follow more subtle and intricate approaches.

There will be limitations in our lives to whatever degree aspects of our personality remain unconscious. We will be limited in not only the way we express ourselves in life, but in the way we connect with the divine and with our own needs. Our conscious self might be quite pure and in this part of ourselves, we may be a beautiful channel. But if we are ignoring unconscious material, this outer channel will be limited. As a result, we will be limited in our perception of our own real needs, including both the needs of our Higher Self and of our body.

False needs will then set in, predominating and confusing us. When this happens, our mind will not be able to sort out which needs are real and which are false. To remain healthy, we need to tune in to the needs of our physical and spiritual bodies. But we can only rely on having the fine perception required when we have the courage to go all the way—to see, become familiar with, and accept all the aspects of ourselves we have brought into this life as our task.

So we must build a bridge to these aspects. We do this by having courage, inner wisdom and faith, all of which we activate through our commitment to our spiritual path. What stops us? What prevents us from making connections with the inner layers of our consciousness? Fear. More specifically, fear of the self, which is the biggest factor stopping us. When we try to spiritualize our being in ways that avoid knowing about the less palatable parts of ourselves, our work cannot be complete. For if we fear some parts of ourselves, we divide ourselves.

Most of us don't even realize we have this fear of self. We are in fact quick to rationalize away this fear. As such, we lose touch with our real needs and instead create false needs: the need to avoid parts of ourselves and the need to escape. Just as we can create false needs on the level of the body—which show up as addictions to drugs, alcohol, harmful stimulants or unwholesome foods—so can our emotional and mental bodies become polluted by the false need to run away from some level of our inner being. Our consciousness then gets tripped up in these false needs.

As we become more thoughtful—more mindful—we open to other possible ways of being. We start to learn—maybe as a first significant step—that there really are parts of ourselves we fear. By simply acknowledging this fear and not pushing it to the side, we start to build a bridge. This is how we start to connect with our inner being which has, until now, remained a stranger to us.

What follows suit from here is no longer quite so hard. Once we know what our fear is, we can begin to question it. We can challenge our fear. And when we do this, we create a strong new pulse on a new level of our soul. This is how we let life enter our spirit where it wasn't able to penetrate before because of our fear—or more correctly because of the denial of our fear. Our denial is what prevents the full beat of the pulse of our incarnation from enlivening all of our being, including every particle of our mental, physical and emotional bodies.

When we learn to overcome our inner fear, and in this way dissolve our inner defenses—defenses which can be quite tricky, subtle and sophisticated—we make room for a whole new expression of life that wants to penetrate our whole being. We open to an entirely new pulse beat.

Inner links are forming now in our world. These are needed by the spiritual movement that wants to complete its total spiritualization of our inner personalities. Then the power of the word of Christ—the power of Christ consciousness—can arrive unimpeded on all levels of our personality. This is what the Spirit World is working for—inspiring us for. Openings are being created in many different ways, even if these sometimes seems disconnected from the spiritual reality we are familiar with.

For example, a century or so ago we experienced an influx from the field of psychology. Granted, while this knowledge has some limitations, it nonetheless pointed out the divergent levels of the personality to us. Without this understanding, total purification and spiritual unification couldn't happen in a genuine and realistic way. So this unfolding was divinely inspired, as it was necessary for the great task ahead of us.

The Spirit World is not content any longer with purification on the conscious level. At this point in time, more is needed. Just as we are now seeing the Lower Self of nations exposed, which are symbolic reflections of our inner world, so the same must happen with each person. It may make us sad at first to see what is becoming visible, but how can true purification take place if we don't become aware of the sadness that's been there all along about the impure—unclean—limited aspects.

These must come to the front of our conscious awareness. Our Lower Self exists, and we must take this seriously—not by fearing it but by meeting it. It is possible to go about this in the right way, trusting and knowing that these destructive energies are fundamentally divine and therefore can be transformed. They are essential and can be altered.

Our job is to make sure no part of ourselves remains denied, rejected and disconnected. For we give great power to any part we deny. This denied part will then come out indirectly and will manage to somehow deprive us of something we need: our health, our vitality, our happiness. Or it will block inspiration from reaching our conscious minds with messages that are extremely important for us to receive.

"My beloved friends, angels of God are filling this space. It is truly an inner space, which is reflected, from your point of view, on the outside. These angels cooperate and are deeply concerned with the task that every one of you has to fulfill, that is waiting for you in a time of great meaning and inner expansion and purpose.

Each of you can be, and many of you will be, carriers, in one form or another, of new truths and new ways. Every one of your tasks is of the greatest importance, and the happiness of each of you is of the greatest importance. Your happiness will be a natural expression of your devotion to the truth of your transformation and of your devotion to the task that is waiting.

So happiness will be a result, and at the same time also a prerequisite. For only the joyous can give joy; only those in truth can bring truth; only the loving and loved ones can give love. Let yourself experience this every day and every hour of your life. The love of the universe permeates all that is, all that ever was, and all that ever will be, all that you are, every level of your blessed being."

–The Pathwork® Guide

Chapter 15

Cause and Effect on Various Levels of Consciousness

It's not easy to talk about cause and effect on this three-dimensional level. But let's try. We can start by saying that at the lowest level of development—on the scale of consciousness—there is no cause and effect, or at least there doesn't appear to be any. As we raise our level of consciousness, we are able to see new horizons. From our new perspective, we are able to see how effects are connected to causes we previously didn't even know existed. When we crest the hill and reach the point where consciousness becomes completely God-infused, cause and effect will no longer exist.

Here we see that, once again, the lowest forms of consciousness have something in common with the highest forms. But there's an enormous difference in what they hold, in terms of attitudes and underlying feelings and thoughts. We can easily understand that primitive consciousness sees the world as an unconnected series of events that are unrelated to cause and effect. It may be harder for us to understand how in the highest realms it doesn't exist at all. And this reality is nearly impossible to convey using human words.

Here on Earth, every act has its consequence. That's not so hard to realize. It's not quite as easy to see that the same relationship exists between our thoughts or our subtle inner attitudes and the overall circumstances of our life. But the more developed we become, the more we will be able to perceive cause and effect on these less obvious levels. On this spiritual path, such perceptions gradually become more acute, and in fact this is very strongly emphasized.

If we commit some overt act—let's say we kill another person—the consequences will be obvious. But we are also killing another person when we malign them. We do this through our questionable accusations, blindness, stubbornness or ill will; when we refuse to give another person the benefit of the doubt; when we don't try to use honest communication or openness to create a different reality. Such secret "killing" has consequences that are just as severe as physical killing.

At first, the effects of this kind of action might be hard for us to perceive. But as we raise our consciousness, we will start to see there's a definite connection between cause and effect, even if the cause was not an overt act but a hidden thought we had previously ignored.

In our current state of consciousness, living in this three-dimensional world, we often find ourselves to be, in many ways, halfway. Our world is not all bad, but it's also not all good. Our personalities too are not all bad, but also not all good. We don't live in heaven, but we also don't live in hell. Our lives represent both extremes.

Many of us do not believe there are other realms—other worlds—and so we also doubt there are other states of consciousness. But by virtue of the fact we are so halfway, this is a clear indication our sphere cannot possibly be the only reality there is. If there is some good in us and in our world, then greater degrees of goodness must exist. So it only makes sense that a plane exists that is all goodness. The same, of course, applies to the bad. If there is a little bad in us and in our world, spheres of consciousness must exist where there is more bad, and eventually, where all is bad.

We're also halfway about cause and effect, or more correctly, in our perception of cause and effect. What changes as we develop is *not* the object of our perception. What changes as we grow is our vision.

An act cannot be reversed. Whatever the momentary consequences are, they are irreversible. Later on, we may be able to modify the act, perhaps by seeing it was a mistake and trying to correct it. We might see the inner current that led us to do the act, and we may use this as material to raise our consciousness and widen our perception and vision. Working in this way, we may be able to neutralize the effects of a negative act. But at the moment it happens, the act is irreversible and the consequences can't be annulled.

If there are consequences in that moment which result from the act, we may be able to eliminate them *in time*, after some time has passed. So we can gradually begin to see the relationship—the connection—between cause and effect and time.

Our state of development creates a reality that corresponds to it. Our current reality contains three dimensions: time, movement and space. What we also experience is a certain degree of cause and effect. If we can't see how our acts lead to specific consequences, we won't be able to use them as the indispensable tools they can be for helping us develop our soul.

For example, if we don't believe a negative thought leads to particular, tangible results, why would we be motivated to correct our thought? But if, over time, we see there is an effect, we can go about correcting the thought so that, once again, *in time* we can eliminate the effects. It's not any different with our positive, truthful, life-affirming thoughts, actions and attitudes. They all have corresponding effects that are desirable.

If we remain unaware of the link between cause and effect in all areas of our lives, believing the effects are haphazard and just coincidences, we won't work to improve the causes we create. We won't be able to perceive that the supreme power in the universe is goodness and love, and therefore the truth of this will not be able to support and strengthen us.

Now let's say we are compelled by our inner forces to impulsively do something destructive. This may cause an instantaneous pain and remorse. We long to be in a state of being where we can undo this act. We want to live as though it never happened. Yet we know that in this world we're living in, that's impossible.

How can it be, then, that there's no cause and effect in higher realms? Maybe we can sense, deep in ourselves, the possibility that "underneath" this current level of cause and effect, a level exists in which we're completely untouched by both the cause we set in motion and the effect we have brought about. What is this part that is unaffected? This is our Higher Self, the divine part of ourselves that does not participate in any of our negative thoughts. It's also not part of our destructive actions and attitudes.

But the layers of our personality that are still mired in false perceptions—and which therefore hold untruthful, unloving attitudes and do destructive acts—have to work themselves out of this quagmire. And this can only happen *in time*. So time and cause and effect are different manifestations of the same reality, and are intrinsically connected. The two cannot be pulled apart.

Making the Connection

Perhaps we're starting to see that this three-dimensional world—with its cause and effect, with its duality, with its limitation of time, space and movement—is directly linked with the distortions, impurities and limitations of our perception and our vision. Our three-dimensional perception is, in itself, an untruthful view of the world. We can add to this untruthful equation the limitation of time, space and movement, together with the struggle that comes with duality, along with the law of cause and effect.

But when we add all this together in the right way, we have the very tools our soul needs to transcend this entire realm of consciousness. Now we start to see that our *perception* is the cause of certain actions, which unavoidably lead to certain effects. But these effects can be the very medicine we need to overcome our distorted perceptions...which create the causes....which in turn create the effects.

There are states of consciousness—the highest states—where only the highest, best, most beautiful and most creative causes are set into motion. Here, in this enlightened state of consciousness, cause and effect are immediately—almost simultaneously—discerned. In such a sphere, there is no gap of time between cause and effect. So the cause *is* the effect. The thought *is* the act.

Even the most secret, subtle attitude creates instant consequences. There is no space in between an effect and its cause. As all becomes one, on this level of being, cause and effect truly become one.

This is why, during certain moments of grace, we can sense the realm deep within in which no matter what happens, we remain untouched. No matter what, we are unalterably pure. No matter what, we are divine. We are good in our essence. For our essence *is* the essence of all. It is God.

On the other hand, there exists a primitive state of consciousness where even the most obvious act appears to be isolated, with no consequences or connection, with no cause and no effect. When a primitive person kills someone, they may truly believe their act will have no further consequences, either for the victim or for themselves. So it won't occur to this person to search for the cause within, to find out what created their desire to commit the act. As such, the act never becomes the medicine that could, in time, cure the disease of evil.

Total Surrender to God

Surrendering to God is an innate movement of our soul. This is our ultimate fate. If we do not do this, we can't fulfill our task and we can't fulfill ourselves. The question is: Do we really have to surrender to God? We all do battle with this central question. And yet our resistance to following this call of our soul is the very thing that causes all our discomfort: our pain, our suffering, our anxiety, and our discontent.

So how does this topic connect with cause and effect? It's like this: Surrendering to God, or our unwillingness to surrender, affects every conceivable part of our life, inner and outer. Let's add some more light to how this could be so.

What are some of the natural effects of surrendering completely to God? Since this *is* our natural soul movement, then to surrender to God is to fulfill our own destiny. Doing so will bring our lives into balance and bring harmony into our whole being.

In our mental body, we will be ruled by truth, having realistic understanding, and clear vision and perception. In our mind we will be at peace. Confusions will clear up and conflicting perceptions will resolve. Frustration then will disappear. With this kind of enlightenment, we will have insight about apparent conflicts that will make all the pieces of the great puzzles in our life fall into place.

On the level of our emotions, our mental reconciliation of opposites is going to create an entirely new way of being, feeling and reacting. For instance, it will no longer appear to us that loving will weaken or humiliate us. Quite to the contrary, we'll discover, loving creates dignity and a healthy sense of pride.

When we become willing to surrender to God, we avoid one of the biggest pitfalls of being human: the temptation to surrender to greater power structures that are negative. But the minute we resist—obstructing our natural soul movement to surrender to God, which is our destiny—we must succumb to a substitute. We will end up in false surrender. Friends, it's very important we understand this.

If we fear someone in authority—it doesn't matter whether this authority really is abusing their power or we only imagine it—it's because we depend on this authority figure in ways that are both tangible and intangible. Because of our dependency and fear, we respond by either submitting and selling out and then hating ourselves for this, or by rebelling blindly against the authority in an effort to avoid hating ourselves. We are trying to preserve our dignity.

But in this situation, this is not true dignity. This is nothing more than a blind reaction based on emotional reflex and stirred up turbulent feelings we are barely aware of. In any case, we are not clear about what's happening. And since we lack true insight, we can't tell whether the authority is really abusive or if we're just acting like a child.

If we are genuinely surrendering to God in all areas of our life, we will easily see an unworthy authority for what it is: someone who wants to subdue us, abuse us, exploit us and trample our dignity. It doesn't matter whether this person is our boss or a mate we depend on financially and whose love we need and crave. If our surrender to God is our key position—our main emphasis and our primary attitude—we will trust God and we will know that trusting God is totally justified.

From here, we will be able to find the courage to risk losing the one we feel we need. When we set God above all, we have the clear vision to see when a human authority is abusive, and then we can make the choice to pay the price needed to gain our freedom. We may have to give up whatever this authority holds out for us, but we will be able to do this if our dignity is more important. Our autonomy can only grow from the rich soil of total inner surrender to God.

Giving ourselves over to God will then have a further consequence. We will need to make a change. For we're going to need to change our situation if we want to get our real needs met without enslaving ourselves as we've been doing. This may mean getting a new position, a new boss, or a new partner. But the new authorities we attract in life will be, like us, autonomous people who are following their call to set God above all else.

They won't need to abuse their power, for they won't be wielding a power built on the backs of needy people. It's also possible we'll now find that the very same people—our boss or our mate—react differently to us with our new and improved attitude. The change in us may engender a change in them, since they too may also have had a conflict between their Higher Self and Lower Self. In resolving their inner conflict, they may discover a new respect for our dignity and set us free, allowing the relationship to become a mutual giving and receiving.

In the event it's our own perception that's distorted—assuming that any and all authority is out to humiliate and abuse us—then our total surrender to God will surface our misconception and we will be able to adjust our perception to match reality. This is how to unwind any compulsion we have to rebel against rightful authority, which is the kind that merely asks us to contribute our rightful share to a mutual venture.

Hiding behind our rebellion to authority is often our own desire to have power over others. Secretly, we want to be the ones who get to abuse power. We may have never thought of it like this, but this is what happens when we let our self-will run the show. Often, embedded in our distorted self-will are feelings of powerlessness and humiliation whenever our self-will is not fulfilled. This leads us to believe that we have two options: become the world's greatest power—God—or be annihilated.

In an effort to avoid being totally annihilated, we may tend to bow to substitute powers, rather than bend to God's will. This is why we may choose to submit to another person who is seemingly stronger than us: a boss, a partner, a dictator. We hope that by serving them, we will gain a superior position ourselves.

Or maybe we'll turn money or position into the power we are seeking. These then become our substitute Gods. Or perhaps we feel powerful when we keep ourselves aloof from other people, never completely opening our heart but always making ourselves desirable, playing directly into the hands of other people's neurotic needs and misconceptions.

Both of these things—submission to substitute authority as well as rebellion against all authority—are effects. They are the results of a cause we ourselves set into motion when we denied and obstructed our natural soul movement of surrendering to God. But as soon as we recognize God as the highest authority, everything falls into place.

Otherwise, if we refuse to do this, we must be confused about what authority we actually do need and should serve. We won't be able to tell when it is appropriate to follow their lead, and when we should step up ourselves because self-assertion is called for.

When our primary stance is surrender to God, we are able to clearly see what is what. With a proper view of things, we can follow suit with a right action that won't be tied to an inner conflict. We will admit that we have needs, that we need a leader or authority in certain parts of our life, that we also have an important role to play and, in accepting our part, we have a heightened sense of ourselves. We feel true dignity.

From this place, when we follow a leader, we won't lose our soul. Because our soul will belong to God, and God returns it to us cleaner, stronger and with even more autonomy. When we refuse to surrender to God and his will, we resist our own destiny and create real guilt that permeates our being and weakens us. So many of our self-punishing patterns—self-doubt, hesitation, weakness—result directly from this.

It doesn't matter how many psychological explanations we may find—and on their level, they may be perfectly true—we can never reverse and transform this self-defeating pattern unless we heal spiritually. And we can only do this when we give over all of ourselves—in every area of our lives, in all ways—to the great creator, God.

When we do this—and of course this is not a one-time event, but one we must do repeatedly, daily, regarding all issues in our life—we will find a new strength and sense of self we never knew we had before. This will almost seem like a paradox. Deep down we have always feared that if we gave ourselves to God, we would lose ourselves. Now we find that—as a very real and palpable reality—Jesus' words were true: We must lose ourselves *in God* in order to find ourselves.

Positive Aggression

With our new strength, we will spontaneously have the wisdom to know when to give in with grace, and when to use positive aggression. From our instantaneous knowing will flow the appropriate act. Energetic, positive, aggressive movements will replace denial and childish, destructive rebellion. We will intuitively know when to gracefully give in by yielding, flowing and accepting—even when our self-will doesn't like it. This will replace humiliating, self-denying submission based on fear and an inability to trust life.

In either case, we will be able to make new choices in a whole new way. Whereas in the past we might have weakly submitted, now we may yield *or* follow, and maintain our dignity either way. Or perhaps we'll find that positive aggression is the order of the day. Then we will be able to stand up for ourselves, rather than blindly and destructively rebel as we might have before.

This time we can act in a new spirit, out of different motives and with a clearer vision. So our stance will have an entirely different effect on others, for the tone of our aggression will change. It could also happen that we come to realize that what the situation really calls for is not fighting, but giving in. We see that it is fair, justified, necessary, right and good for everyone involved. We now understand there was no injustice or abuse after all, so there's no need for aggression.

Positive aggression, however, is not only used for the purpose of exposing injustice and abuse. It's not only an action we take in response to something, it is also an initiating action. Whether within ourselves or out in the world, this kind of action—positive aggression—is needed to expand, to move out, to create, to improve. Without this energetic movement surging ahead, we can't transform our negative material.

Such an organic, healthy surging movement is not depleting or effortful. Rather, it's a freeing release that energizes our whole being. But this only happens when our organic, appropriate aggression aligns with God's will. The positive new reality we are striving for can only come to pass when we have freed ourselves from the confusions that accompany our denial of our soul movements—of our inner call to give ourselves over to God.

When we step into the new reality, we won't have to ask if we should stand up and assert ourselves or give in and follow. We won't doubt the nature of those we need and depend on. We won't question the motives of authority. We won't have to grapple with our intellect alone, which could never give us the insight we want. We will enjoy spontaneity. The knowledge we need will land in our lap, strong and clear, without nagging doubt.

We will flow from the center of ourselves where God lives and reigns, where Christ is king, and where all is right in our world: in our actions, in our perceptions, in our knowledge, in our reactions and in our feelings. The peace and single point of focus we long for lies in this key: total surrender to God. Friends, use this key.

"My beloved friends, the blessings extended to all of you are specifically directed at this time toward helping you to give over to Him Who holds you, Who contains you, Who makes you safe and secure, Who infuses His truth and His love into all your being, so that you become an instrumentality for Him. Make it a reality. Be blessed."
–The Pathwork® Guide

Chapter 16

Three Aspects of the New Divine Influx

"Blessings, my dearly beloved friends. God's light envelops you all. This light contains all you need. Try to perceive it, try to feel its reality. It is always there for you, and to the degree you refine your inner being through the purification process, you cannot help being aware of this light that flows through all the universe, through all of creation. Those of God's children who have chosen to make the very best of their lives through such a path are especially blessed. For with this opportunity to purify themselves and serve God, they fulfill a great need in the Plan of Salvation."
–The Pathwork® Guide

The term New Age has been used a lot. Some people have used it with the correct understanding, others have managed to turn it into a cliché. This is unavoidable. It happens with truthful concepts due to people's tendency to be lazy and glib, using a label so they don't have to feel the reality of a certain truth. But for those who can avoid this trap, they should not give up altogether on using a term that conveys a true idea.

It is due to this tendency that different words are used in these teachings to express the same truth. Also, from time to time, the true meaning of a particular word is given in an effort to keep its true concept alive. As far as the New Age is concerned, it has been stated already that at various intervals in history, our world is swept with a new influx that comes streaming in. When this happens, it is because humanity has grown enough to be ready for it. This is what is happening now.

As we enter fully into this new era, the consciousness of the Christ spirit is now permeating this world, attempting to penetrate each person's consciousness to a greater and greater degree. When this powerful influx arrives, it is accompanied by certain things that may not be pleasant, agreeable, welcome or even constructive. Events happening on Earth right now that most people consider to be downright undesirable are a direct result of the influx of this energy.

But in truth, without this, the expansion and growth in consciousness inherent in this new era couldn't happen.

Our minds are still very much geared to the immediate future. We believe that what is right and good in this moment will also be right and good in the ultimate end. If something appears right now to be evil, it must also be evil in the long run. This, however, is seldom the case. Sometimes, what appears to be an outright negative manifestation was actually needed for full development to happen. This applies to each person as equally as it applies to humanity as a whole, or to put it another way, to the entity that is Earth.

Communication

There are some specific things that accompany this new influx. One of them is communication, which develops as a consciousness evolves. To the extent a spiritual being has grown, there will also be an ability to communicate, which includes the ability to listen and to express ourselves appropriately and adequately. If our development is impaired, our ability to communicate will be limited.

So it is that we see many people who cannot or will not even try to express in words what they are thinking and feeling. Such individuals either have too much pride, or they demand that others understand them without their having to make an effort to be understood. For making ourselves understandable does require some labor. But the art of communication can and must be learned by everyone. Doing so will ask us to cooperate, using our goodwill and positive intentionality.

Let's examine this some more, starting at the outermost level. It's not a co-incidence that a major outcome of today's technology is communication. Even if this level of communication only applies to outer events, it still has a big im-pact on the inner levels of our souls. First off, it brings us much closer together. In bygone eras, there was a much greater sense of separation because of how far apart people were. Their inability to communicate created the illusion that other people were inherently different—alien. Enemies, therefore, were not to be trusted. But when we discover that, regarding the basics of life—suffering and longing, living and dying—others are just like us, then much of the fear is eliminated. Then the illusion and the enmity go away. This contributes greatly to humanity's growing movement toward unity.

Our spiritual growth is fueled by our knowledge of what is happening in the world. In the past, our isolation and separateness made the world seem vast—too vast for us to take it in. Our personal tragedies seemed unique, so we had no sense of sisterhood or brotherhood. Today, even the most unspiritual people are able to experience the whole world in a different way. The planet doesn't seem so foreign or strange. Just knowing about the events happening in other parts of the world right now creates an expanded overall awareness, and that has an impact on the development of a soul.

Technology, then, is not in opposition to living a spiritual life or to becoming spiritually developed. Too often though it is misdirected and abused, and so it is viewed as being an obstacle to our spirituality. Once again we can see how everything on Earth and in the universe is an expression of divine will. This is how creation can and does serve the great plan. It's not possible to create something here that doesn't have roots in the Spirit World. All evil—all demonic manifestations—can only be misused divine creations. They are always distortions and can never be self-creative.

We now have the ability to witness the events happening for brothers and sisters around the globe, and our ability to share their experiences with them has an important impact on us. Plus, our ability to move fairly quickly from one corner of the world to another allows us to approach the laws of the world of spirit, where movement is one with thought and therefore simultaneous.

Communication is indeed a highly important byproduct of becoming more spiritually advanced. As we grow, we also improve our ability to communicate on more subtle levels. We can follow psychological approaches that enhance our awareness of ourselves, and when we understand ourselves better, we can communicate better. For as long as we're in the dark about our own feelings, needs and true reactions—not to mention clueless about what is going on in someone else—it's not possible to create a bridge with them in any significant way.

It's essentially the same for a child who, when very young, doesn't really know that it is lonely or hurting. A child doesn't know that what it needs is more love, or attention, or understanding. If the child could articulate all this, it would only be a small step to sharing these feelings with someone. So without adequate communication, we remain in the dark, living in a fog of confusion and cut off from others. The spirit of Christ represents the opposite of this. It ushers in the light of awareness, of brotherhood and sisterhood, and of communication.

Clearly, to have true communication with another, we must be able to communicate with ourselves. We must be able to access inner levels we couldn't reach before. So self-knowing is the foundation, the groundwork. For how can we communicate something we don't know? This is why this spiritual path is primarily focused on self-knowledge and self-exploration. But we must not stop there. Self-knowing is only the first part of the path.

From here we will organically learn to take the next step into the art of communication. We will have to give up the state of being half-awake, and opt instead to think, practice and observe ourselves. It will no longer work to assume anyone should just know how we feel. An effort will be required to lovingly reach out, explain, and patiently search through the mazes of misunderstanding.

The more we practice doing this, the more spontaneous our communication will be. We will automatically be able to outwardly be what, in the past, we were only secretly and inwardly able to be. Imagine what enormous difference such a shift could make in our communications. Isn't it true we often think someone is being mean when, in reality, the other person fears us and is using coldness as a defense? If we know this, it removes our own fear, anger and false pride. If we know this, we might be able to meet this person in a whole new way. This in turn can help them dissolve their negative defenses that are alienating us.

This is how communication works to bring souls together. It dismantles the wall of fear that creates hate between people. Communication, then, is an integral part of a good life.

Learning the Art of Communication

All of that said, attempting to explain ourselves is not enough. The *way* we reveal ourselves is what makes communication an art. If we communicate our explanation in a way that accuses and blames, we will only build a bigger wall. But if, instead, we focus on simply telling the other what we feel and what we need, sharing our assumptions and impressions in an open, questioning spirit—without an insistence that our perceptions are in truth—then we will be able to find true understanding. We can communicate in a way that establishes truth while being clear and standing in the light. By practicing communicating, we learn the skill of communicating well, and in this way we foster unity and love.

If we don't have any bridges connecting us to others, how can we stop feeling lonely? If we don't overcome the misconception that others are our enemy, how can we lose our fear of people? The only way to get what we want is to go through the trouble of exploring ourselves adequately so we know what we really feel.

Often we believe we feel one way, yet that's not at all what's really going on. We need to try to explain ourselves, and this will feel like we are taking a risk. Also, it can seldom be done in a single stroke. We must enter into an ongoing dialogue, using all the goodwill we can muster to let go of blame and shed our pride. This, at an emotional level, is what effective communication involves.

This is how we can work together to establish the great oneness among all people. This is how we will free ourselves from hate and fear, which are nothing but war on every level. In other words, it will be through communication that we will help bring the Kingdom of Heaven to Earth.

In addition, there is a deeper level of communication we've been ignoring. Now, it is obscure, but once we turn the lens of our attention toward it, it will show itself clearly to us. For every human interaction will ultimately help us reach our final goal: love, understanding, truth, brotherhood, oneness. In the end, even our most negative and challenging interactions serve this aim.

Whenever two entities—they can be individuals or collective groups—get tangled up in a negative interaction, they are fulfilling a deeper purpose. This is the case even when the outcome is unpleasant. For the Higher Self of each person is always involved and working hard. It's not quite right to say the Higher Self created the negative interaction, but it is able to use what is already there—which is negativity—for the purpose of dissolving the negativity.

The only way for the negative material to be dissolved and transformed is by first allowing it to fully manifest. So even if both parties are completely in the dark about how they are contributing to the struggle, and even if they are locked in self-righteousness and one-sidedness, nonetheless, these things are serving a higher purpose. Exposing the untruth, which is currently hiding from their view, will be significant when they recognize the whole truth of the difficult interaction.

So when there is a conflict, there is a Higher Self exchange simultaneously happening below the Lower Self exchange. This is important for us to take in and contemplate.

If we imagine two people or groups of people fighting, a war is taking place on the surface. The two accuse each other and hate each other. They only wish to see the worst in each other, and they want to harm each other. But at the same time—on another deeper level—these two entities agree. In their deeper selves, they are aware that whatever happens on the surface, it is serving a common good. And our common good is always serving truth, love and unity.

On this spiritual path, when two people are at odds and are able to work deeply to reach the truth, there is often a wonderful reconciliation in which the two are united in love. These are the same two people who were just hating and blaming each other. We can witness the sequential way—in time—that conciliation happens on this plane of existence. First the hate, then the search to find truth, then unity and love. On the deeper levels of our being, such sequences don't exist. In our deep consciousness, truth, unity and love all exist simultaneously.

Going forward, we need to take this into account. Doing so will help us perceive that in every situation—regardless how negative it seems and how hopelessly confused we have become—the conflict also simultaneously holds inner truth, inner unity and inner love. By understanding this, we will be able to move through difficult interactions with greater ease on the level of sequential time. Then hate/search/truth/unity/love will follow each other in quick succession. Or at least quicker.

This influx of the Christ consciousness is bringing more laws and spiritual values to planet Earth. Many spiritual laws and values are known by many through religions, but not many truly understand them and experience them in their depth. Fewer still live them on their innermost levels. Humanity continues to take these laws and, in distorting and confusing them, cause people to reject them. For when they are distorted, they make no sense. So then people either disregard them altogether, or they hypocritically obey them on a surface level that does not reach their core.

The more we humans grow, the greater can this influx of the light of Christ be. With this light, we will be able to weave true spiritual values into the fabric of our collective human consciousness.

We began this teaching talking about the law of brotherhood and sisterhood. Without brotherhood and sisterhood, we cannot have love. And without love, we cannot have brotherhood and sisterhood. Whereas love is union, hate is isolation, dissension and being split. Love, on the other hand, means mutual understanding.

But in order for understanding to grow and increase, we will need to have goodwill and we will need to make an effort. Love then doesn't happen by magic. It's not a miracle, nor is union. We are not able to experience union with God as long as we are unable to experience union with our sisters and brothers—even those we now think of as our enemies.

It's possible that on the surface level, we are not going to become friends with them. Because for that to happen, both sides have to really desire to be in union and truth. But it's still possible for us to become consciously connected with their Higher Self on the inner level.

Don't forget, love—which is union with God and others—is what results from communication. And communication can only result from serious effort. Our work is to commit to focusing our energy and our attention to making ourselves understood in the best way possible, and to also understand the other.

For any of this to happen, we will need to empty our mind of all the preconceived ideas our Lower Self has invested in. We will have to set down our distrust and hateful feelings. We will need to open our inner ears and learn to listen. We will need to help others see our goodwill and our desire to be in truth. We will need to step into maturity, realizing that other people don't know what we're thinking, feeling, meaning, wanting.

We need to explain ourselves in the deepest and most sincere way we can. If we walk in the world like this, we'll be able to resolve all the problems between ourselves and others. From this will come deep self-esteem and great strength.

But first, we must become willing to sacrifice our stubbornness. We must give up our pride and our pleasure in building a case against someone. We must let go of the fear we'll find out we are bad and wrong. All this we must be willing to put aside. This is how we will contribute to an ever-increasing flow of information that is unprecedented in the history of humankind. This is the way to herald a key aspect of the Christ consciousness—using our own selves and inviting our brothers and sisters to join us. When we do this, we are truly working as a servant to God's plan.

We must resist the temptation to keep ourselves locked up in isolation and resentment. We must also resist the temptation to blame and accuse. We must make ourselves neutral—at least for a time—until we've had the chance to sort things out and find the truth. Don't fear truth. It truly holds the key for setting ourselves free.

The truth will let us off the hook of our secret self-accusations and in doing so free others from our accusations. We may well uncover imperfections in them and in us, but when we start seeing our faults in a new light, this new connotation will free us from the need to hurt and shame anyone, anymore—ourselves included.

Group Consciousness

This new influx of Christ consciousness is sweeping through our planet with fantastic force, yet we don't always see how it is manifesting. It starts by first reaching the inner consciousness of humanity. Wherever there is even the slightest crack, the light gets in. Then consciousness starts to change, even if ever so barely at first. Perhaps we will have a new way of thinking about life. Maybe we will want to start understanding ourselves and our life in a more profound way.

Even people who aren't as ready and not so well developed can lend a hand to the Great Plan, although perhaps unwittingly. They become instruments, even if their instrument is only tuned to negativity. Through their actions, they affect those around them, and this then conspires to bring about new conditions. It is their Higher Self, as already said, working in concert with the Plan, allowing their outer negative will to contribute something positive to the bigger picture.

This new influx began with the dawning of the New Age. In the new era we are now entering, this energy will affect outer events, often in the most obscure way. Something that appears entirely undesirable—a negative occurrence—will be shown to be, in reality, a necessary event. It is what will move us to establish new values and reestablish life in a way that is based on the spiritual premises of truth and love. Another way to say this is that destructiveness has advanced so far it can no longer be molded, changed or transformed. It needs to be destroyed before we can build a new and better structure.

It's like this with many destructive events of this kind on Earth. We need to sort out the difference between events that are flat-out unnecessary since they oppose life—these are expressions of evil—and those that are in the category just described. The distinction isn't always clear. But as we train our inner vision and see how creation really works, we'll see everything more clearly.

If we look around, we may see that these values are springing up all over, laboriously working their way through our thickets of old, obsolete values. Those are our destructive attitudes that we inflict on life. The new values are just sprouting, so they are new and delicate plants. We can nurture them with our courage, with our commitment to a larger cause, and with our much needed self-honesty, all of which fosters our development and therefore expands our consciousness. The more we tend to what is trying to grow, the stronger these new plants will become on our planet.

This process—which is based on a cellular structure—begins with a single cell. This is the individual consciousness that is needing to be changed. But this change can't happen in the vacuum of isolation. It always works in conjunction with others. For individual consciousness nests within the greater consciousness, the collective whole.

The way for us to measure our development and individual values is by looking at our interactions with others. Through communication, our interactions can be improved and healed until there is no more separation. The more each cell of consciousness purifies, becoming more and more aligned with divine will, the more we affect all of the earth entity. The cells meld together and form one structure, although each will continue its individual life.

Many of us feel a lot of ambivalence about this melding. On one hand, we fear giving up what we call our individuality. We believe our uniqueness— our particular manifestation of the divine—depends on our separation. We assume—falsely—that if we become one with the whole, we will give up what makes us unique. In reality, it works the other way around.

So we are all struggling against the inherent fate of all created beings—the push toward oneness. We fight and we resist, much to our chagrin. For our longing to experience oneness will never be relieved until we achieve oneness. This longing in our soul is desperate, and the pain of not fulfilling our longing is excruciating. But to not know of this longing and to not feel this pain is even worse. Our confusion, apathy and lack of aliveness then become a secondary pain. We can never understand this state, because it's the result of long, winding chain reactions that originated from the precise pain of denying oneness.

The Aquarian Age we have entered into, which is also called the New Age, has brought about the formation of groups and therefore the emergence of group consciousness. This is the first time such a process has existed. Of course we could say humanity as a whole is a group on a large scale, and our societies couldn't exist without at least some degree of group consciousness. But until now people have been primarily concerned with their own interests, even if this self-concern negatively affects the rest of the world.

It's not that this attitude is now gone. Far from it. But now there is a new, growing awareness that if we pursue nothing but our own self-interest—to the downfall of others—we are going way past the point of violating spiritual laws, values and morals. We are starting to see that we are the ones who must eventually suffer. By adopting a self-serving attitude, we will suffer as much if not more than those we disregard with our selfish shortsightedness.

Our human family cannot exist without a group spirit. But most of the world's societies have not yet put adequate emphasis on spiritual values. So people are not aware of this new influx, and they plunge ahead with old values and standards. But these are based on shortsighted goals and a desire for immediate results.

It's not a coincidence that in recent decades new groups of all sorts have sprung up, and many of them are misguided. They are being influenced by evil spirits and their destructive forces. It can't be any other way than it is, on this plane of existence. Anywhere there is a divine influx, the demonic forces send out their cavalry to influence and corrupt those who are not yet purified. They do this by tempting them. Their goal is to destroy them.

At the same time, new communities representing new values must spread, and this does not change that fact. These new communities will become the models for new ways of life. The point is we must be wakeful, and we must not neglect to do our work of self-purification. This is our key to safety. If we keep painstakingly doing our work—working in a spirit of glad service to the will of God—then the evil forces will not be able to confuse us. We will find answers and we will stay clean, even if our Lower Self breaks out into the open now and then.

Exposure

There is another important thing arriving with this new influx: exposure. Once again we can see this aspect showing up in both individuals and in the collective. It's so obvious, it would be hard to miss this one. Through the developments in psychology and more recently, through people doing profound spiritual work, exposure of the self has gone to depths never before seen. The exceptions are the small number of initiates who have been forming small groups of followers in different cultures all along.

Now we are ready to expose deeper levels of ourselves than we have done before, by a large margin. Even those with the least amount of self-knowing have achieved a certain amount of awareness, such that these deeper levels can now help determine their lives. Many of us may at this time take this for granted, but it has by no means always been this way.

It is through the combination of communication and exposure that we now have a greater ability to explore ourselves. Our willingness to explore is what opens doors to communication and our ability to communicate leads to oneness—to align with the great force of Christ spirit that is sweeping through our world.

It's clear that our refusal to expose our inner selves leads to isolation. And so the resistance to exposure persists. What does it mean when we refuse exposure? It is always a sign we have a stake in propping up a rotten structure—a structure that needs to be torn down and replaced. In our unwillingness lies a clear wish to keep living a lie. What's the way out? Dedicating ourselves to the truth. This is what will bring us the courage we need to expose and change.

If we don't do it willingly, it will be done for us, as secret matters will be exposed by means of outside forces. A crisis will occur that will bring them to the surface. Once the new influx is set into motion, the force of it cannot be halted. The more opposition it runs into, the more painful will the crisis be.

We can now clearly observe this in public life. In recent times, we are seeing hidden destructiveness being exposed and then communicated with the public. Again it is obvious that something new is happening. We have never seen it happen to the same degree before, or in the same way. And it is continuing. We can see that something new has been set into motion. Through a combination of communication and exposure, the entire world now knows of political misdeeds that would have been kept secret in the past.

As group consciousness evolves, there is a great interaction and interplay unfolding that is allowing all of humanity to join the drama of development. It's important we start to view world events through this lens. This is exactly the process we follow as we do our personal work of self-development: we expose our Lower Self, we share what we have found, and then we communicate this to others. Is there any better way to establish close connections that build trust and generate love?

Over and over we have been looking at the parallels between developing ourselves as individuals and developing the planet. Everything we learn to apply to ourselves also applies in some way on the level of the collective. Exposure has never existed here like this before. As masks are starting to crumble, Lower Self aspects are beginning to show through with less ability to be concealed than in the past. So now we can see events and intentions for what they actually are, without all the camouflage of lies that causes such tremendous suffering and confusion.

So we can see then that exposure—a direct result of the Christ consciousness sweeping our planet—is very much part of the new influx. If we hope to develop spiritually without exposure, our half-measures will eventually lead to stalemate. At the same time, if exposure isn't infused with love, our work will be self-defeating. The ones who deserve our respect are the ones with the courage to do it willingly. We must not allow the ones who refuse to do it willingly to destroy their environment and to use concealment to influence events.

It is our inner conviction to serve a larger cause that gives us the strength and courage we need to bring what needs to be exposed out in the light, and to do so in an appropriate way. In other words, we need to work in a loving way. As we expose more and more of ourselves to ourselves—and then subsequently also to others—the more will we discover our true inherent worth. And we will know it is our Higher Self—the part of us that is already developed—that is the part making the exposure possible.

It's the same with the entity of the planet. It is the Higher Self of Earth that is orchestrating all the exposure we now see on the political front. We should not think of the New Age as some vague, generic force. It is, in itself, a consciousness. As the need arises, specific aspects manifest in various parts of the world.

As with all kinds of consciousness, the consciousness of this new era is made up of many aspects that create one harmonious whole. We have just been looking at three of its aspects: communication, group consciousness and exposure. In addition, we looked at the intrinsic parallels between the way these particular aspects manifest at the levels of the collective and the individual.

Those of us who have been working with the teachings of this spiritual path—or another like it—are well versed in the individual level. This has been our focus all along. While we may still have some resistance to work with and some obstacles to get through, we are on board in principle with how this process works. We understand its value and see why it is needed. When we are able to observe the same process occurring at the collective level, our individual work will deepen.

"Look at this beautiful world with the eyes that see the whole, that comprehend the Lord's working behind all that is. Let your hearts be filled with the freshness of life's healing power that flows from the Source that encompasses all that ever was created and ever will be created. This Source resides right in your own center, even when you are unable to connect with it or to experience its reality through your confusions and your momentary suffering. It is always there.

You are all surrounded by the great force that flows with such renewed vigor through your universe. Be blessed, my beloved ones. Pursue your commitment to the end, never let up in your devotion to serve God."

–The Pathwork® Guide

Chapter 17

Inner Space, Focused Emptiness

"My beloved friends, you are blessed in body, soul and spirit. Your path is blessed every step of the way. You may at times doubt this when the going gets rough. But when this is so, it is not because blessings are withheld from you. It is because you encounter parts of your inner landscape that need to be successfully traversed. To traverse difficult inner terrains it is necessary to understand its meaning for your own being and thus to dissolve the roadblocks you find on your way."

–The Pathwork® Guide

At this point in time, many people are as comfortable with the term "inner space" as they are with outer space. But most people think of inner space as merely a symbol of a person's state of mind. This is not the case. Inner space is actually a real world—a vast reality. This in fact is the real universe and outer space is a mirror image of it—a reflection. This is the reason outer reality can never quite be grasped. Life can't be truly absorbed, experienced and understood when we only view it from the outside. That's why life is so frustrating—and often so frightening—for so many.

It's not easy to understand how it's possible that inner space could in itself be a world—*the* world. The difficulty lies in the limited time/space continuum of our three-dimensional reality. We perceive everything we touch, see and experience from a limited perspective. Our minds are conditioned to perceive things a certain way and at this juncture, we're not capable of perceiving life another way. But that doesn't mean our current way is the right way, the only way, or complete way.

The goal of any spiritual path is to perceive life in a way that goes beyond the outer reflection. Our aim is to focus on the new dimensions we discover in *inner space*. In some spiritual disciplines, this may be clearly stated as the intention, and in others it might never be mentioned as such.

But when we reach a certain point of development on our path of purification, a new vision wakes up, sometimes gradually and sometimes more suddenly. Even when it seems to happen suddenly, this is only an illusion. All awakening happens as a result of taking many steps on a spiritual path and fighting many inner battles.

Scientists have discovered that each atom is duplicated in the outer universe, as we know it. This is an important recognition. As we have come to understand, time is a variable that depends on the dimension from which it is experienced. It's the same for space. In the same way that there isn't an objective, fixed time, there isn't an objective, fixed space. So our real being can live, move and breathe—and cross vast distances—within an atom, according to our outer system of measurement.

Just as the relationship to time changes in different dimensions, the relationship of measurement changes when a spirit withdraws into the inner world. This explains why we seem to lose contact with what we call "dead" people. Our awareness changes because they now live in the inner reality, which for us, can only be an abstract idea. And yet the thing that is really abstract is outer space.

When a person dies, the spirit—that which is alive—does not go to heaven, as we erroneously assume, but rather *withdraws* into the inner world. Our spirit does not lift out of the body and float into outer space. When someone with extrasensory perception sees something like this, what they are seeing is only the mirror image of an event that is happening in the inner landscape.

For a long time, a majority of humans have been looking for God up in heaven. Then Jesus Christ came and tried to teach us that we must look for God within, because God lives in the inner spaces. As such, all meditation exercises and practices guide us to focus on inner space.

In a previous teaching, we talked about the value of a meditation exercise in which we don't think. We simply make ourselves empty. Most who try this find how difficult it is to do this. The human mind is often completely filled with its own material, and so it can be very difficult to still the mind. There are several approaches we can take. In Eastern religion, the approach usually involves long practices and lots of discipline. If we combine this with solitude and sitting still, we may eventually produce a state of inner stillness.

But on *this* spiritual path, we take a different approach. The goal of these teachings is not to take us out of our world. Our goal is actually the exact opposite: We want to be *in* our world, in the very best possible way. We want to create by understanding and accepting in a way that is productive and constructive.

We will only be able to do this when we fully and truly know and understand ourselves. To do this, we have to traverse the difficult inner spaces, but doing so will make us better equipped to function in this three-dimensional reality. For then there won't be a split between our inner space and our outer world.

Our perception of outer truth will increase the more inner truth reigns. We will understand the outer world when our understanding of our inner selves grows. We will be able to restructure—to transform—our outer life as soon as we learn to re-mold whatever is in us that is imperfect, or faulty.

Our vision will expand and we will have a greater appreciation of the beauty of creation when we are able to see our inner beauty as a manifestation of the divine. We will become at peace in this world to whatever extent we find inner peace. This will be true, even in the presence of life's difficulties.

In other words, we don't need to find a secluded mountaintop to reach inner space. On this path, we take a different route to reach our destination. We go directly through whatever seems to be our biggest obstruction: the imperfections within us and around us. By approaching them, we deal with them, until they lose their fearsome roar. This is our path.

Focused Emptiness

While it can be a helpful exercise to sit and focus on inner emptiness, that must not be our sole approach to self-realization. Likewise, dealing with outer troubles in our world must never be our only approach to our own salvation or the salvation of this world.

Focused emptiness will grow—spontaneously and deliberately—as we face and remove our inner obstacles. In the early stages, we are going to have to be with the experience of nothingness and emptiness. For when our mind quiets, we first encounter the void, and this is what makes the attempt so frightening. It seems to confirm our suspicion that we are indeed only our outer mortal self, and there's nothing inside.

This is why our minds make themselves so noisy and so busy, in an effort to blot out the quiet that appears to signal…nothing. Here again courage will be needed to go all the way through this tunnel of uncertainty. We must take the risk of being in this great quietude, which at first seems devoid of anything that spells consciousness, and which seems empty of meaning.

Many people have experienced how the voice of our inner God—our Higher Self—slips inspirations into our mind when we least think of it. It doesn't happen during meditation or prayer, or even right after. It waits until our mind is relaxed enough and free enough from self-will for the inner voice to be heard. It works the same way when it comes to experiencing the inner universe, which is the real world.

Focused emptiness allows what was hidden to emerge. This includes errors, distortions, and other Lower Self material. Eventually, it will bring us in touch with the reality of our Higher Self and the vast, eternal world where it dwells. As such, focused emptiness connects us with all levels of our being. We will need to travel through many stages and phases. We can only reach the later stages when a certain amount of purification and integration has been accomplished.

So whereas *focused* emptiness is a heightening of our consciousness, *unfocused* emptiness is a lessening of our consciousness. When we are unfocused, we tune out and our mind wanders vaguely. This may lead us to mindless emptiness. The final stages of this are sleep or other states of unconsciousness. By contrast, in focused emptiness we are fully there—aware and concentrating.

If we focus exclusively on our inner world—at the exclusion of our outer world—we create a split. Worse, we forfeit the whole reason we incarnated. For how can we complete our task—whatever it is—if we don't use our outer world for this purpose? If it wasn't necessary for us to have come to this dimension, we wouldn't have come here.

So we need to make use of our time here, bringing our inner and outer conditions into a healthy, meaningful relationship with each other. And that is just what we learn to do on this path. All our experiences in life relate to our personality—to all the various levels of ourselves. It is always the inner being that creates the outer conditions, a truth we quickly come to see as we start doing our work.

If we are not regularly relating our inner world to our outer life, this will create an imbalance, and the result won't be good. For example, sometimes we see people who are doing a lot of outer good work lose their way as easily as those who don't give other people a second thought. This happens because our outer good intentions and good works must arise from an inner focus if we want to avoid creating disharmony and a dangerous split in our personality.

Through focused emptiness we eventually arrive in the eternal light. If we are willing to oversimplify things, we can say there are basic stages we will go through. Note, in practice these stages will overlap and not happen in neat succession as outlined here for the purpose of clarifying the work.

1) We will experience the busyness and noise of our mind.

2) As we quiet the noise, we will encounter nothingness, emptiness.

3) We will start to see connections between aspects of our inner self and our outer experiences. With our new understandings about levels of ourselves we haven't recognized before, new Lower Self material will appear. This is not merely an experience of Lower Self—this is a ray of divine guidance. For recognizing the Lower Self is always a manifestation of guidance from our Higher Self.

4) Higher Self messages will begin to manifest directly. We could also say our channel opens. In this way, we will now receive encouragement, advice and

other words intended to bolster our courage and give us faith. In this phase, divine guidance is operating mostly through our mind. This isn't necessarily a totally emotional and spiritual experience. We may be excited and gladdened by it, but we are reacting as a result of our mind receiving knowledge it has absorbed and found convincing.

5) In this final stage, we have a direct and total experience that is spiritual and emotional. Our whole being becomes filled with the Holy Spirit. Now we *know*, not through our mind, but through our whole being. When we know something through our mind, the knowledge is *indirect*. It has been *relayed* to us. This is the human mind we need to function on this level of consciousness. *Direct knowing* is different.

The final phase has many stages within it. For there are limitless possibilities—truly infinite possibilities—in how we can experience the real world. One of them is simply *total knowing*, which reaches every fiber of our being and every level of our consciousness. We can also experience the real world through visions of other dimensions, but they are never just about what we see. The whole person will always be affected by a total experience.

Every sense perception is total in the real world, unlike what we experience in our fragmented world. So seeing isn't only seeing, it's also hearing, feeling, smelling and tasting—plus many perceptions we know nothing about on this level of being—all rolled into one. In this fifth stage, knowing, feeling and perceiving are bundled with hearing and seeing, in one all-inclusive package. Every capacity God has created is included. We can't even imagine the limitless possibilities—not to mention the richness and variety—of having all these capacities.

The ideal state to be in to be filled by the Holy Spirit is focused emptiness. What is the Holy Spirit? It is the whole world of God, in all its glory and magnificence. We don't have words in the human language adequate to convey it. It's not possible to describe what exists beyond the bounds of fear, distrust and doubt, after death, evil and suffering are overcome. But we can reach all the splendor and fullness of the Spirit World by crossing over the threshold of focused emptiness.

Practicing Focused Emptiness

Many begin a practice, such as the practice of focused emptiness, with the expectation of immediate results. In fact what's really necessary is to have no expectations at all. For expectations create tensions that prevent the inner and outer relaxation we are looking for. What's more, expectations are unrealistic. It may take us many incarnations to reach the fifth stage. So rather than set ourselves up for disappointment—which can set off chain reactions of other negative emotions like fear, doubt and discouragement—it is better to let go of any and all expectations.

In our work, we want to infuse patience, humility and awe into our approach at each stage. For these experiences will open us up to vast inner space. Many worlds, universes and spheres exist, with unending mountains, seas and plains. We need to know that these inner spaces are not abstract or symbolic. They are more real than the outer, objectified world so many believe to be the only reality.

In inner space, measurement is not the same as here in the outer world. There is a different relativity between measurement and time/space/movement. If we can even capture a vague or hazy sense of this, it will change our outlook and help us go further on our path. We don't need to sit for hours and hours practicing focused emptiness. That's not the point of it. But each time we pray and meditate, we can attempt it to some degree.

So what *is* the main point? We want to reach autonomy, in every sense of the word. Everything in life depends on our ability to respect ourselves and discover our values. We must discover our capacity for loving and reach the fulfillment we long for. We need to fulfill the task we agreed to when we decided to incarnate. We want to experience God living in us and all around us.

We need to develop the ability to be a true leader as well as a follower. And last but not least, we want to develop the ability to let go of our mind and find the inner space that is our real home. For only by finding our true inner home can we find eternal life. This is the only way to remove all our fears, forever.

Taking Self-Responsibility

We can't surrender to God's will until we are in full possession of ourselves. At the same time, we can't find and be all of ourselves unless we surrender to God unconditionally. To resolve this paradox, it's important we look at our resistance to reaching the all-important state of autonomy.

Too often, what we really crave is an authority figure who is going to take over for us when life becomes hazardous; when we have to pay the price for our mistakes; when we have to experience the conditions we created with our imperfections. So many people crave a "perfect life" where we don't have to deal with any of that. We delude ourselves into thinking we can avoid ever making mistakes and avoid paying the price when we do. This is a dangerous illusion, made especially so because it's so subtle we can easily gloss over it. By rationalizing it, we are able to deny it.

If we feel confused about ourselves, our lives, or by what's happening around us, this is a sign we're suffering from this delusion and are deliberately avoiding growing up. If we are rebelling against authority figures, this is a sign we're still craving the "right" authority. We want a super-person to come protect us from the troubles of life, so we don't have to experience our reality. When we are autonomous though, we no longer need to rebel against authority. We are no longer confused. We can clearly see what's true and what is not true, so we can decide to agree or not agree. We don't need to resort to rebellion or fearful submission.

So how do we get there? What is the road to clarity and the ability to make good decisions? We must become willing to probe, search, question, explore and be open. Following such a course requires patience to sort out the issues in our life. There are no quick, ready-made answers.

The dependent, childish person abhors being patient and doesn't want to work to find out more, because that means work. The dependent, childish person wants easy answers and is quick to jump to conclusions. When we're afraid to make a mistake, we don't question our hasty conclusions. Instead, we stiffly insist we are right and this bars the door to truth and clarity. The result? Inner confusion, which breeds confusing experiences. If we can't connect the dots and see how we have created these negative, confusing experiences, then life will appear unfair and too hard. So then we demand a perfect authority to come put things right.

But the more loudly we claim we want to be independent, the more suspect our real intentions are. The more we feel the need to prove we're a free agent and can't be influenced, the more likely it is we're running away from real autonomy. The truth is, we're not willing to take full responsibility for our decisions, our experiences, or our life.

The bigger our rebellion against those in authority whom we say are denying us our rights, the more we secretly resent them for not living up to our impossible demands. And what are those demands? That we not have to make mistakes and pay any price for them; that we not have to deal with the consequences of our errors, unwise decisions, negativities or distortions. We want to be handed an infallible key that gives us this kind of magic, and allows us to remain free forever.

What is our idea of freedom? To be able to do whatever we want, whether or not its desirable for others or for our Real Self. We never want to be frustrated or disciplined. When we aren't able to reach these goals, we blame authority figures and then resent them. Then we accuse them of doing the opposite of what we expect them to do. To be more specific, we blame them for blocking our freedom by setting limits. We refuse to see that these are life's laws—these are the limitations of reality. We deliberately, albeit unconsciously, create confusion by distorting the limitations as though having boundaries means we're enslaved.

We must start to see how and to what extent we are showing up in life like this. Then we need to ask ourselves some seriously probing questions. Am I willing to assume self-responsibility, with all this requires? Can I accept that I am still imperfect, and that I am going to make mistakes? When I do, am I willing to pay the price for them? The more willing we are to pay the price, the lower the price will be. In fact, the price will turn into a stepping stone, a necessary lesson, a threshold.

We can gain the strength to walk this path only from our willingness to surrender to God's will. Then we will be able to truly stand in the middle of life as it unfolds around us, not denying it, not fleeing from it, and never using spirituality as a way to escape from it.

When our surrender to God is genuine, all dualistic confusion will dissolve and we will be able to step into full autonomy. By following through on our path, we will clear up any confusion about becoming an individual versus being a member of a community. We won't be confused about self-surrender versus real independence. For true selfhood allows us to become a social being who is at peace with our surroundings. We will learn how to be intimately connected with others and always contribute to them.

When we become a truly autonomous person, we can be a strong leader and also a willing follower, because our vision will be clear and our being will be centered in divine reality.

The thing that most prevents us from walking through these gateways is that we want to avoid full self-responsibility. We aren't willing to be accountable. Our freedom is directly dependent on this. Our ability to let go in strength, not weakness, depends on this.

Of course autonomy, like so many things, is a question of degree. Some people are able to stand on their own two feet when it comes to earning a living. We may even do so in a way we generally enjoy. In this area of our life, we may be able to accept that there will be challenges to face, there may be boredom or strife. During difficult times, we're willing to give our best. And this is precisely why we are able to enjoy our work and be successful.

But there may be other areas, perhaps less noticeable, where we still depend on others and won't be our own self. Our work is to explore these areas. A few telltale signs are whether we can distinguish between those we can trust and those we can't, and how we feel about authority figures in our life. Then where do our intense feelings go? It's entirely possible we aim our positive feelings toward those who are not to be trusted, while viewing with suspicion the people who are encouraging our autonomy and who deserve our trust.

If we are not able to trust ourselves, we will never be able to sort out who is trustworthy. And why can't we trust ourselves? Because we don't know which parts of ourselves deserve our trust. Too often, we insist the childish part—

the most shortsighted, destructive part—is the part of ourselves that's most independent. We like to believe that doing what feels most pleasurable in the moment and always following the line of least resistance amounts to autonomy. It might be so on occasion, but it most certainly is not always so.

We can only trust ourselves if we have learned to listen for the voice of the true inner authority. That's the one capable of saying no to instant gratification because in the long run that defeats us. To live a healthy, full, satisfying life, we must step into true maturity. This is what creates the underpinning for spiritual self-realization. Without maturity, our spirituality will sooner or later twist into a distortion, no matter how good our intentions were starting out.

On the other hand, it's not possible to reach full independence and health by way of only psychological means. To reach our goals, we will need to learn that there are several different voices inside to listen to. We will need to learn which voices to trust and which to reject. We will need to explore all there is to uncover within, or our goals will remain elusive and all this a beautiful theory.

At the beginning, the voice of the Higher Self will be the hardest to hear. Yet this is the voice we must listen to more than all the loud clamoring of the other voice—the one that never wants to tolerate any frustration.

The only way for a community to become autonomous, safe and creative as a group entity is for the members of the community to gain autonomy. In the new era we are now entering, everything will tend to move in this direction. To whatever degree individuals develop—reaching emotional, mental and spiritual maturity—whole societies can be transformed.

When the overall attitude of a society reaches this state, then even those who come from the lowest spheres—with spiritual ignorance or a destructive intent—will not be able to wreak havoc on Earth. Their negative influence will melt away like snow in the sun. This is not the case now. Too many people hanker after leaders who will allow everything and not forbid anything, and who make promises about taking away the hardships of living.

Only when people step into true autonomy will they be able to have deep, realistic, intense contact with the Christ consciousness in an extended way. If we remain immature, the road will be blocked, the voices confusing, and the experience inaccessible. Then the idea of surrendering to God seems confusing. For the wish to surrender to false authority—someone who permits everything, sets no limits about following the line of least resistance, imposes no frustrations, and offers this kind of utopia—creates a fear in us. For in our inner being we know the dangers of such a surrender.

As it says in the Bible, the weaker ones will surrender to false prophets. When we are in an unfinished state in our development—only partially striving for autonomy—we will fear all forms of surrender. What we really fear and distrust is our own desire for a false prophet who will promise what they should never promise.

These promises may not be stated in so many words, but they are implied in the messages being communicated. These messages connect with the consciousness of those who are most vulnerable due to how unwilling they are to take responsibility for their own lives.

What this all boils down to is that no matter how willing we may be to surrender to God's will—desiring God's guidance in whatever form it might be given to us—our resistance to surrendering cannot be overcome if we are not able to take responsibility for all aspects of our being.

From the point of view of evolution, spirit can penetrate into matter to whatever degree spiritual laws are followed and truth is found. A person's level of self-responsibility is the key. More spirit can be born into flesh—more life can penetrate matter—when our spiritual self grows stronger.

As more of our real being is born into our body, talents may come to the foreground we knew nothing of before. Suddenly a new wisdom may manifest, a new understanding may unfold, a new capacity to feel and love may arise. All these things come from our Real Self that lives in the inner space. That is the real world.

As we make room for these aspects to push into the life of matter, we will be fulfilling our part in the scheme of evolution. These divine attitudes can't grow in us from the outside. They cannot be added onto us. They only can blossom in our outer world when we make room for our inner being, which has yet to fully manifest.

This is what happens as a result of our growth process, when we undertake the hard work we must do on this path. After we have made some headway in our development, our progress will be helped along by our focus on inner emptiness. We must discover that the emptiness is an illusion. The truth we will discover is a fullness—a rich world filled with glory. If we tap into it, we can receive everything we need from this inner source and translate it into our outer experience.

Live a Spiritual Life

Throughout the ages, Christ has come many times, in many different forms, as various enlightened ones. But he has never come as completely and fully—as freely—as in Jesus. So here too it is a question of the degree to which spirit flows into matter. The maximum of spirit, of life and of consciousness can only manifest in matter that is unobstructed.

Eventually we will reach the point in our evolution on this sphere—on this planet we call Earth—when matter will yield to spirit so completely that matter will be totally spiritualized. Matter will then no longer be an obstruction to spirit. We will have completely filled the void with life.

There is no aspect of our personality that is insignificant in terms of evolution and creation. There is no such thing as a "merely psychological aspect." Every thought, every feeling, every attitude, every reaction, reflects how much we can participate in the greatness of life. When we know this, we will find it easier to give ourselves completely to doing this work. We will learn how to unify every duality, so our spiritual life and our worldly life become one.

"Make room for unobstructed life, for unencumbered spirit! Let it fill every part of your being so that you will finally know who you really are. You are all blessed, my very dearest ones."

–The Pathwork® Guide

Ways to learn more

1 The function of the ego in relationship to the Real Self
- *PEARLS*, Chapter 9: Why flubbing on perfection is the way to find joy
- *PEARLS*, Chapter 17: Discovering the key to letting go & letting God

2 What blocks the ego from connecting with the Real Self
- *SPIRITUAL LAWS*: Hard & fast logic for forging ahead
- *BLINDED BY FEAR*: Insights from the Pathwork® Guide on how to face our fears
- *LIVING LIGHT:* On Seeking and Finding True Faith, Chapter 15: Shame of the Higher Self: We're ashamed of our best self. Crazy, right?
- *SPILLING THE SCRIPT*, Chapter: RUNNING FOR COVER | Masks & Defenses
- *BONES*, Chapter 4: Three basic personality types: Reason, will and emotion

3 The ego's cooperation with or obstruction of the Real Self
- *BONES*, Chapter 15: Learning to speak the language of the unconscious mind

4 How unconscious negativity stops the ego from surrendering
- *BONES*, Chapter 17: Overcoming our Negative Intention by identifying with our spiritual self

6 Self-identification through the stages of awakening consciousness
- *FINDING GOLD*, Chapter 13: Being values versus appearance values
- *LIVING LIGHT*, Chapter 14: Shame: The right and wrong kind
- *BONES*, Chapter 12: Finding tut the truth about ourselves, including our faults
- *PEARLS*, Chapter 14: Meditating to connect three voices: The ego, the Lower Self & the Higher Self

7 Inner and outer experience
- *BONES*, Chapter 2: The importance of feeling all our feelings, including fear
- *BONES*, Chapter 8: How and why we recreate childhood hurts
- *BONES*, Chapter 7: Love, power and serenity in divinity or in distortion
- *BONES*, Chapter 9: Images and the deep, deep damage they do
- *BONES*, Chapter 19: The giant misunderstanding about freedom and self-responsibility

9 Moving the mind to push the divine light spark into the outer regions
- *SPILLING THE SCRIPT*: Meeting the Selves
- *HOLY MOLY:* The Story of Duality, Darkness and a Daring Rescue
- BONES, Chapter 13: The ubiquitous faults of self will, pride and fear

11 The era of new consciousness
- *PEARLS*, Chapter 15: What's the real spiritual meaning of crisis?

13 Changing from outer to inner laws in this new era
- *PEARLS*, Chapter 10: Two rebellious reactions to authority
- *GEMS*, Chapter 6: Finding balance within instead of banking on outer rules

14 The pulse of life on every level
- Part I of **Understand these Spiritual Teachings**: The Work of Healing
- *SPILLING THE SCRIPT,* Chapter: Finding the Treasure
- *DOING THE WORK:* Healing Our Body, Mind & Spirit by Getting to Know the Self

What is Pathwork®?

This remarkable collection of spiritual teachings has been selected by Jill Loree from the body of material collectively known as the Pathwork spiritual materials. The teachings of the Pathwork are contained in about 250 lectures that were given in the 1950s, '60s and '70s by a Vienna-born New Yorker named Eva Pierrakos. The teachings are unparalleled in their wisdom, scope and practicality, and therefore also in their effectiveness.

By following these Pathwork teachings, we embark on a lifelong spiritual journey of self-discovery that allows us to heal our emotional wounds, understand the true workings of life, and foster harmony and balance within our own being, as well as with others and God.

Perhaps the least interesting thing to know about these lectures is that they were channeled. This relevant-yet-insignificant fact is often one of the first things that tumbles out when one tries to explain the Pathwork. It is a relevant point of interest because this material is often of great interest to people who have curious minds and would like to understand the origin of these teachings. At the same time, it is insignificant because it doesn't really matter where they came from. As the Guide often said, you shouldn't believe anything—no matter who said it—unless it makes sense to you.

Who is the Pathwork Guide?

The Guide is the entity who is actually speaking, using Eva as the medium, or channel, through which he spoke. Owed to Eva's dedication to her task—including her willingness to do her own work—the material continually evolved and deepened over the course of the 22 years she gave monthly lectures.

Pathwork is a trademarked word owned by the Pathwork Foundation, a non-profit organization. It was coined along the way by Eva and other followers of the Guide based on the fact that he so often spoke of "being on a path," and the reality that it is hard work to follow such a path.

In truth, every human being is on a spiritual path, whether they know it or not. Today, however, many more people are becoming conscious about their spiritual journey. For hard as it may be to look directly at our own faults and negativity, at some point we realize we can't keep looking away from ourselves and hope to find solutions. And that, in a way, is the heart of what the Guide teaches: The only way to get to the other side of our struggles in life is by stepping through the gateway of self-responsibility.

The lectures are all now available online in the form of printed transcripts, free audio recordings and, for a fee, the original recordings by Eva:

www.pathwork.org

What is Phoenesse®?

The Guide offers profound teachings that are only valuable if they are put into service in understanding and unwinding our everyday disharmonies, both large and small. One has to actively apply the Guide's teachings to be served by them. That's really the key.

But the lectures are long—roughly 10-12 pages each—and dense, so it takes some mental stamina to get through them. This is where Phoenesse can help.

Doing the Work

Inspired directly by the Guide, Phoenesse offers a fresh approach to these timeless spiritual teachings. Phoenesse—pronounced "finesse"—is a registered service mark of Phoenesse LLC, founded by Jill Loree.

In the *Real. Clear.* seven-book series, Jill Loree has rewritten nearly 100 of the teachings using easier-to-read language, and organized them by topic. Podcasts of each teaching are also available online.

In the *Self.Care.* How-to-Heal teaching series, Jill Loree offers a high-level overview of the work, identifying the various parts of the self and showing how to actually go about doing the work of healing.

You can also read an overview of the Guide's teachings on the Phoenesse website:

www.phoenesse.com

phoenesse
FIND YOUR TRUE YOU.

What is The Guide Speaks?

After each lecture, attendees were encouraged to ask questions. In addition, once a month Eva and the Guide would hold dedicated Question & Answer sessions. Unlike the original lectures, which were prepared by a council of spiritual beings, the Pathwork Guide answered these questions himself. For this reason, the Q&As embody a somewhat different energy from the lectures, which—in addition to their shorter length—makes them easier to digest.

The Q&As were either related to the lecture just given, to a person's personal issues, or to life in general. They offer a wisdom and perspective that has the potential to change a person's worldview. Jill Loree has sorted the thousands of questions into topics to make the answers more accessible, and has made them available for free online:

www.theguidespeaks.com

About the Author

Jill Loree | Founder of Phoenesse

Jill Loree
Founder of Phoenesse

A neatnik with a ready sense of humor, Jill Loree's first job as a root-beer-stand carhop in northern Wisconsin was an early sign that things could only get better.

She would go on to throw pizzas and bartend while in college, be-fore discovering that the sweet spot of her 30-year sales-and-marketing career would be in business-to-business advertising. A true Gemini, she has a degree in chemistry and a flair for writing. Her brain fires on both the left and right sides.

That said, her real passion in life has been her spiritual path. Raised in the Lutheran faith, she became a more deeply spiritual person in the rooms of Alcoholics Anonymous, a spiritual recovery program, starting in 1989. In 1997, she was introduced to the wisdom of the Pathwork, which she describes as "having walked through the doorway of a fourth step and found the whole library."

She completed four years of Pathwork Helpership training in 2007 followed by four years of apprenticing and discernment before step-ping into her full Helpership in 2011. She has been a teacher in the Transformation Program offered at Sevenoaks Retreat Center in Madison, Virginia, operated by Mid-Atlantic Pathwork, where she also led marketing activities for over two years and served on the Board of Trustees.

In 2012, Jill completed four years of kabbalah training in a course called the Soul's Journey, achieving certification for hands-on healing using the energies embodied in the tree of life.

Not bad for a former pom-pom squad captain who once played Dolly in Hello Dolly! She is now the proud mom of two adult children, Charlie and Jackson, who were born and raised in Atlanta. Jill Loree is delighted to be married to Scott Wisler, but continues to use her middle name as her last (it's pronounced loh-REE). In her spare time she enjoys reading, writing, yoga, golf, skiing and hiking, especially in the mountains.

In 2014, she consciously decoupled from the corporate world and is now dedicating her life to writing and teaching about spirituality, personal healing and self-discovery.

Catch up with Jill at www.phoenesse.com.

phoenesse®
FIND YOUR TRUE YOU.

More from Phoenesse

Get a **Better Boat**

Get a Better Boat
Trustworthy Teachings for Difficult Times

If we build our house on sand, it might last for a while. But eventually things will start to crumble and collapse. We may even have forgotten we decided long ago to build on sand. That doesn't change the reality of the situation though.

Over time, anything not built on a solid foundation of truth is bound to eventually collapse. It must. So it can be rebuilt the right way.

The era that's now arriving is going to further shake whatever is not sound, whatever has been built on sand. We must collectively come to realize that the only way to get to the other side of our challenges is by waking up and stepping through the doorway of self-responsibility. And that's exactly what the Pathwork Guide is showing us how to do in this collection of 33 spiritual essays.

Jill Loree began working deeply with the Pathwork teachings in 1997. In 2014, she began working full time to make them easier to access. Now, in Get a Better Boat, she crafts a clear message—a beacon of light—to help us navigate these difficult times.

The spiritual teachings in this book are now 50 years old. Yet these timeless teachings are proven and deeply trustworthy. They chart a highly spiritual—and very practical—way to journey through the seas of life. If you let them, they can become your better boat.

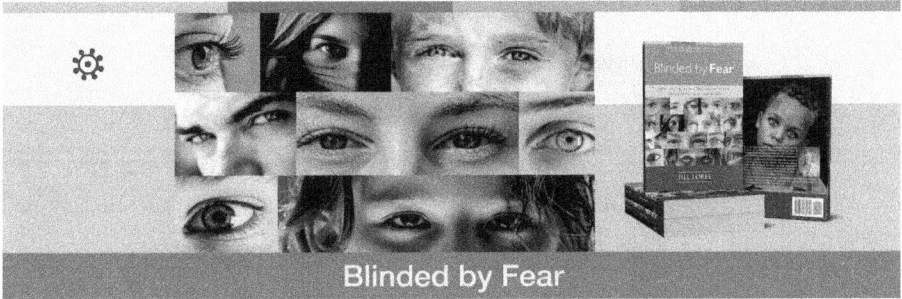

Blinded by Fear

Blinded by Fear
Insights From the Pathwork® Guide
on How to Face Our Fears

It's an error to think that becoming aware of our fears—of turning towards them and facing them in the light—will give them more power. Yet too often we turn a blind eye, hoping to avoid something unpleasant.

In truth, it's not awareness of our fears that causes us problems, but our fearful attitude about even looking at them. By not facing our fears, we keep fighting the parts of ourselves that happen to be in fear, right now. We cramp up our whole being—including our bodies—bracing ourselves against feelings of fear.

In this collection of insights, fear is illuminated from many perspectives. Because it's only by bringing our fears into the fresh air of our conscious awareness that they lose their terrible roar.

Understand These
Spiritual Teachings

Read Online

Learn About **Self-Transformation**

Understand these Spiritual Teachings

Read an overview of the Pathwork Guide's teachings about personal self-development on the Phoenesse website. This profound spiritual wisdom is presented in three parts:

• **The Work of Healing**: Learn about the work of incarnating as a human into this land of duality, and the steps we can take to unwind our difficulties and free ourselves from struggle.

• **The Prequel**: Learn about the series of events that unfolded in the Spirit World, landing us here in this difficult dimension.

• **The Rescue**: Learn what happened when we lost our free will, how we got it back, and who we should thank.

www.phoenesse.com

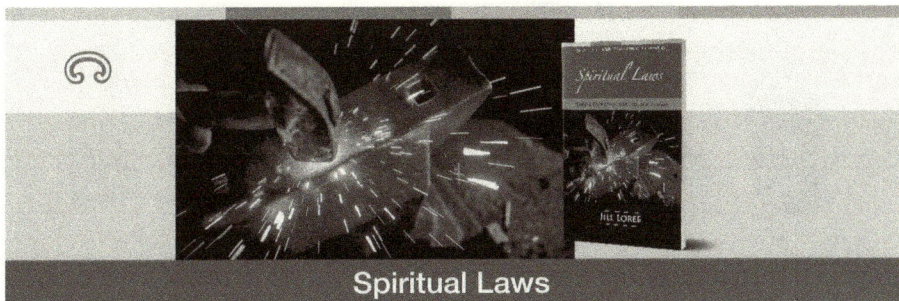

Spiritual Laws

Spiritual Laws
Hard & Fast Logic for Forging Ahead

Just what are the laws that rule this precious land? Turns out, there are an infinite number of laws that govern everything that happens. And while *Spiritual Laws* does not claim to be comprehensive in covering them all, this sampling of teachings from the Pathwork Guide does a nice job of explaining how this sphere works.

Understanding this will help us grasp the truth that behind our trials, there is a method. That someone or something is behind life, working out a plan. So gather round and listen up, because there are important guidelines we could all stand to know more about, and the hammer is about to drop.

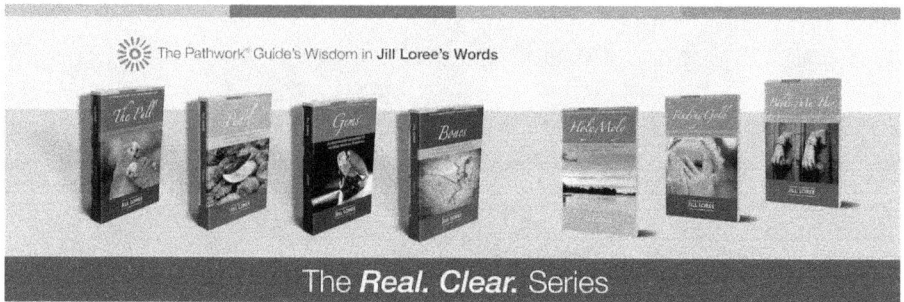

The *Real. Clear.* Series

The *Real. Clear.* Series
A Seven-Book Series for Spiritual Clarity

The *Real. Clear.* series offers a fresh approach to timeless spiritual teachings by way of easier-to-read language; it's the Pathwork Guide's wisdom in Jill Loree's words. Each book is written with a bit of levity because, as Mary Poppins put it, "A spoonful of sugar helps the medicine go down."

HOLY MOLY: The Story of Duality, Darkness and a Daring Rescue

There's one story, as ancient and ageless as anything one can imagine, that lays a foundation on which all other truths stand. It exposes the origin of opposites. It illuminates the reality of darkness in our midst. It speaks of herculean efforts made on our behalf. This is that story.

FINDING GOLD: The Search for Our Own Precious Self

The journey to finding the whole amazing nugget of the Real Self is a lot like prospecting for gold. Both combine the lure of potential and the excitement of seeing a sparkling possibility, with needing to have the patience of a saint.

It helps to have a map of our inner landscape and a headlamp for seeing into dark corners. That's what Jill Loree has created in this collection of spiritual teachings called *Finding Gold*.

BIBLE ME THIS: Releasing the Riddles of Holy Scripture

The Bible is a stumper for many of us, not unlike the Riddler teasing Batman with his "Riddle me this" taunts. But what if we could know what some of those obscure passages mean? What's the truth hidden in the myth of Adam

& Eve? And what was up with that Tower of Babel?

Bible Me This is a collection of in-depth answers to a variety of questions asked of the Guide about the Bible.

THE PULL: Relationships & Their Spiritual Significance

The Pull is about discovering the truth about relationships: they are the doorway through which we ultimately can come to know ourselves, God and another person; through them, we can learn to fully live. Because while life may be many things, more than anything else, it is all about relationships.

The Pull walks us through the delicate dance of intimate relationships, helping us navigate one of the most challenging aspects of life.

PEARLS: A Mind-Opening Collection of 17 Fresh Spiritual Teachings

In this classic, practical collection, Jill Loree strings together timeless spiritual teachings, each carefully polished with a light touch. Topics include: Privacy & Secrecy • The Lord's Prayer • Political Systems • The Superstition of Pessimism • Preparing to Reincarnate • Our Relationship to Time • Grace & Deficit • The Power of Words • Perfectionism • Authority • Order • Positive Thinking • Three Faces of Evil • Meditation for Three Voices • The Spiritual Meaning of Crisis • Leadership • Letting Go & Letting God

GEMS: A Multifaceted Collection of 16 Clear Spiritual Teachings

Clear and radiant, colorful and deep, each sparkling gem in this collection of spiritual teachings taken mostly from the final 50 lectures out of nearly 250, offers a ray of light to help illuminate our steps to reaching oneness.

BONES: A Building-Block Collection of 19 Fundamental Spiritual Teachings

This collection is like the bones of a body—a framework around which the remaining body of work can arrange itself. Sure, there's a lot that needs to be filled in to make it all come to life, but with *Bones*, now we've got the basic building blocks in place.

NUTSHELLS: Short & Sweet Spiritual Insights

Nutshells are short-and-sweet daily spiritual insights carved from three books: *Pearls*, *Gems* and *Bones*. Meaningful inspirations and memorable phrases are woven together to create a new creation that largely resembles the original form. Like the acorn that contains the potential for the oak tree, these nuggets of wisdom hold the power to change our whole perspective on life.

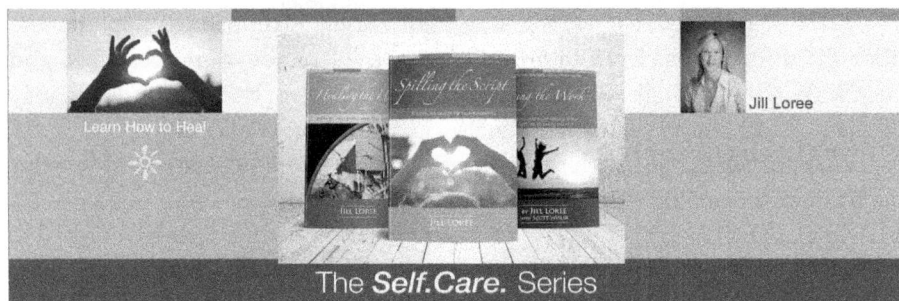

The *Self.Care.* Series

The *Self. Care.* Series
A Three-Book Teaching Series

The *Self. Care.* How-to-Heal series offers a bird's-eye view of the Pathwork Guide's teachings and shows us how to apply them in working with ourselves and others.

SPILLING THE SCRIPT: A Concise Guide to Self-Knowing

Now, for the first time, powerful spiritual teachings from the Guide are available in one concise book. Jill Loree has written *Spilling the Script* to deliver a clear, high-level perspective about self-discovery and healing, giving us the map we need for following this life-changing path to oneness.

The goal of this spiritual journey is to make contact with our divine core so we can transition from living in duality to discovering the joy of being in unity. For even as we believe ourselves to be victims of an unfair universe, the truth is that we are continually guarding ourselves against pain, and through our defended approach to life we unknowingly bring about our current life circumstances. But we can make new choices.

Bit by bit, as we come out of the trance we have been in, we begin to see cause and effect, and to take responsibility for the state of our lives. Gradually, our lives transform. We once again can sense our essential nature and eternal connectedness with all that is.

"You will find how you cause all your difficulties. You have already stopped regarding these words as mere theory, but the better you progress, the more will

you truly understand just how and why you cause your hardships. By so doing, you gain the key to changing your life."
–Pathwork Guide, Lecture #78

HEALING THE HURT: How to Heal Using Spiritual Guidance

The work of healing our fractured inner selves takes a little finesse, a lot of stick-to-it-iveness, and the skilled help of someone who has gone down this road before. Being a Helper then is about applying all we have learned on our own healing journey to help guide others through the process of reunifying their fragmented hidden places.

That may sound simple, but it's surely not easy. It's also not easy to be the Worker, the one who does this work of spiritual healing. Now, with *Healing the Hurt*, everyone can understand the important skills needed by a Helper to assure Workers find what they're looking for.

DOING THE WORK: Healing Our Body, Mind & Spirit by Getting to Know the Self | By Jill Loree with Scott Wisler

Many of us have an inkling there can be more to life: that more meaningful moments are possible, and more satisfying experiences are attainable. Well, we're right. And fortunately, the tools for bringing this about are not really a secret. They're just not obvious. Herein lies the crux of the problem. We must come to realize what we have not been willing or able to see before.

Truth be told, no one gets out of planet Earth alive. But we can come out ahead by learning to make the best use of our time here. And that starts the day we begin doing the work. So let's get at it.

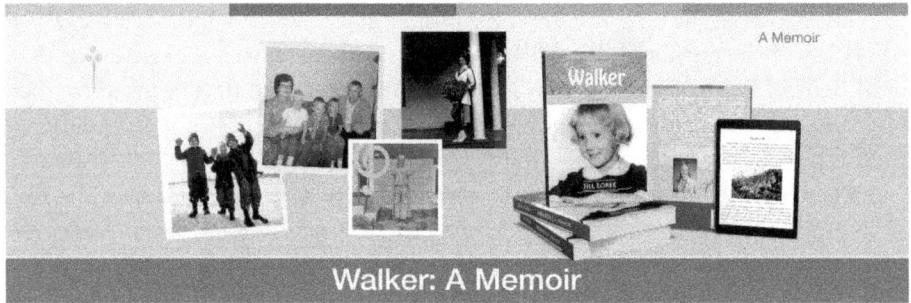

Walker: A Memoir

Walker
A Memoir

Walker is a memoir about one woman's spiritual journey to open her heart and develop compassion. Through it all, her own gumption would be her steady companion.

It starts out with a young girl raised in a singing Lutheran family where things looked good on the outside. But inside, Jill Loree was struggling. Later, she would "trudge the dreary road of happy destiny," as the AA Big Book puts it, getting sober at 26 and picking up only one white chip. That's not nothing, considering that most of Jill Loree's childhood memories are infused with her father's drinking. Her mother, on the other hand, had a controlling, co-dependent streak that wouldn't end. Sounds dreary indeed, right?

In this spiritual memoir however, Jill Loree artfully lifts the story out of the ditch and finds the grace weaving between the lines. *Walker* also merges in a touch of poetry—her own, her sons' and even her Dad's—adding heart, depth and levity to the telling. Her gentle wit and brisk writing pace keeps things moving along. True to the title, there's no need to sit and stew in misery.

Today, Jill Loree's spiritual path is filled with the light of Christ, which is what she has discovered emerges from the core of one's being after clearing away the detritus accumulated in youth—just as the Pathwork Guide said it would. That's the deeper message she is now passionate about sharing, and which shines through in this warm telling of the story of her life.

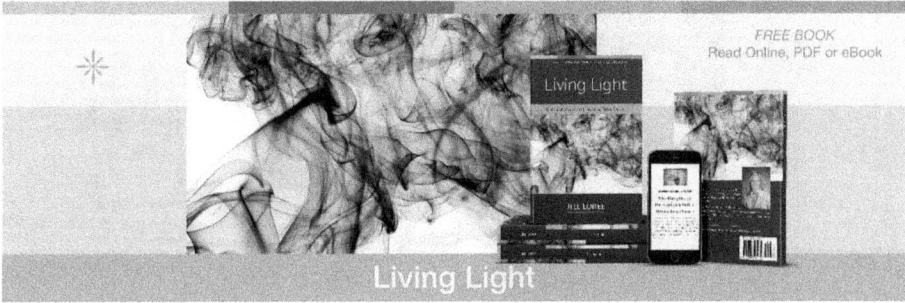

Living Light
On Seeking and Finding True Faith

What greater gift could we give ourselves than to wake up and bring forward the Christ consciousness that dwells within. To become a living light. Indeed, every time we listen for the truth, we will find the light of Christ within. And there is nothing greater for us to uncover than this, and to find true faith. For that's the moment we'll know there is truly nothing to fear.

By Jill Loree & Scott Wisler

Word for Word

Word for Word
An Intimate Exchange Between
a Couple of Kindred Souls

By Jill Loree
and Scott Wisler

What does it really look like, not just to talk the talk, but also to walk the walk of a spiritual path?

Surprisingly insightful and at times pretty funny, *Word for Word* is a unique collection of text and email messages written back and forth between a couple of died-in-the-wool spiritual seekers, Jill and Scott, as they walked head-long into a new relationship that would prove lasting.

Typos and punctuation have been cleaned up to aid readability, but believe it or not, nothing has been added or subtracted nor has any-thing been tweaked so the two don't look too strange. You'll see.

Questions & Answers with the Pathwork® Guide

The Guide Speaks
The Complete Q&A Collection

By Eva Pierrakos
with Jill Loree

On *The Guide Speaks*, Jill Loree opens up this fascinating collection of thousands of Q&As answered by the Pathwork Guide, all arranged alphabetically by topic. This website includes hard-hitting questions asked about fears, hate, anger, health, relationships and so much more.

Keywords
A Collection of Jill's Favorite Q&As

Jill Loree has combined her favorite questions about religion, Jesus Christ, the Bible, reincarnation, the Spirit World, death, prayer and meditation, and God into a single "Best Of" collection. You can read this collection online or download *Keywords: Answers to Key Questions Asked of the Pathwork® Guide*.

"There are so many questions you need to ask, personal and general ones. In the end they become one and the same. The lectures I am called upon to deliver are also answers to unspoken questions, questions that arise out of your inner yearning, searching, and desires to know and to be in truth. They arise out of your willingness to find divine reality, whether this attitude exists on the conscious or unconscious level.

But there are other questions that need to be asked deliberately on the active, outer, conscious level in order to fulfill the law. For only when you knock can the door be opened; only when you ask can you be given. This is a law."
– The Pathwork Guide in Q&A #250

www.theguidespeaks.com

phoenesse
FIND YOUR TRUE YOU.

www.ingramcontent.com/pod-product-compliance
Lightning Source LLC
Chambersburg PA
CBHW051725040426
42447CB00008B/978